BATTLE OF THE SPIRITS

G. Edward Reid

▼

OMEGA PRODUCTIONS
P.O. Box 600
Fulton, MD 20759

DISTRIBUTED BY
Review and Herald® Publishing Association
55 West Oak Ridge Drive
Hagerstown, MD 21740

This book was
Edited by Lincoln E. Steed
Designed by Bill Kirstein
Electronic makeup by Shirley M. Bolivar
Cover photo: © Allan Davey/Masterfile and © PhotoDisc (Digitally modified)
Typeset: Times 11/13

PRINTED IN U.S.A

05 04 03 02 01   5 4 3 2 1

ISBN 0-9711134-0-8

Contents

CHAPTER 1

Not Against Flesh and Blood

We are fighting for our lives—with an invisible enemy. "For we do not wrestle against flesh and blood, but against principalities, against powers, against the rulers of the darkness of this age, against spiritual hosts of wickedness in the heavenly places" (Ephesians 6:12). These supernatural powers are now mustering their forces for earth's final battle. They will not be fighting over oil in the Middle East, or to defeat Communism, or to oppose the Capitalist West. The battle will be an all-out war for the souls of men, women, and children—their eternal destiny.

This is not a time to be frightened. But we must be awake and vigilant. We have many promises that God will be with His faithful people. "When the enemy comes in like a flood, the Spirit of the Lord will lift up a standard against him" (Isaiah 59:19).

The "bad guys" are all around us. "Could the veil be lifted, we would see evil angels pressing their darkness around us and working with all their power to deceive and destroy. Wicked men are surrounded, influenced, and aided by evil spirits. The man of faith and prayer has yielded his soul to divine guidance, and angels of God bring to him light and strength from heaven" (*Testimonies for the Church,* vol. 5, p. 199). In this warfare no one can take a neutral position and watch from the sidelines. "We must inevitably be under the control of one or the other of the two great powers that are contending for the supremacy of the world. It is not necessary for us deliberately to choose the service of the kingdom of darkness in order to come under its dominion. We have only to neglect to ally ourselves with the kingdom of light. If we do not co-operate with the heavenly agencies, Satan will take possession of the heart, and will make it his abiding place. The only defense against evil is the indwelling of

Christ in the heart through faith in His righteousness. Unless we become vitally connected with God, we can never resist the unhallowed effects of self-love, self-indulgence, and temptation to sin. We may leave off many bad habits, for the time we may part company with Satan; but without a vital connection with God, through the surrender of ourselves to Him moment by moment, we shall be overcome. Without a personal acquaintance with Christ, and a continual communion, we are at the mercy of the enemy, and shall do his bidding in the end" (*The Desire of Ages,* p. 324).

The struggle is real and unrelenting. The stakes are as high as they can get. We are fighting for our lives—our eternal lives! This struggle between good and evil in the invisible world is plainly revealed in the Bible and evidenced in human history. Many today believe that the "spirits" are the spirits of the dead. But the Bible clearly teaches the existence of angels both good and bad, and it also presents clear evidence that the spirits are not the disembodied spirits of dead men.

Millions of Angels

The Bible writers tell of a vast number of angels. A number that is beyond counting. They are described as "ten thousand times ten thousand [that alone is 100,000,000] and thousands of thousands" (Daniel 7:10). That is the number of angels that Daniel saw that were just around the throne of God! The apostle Paul declared that the angels are "an innumerable company" (Hebrews 12:22). And the good news is that this vast company of angels are "all ministering spirits sent forth to minister for those who will inherit salvation" (Hebrews 1:14).

God informs us that the angels are strong and fast. Many of the awesome angel feats recorded in the Bible are performed by only one angel! For example, we know that when God sends forth His messengers they appear as "a flash of lightning" (Ezekiel 1:14). The lone angel that appeared at the tomb of Jesus on the resurrection morning caused a great earthquake by his descent from heaven. He looked like lightning, and the large group of trained soldiers that were guarding the tomb "became as dead men" (Matthew 28:2-4). And when God destroyed the army of the Assyrian king Sennacherib, 185,000 men, including "all the mighty men of valor," were killed in one night by one angel. (See 2 Kings 19:35; 2 Chronicles 32:21.)

Angels Inform and Protect

God is so eager to inform and protect His children that "angels are sent on missions of mercy to the children of God. To Abraham, with promises of blessing; to the gates of Sodom, to rescue righteous Lot from its fiery doom; to Elijah, as he was about to perish from weariness and hunger in the desert; to Elisha, with chariots and horses of fire surrounding the little town where he was shut in by his foes; to Daniel, while seeking divine wisdom in the court of a heathen king, or abandoned to become the lions' prey; to Peter, doomed to death in Herod's dungeon; to the prisoners at Philippi; to Paul and his companions in the night of tempest on the sea; to open the mind of Cornelius to receive the gospel; to dispatch Peter with the message of salvation to the Gentile stranger—thus holy angels have, in all ages, ministered to God's people" (*The Great Controversy,* p. 512). There are many more such experiences that we could mention. Angels walked and talked with Jacob on his way back home after his 20-year exile. An angel appeared to Gideon when he was commissioned to deliver Israel. An angel appeared to Zacharias to announce the birth and mission of John the Baptist. And an angel appeared to Mary to inform her that she had been chosen to be the mother of Jesus.

Angels were present in force at the birth of Jesus. A choir of angels brought the good news to the shepherds who were watching their sheep at night. On that occasion they sang praises to glorify God and gave instructions as to where Jesus might be found. That same shining angel band appeared from a great distance away to be a bright star that guided the wise men from the East to the Christ child. Then an angel appeared to Joseph to give instructions that Jesus should be taken to Egypt for safekeeping until the death of Herod. And we can add to all this the exploits of the angel Gabriel who appeared to Daniel (in addition to his visits to Zacharias and Mary) and explained the great time prophecies that reveal the hand of God in the affairs of nations.

Guardian Angels

A great source of comfort in the battle of life is the fact that God has sent the angels to minister to us. In fact, we know that each person has been assigned at least one guardian angel. Satan knows this, and in his conversation with God about Job he said, "Does Job fear God for nothing? Have you not made a hedge around him, around his household, and around all that he has on every side?" (Job 1:9, 10). According to the Bible, this hedge that protects God's people is the guardianship of angels. "The angel of the Lord encamps all around those who fear Him, and delivers them" (Psalm 34:7). And Jesus said when warning those around Him not to despise the children, "Take heed that you do not despise one of these little ones, for I say to you that in heaven their angels always see the face of My Father who is in heaven" (Matthew 18:10).

Ellen White mentions guardian angels more than 50 times in her writings: "A guardian angel is appointed to every follower of Christ. These heavenly watchers shield the righteous from the power of the wicked one. . . . His angels are appointed to watch over us, and if we put ourselves under their guardianship, then in every time of danger they will be at our right hand. When unconsciously we are in danger of exerting a wrong influence, the angels will be by our side, prompting us to a better course, choosing words for us, and influencing our actions. Thus our influence may be a silent, unconscious, but mighty power in drawing others to Christ and the heavenly world" (*My Life Today,* p. 302).

"Every redeemed one will understand the ministry of angels in his own life. The angel who was his guardian from his earliest moment; the angel who watched his steps, and covered his head in the day of peril; the angel who was with him in the valley of the shadow of death, who marked his resting place, who was the first to greet him in the resurrection morning—what will it be to hold converse with him, and to learn the history of divine interposition in the individual life, of heavenly co-operation in every work for humanity!" (*Education,* p. 305).

"Angels are commissioned to watch in every family. Each one has the watchcare of a holy angel. These angels are invisible, but sometimes they let their light shine so distinctly that it is recognized" (*This Day With God*, p. 160). God's promise is: "Because you have made the Lord, who is my refuge, even the Most High, your dwelling place, no evil shall befall you, nor shall any plague come near your dwelling; for He shall give His angels charge over you, to keep you in all your ways" (Psalm 91:9-11).

Now the Bad News

It is such a comfort to learn and understand the work of the heavenly angels—to learn of their vast numbers, their strength, their speed, their information, their protection.

The devil also has a large number of angels, "spirits" if you please, on his side. As a result of the Lucifer-inspired rebellion in heaven one third of the angels defected with him and were cast out of heaven (see Revelation 1:4). In their new sinful nature these fallen angels became "evil spirits." Created sinless, and equal in nature, power, and glory with the holy beings that are now God's messengers, they are leagued together for the dishonor of God and the destruction of men. "United with Satan in his rebellion, and with him cast out from heaven, they have, through all succeeding ages, co-operated with him in his warfare against the divine authority. We are told in Scripture of their confederacy and government, of their various orders, of their intelligence and subtlety, and of their malicious designs against the peace and happiness of men" (*The Great Controversy,* p. 513).

Satan and his evil angels are devoted to the work of deception, discouragement, enticement to sin, and the overthrow of God's kingdom. Apparently, just as men can be filled with the Holy Spirit they also can be filled with the spirits of Satan. It is clear in the New Testament record that men were possessed with demons. A vivid example of their number, power, and attitude, and also of the power of God to overcome them is given in the biblical account of the healing of the demoniacs at Gadara. Those poor madmen were not able to be restrained. They were writhing, foaming, raging, and filling the air with their cries. They were hurting themselves and were a threat to all who dared to approach them. Their bleeding and disfigured bodies and twisted minds presented an awesome and frightening spectacle—a prime example of the work of Satan. One of the demons cried out, "My name is Legion, for we are many" (Mark 5:9). A legion in the Roman army consisted of from 3,000-5,000 men. When Jesus cast the demons out of the men they were permitted at their request to enter a large herd of pigs. The pigs in a herd of about 2,000 immediately went wild and stampeded into the sea.

There are many other incidents of demon possession mentioned in the Bible. Perhaps of greatest significance to us today is not the overt devil possession of those who are openly Satan worshipers, but the "Christianized" version of devil possession and deception. This is the type that "works miracles." Because many Christians are more inclined to accept feelings than biblical fact and impressions and opinions rather than the Word of God, many are being and will be deceived.

Paul warned, "For such are false apostles, deceitful workers, transforming themselves into apostles of Christ. And no wonder! For Satan himself transforms himself into an angel of light. Therefore it is no great thing if his ministers also transform themselves into ministers of righteousness, whose end will be according to their works" (2 Corinthians

11:14, 15). And in Revelation, John warns of a false religious power that makes fire come down from heaven and works miracles to deceive the whole world (see Revelation 13:13, 14; 16:14).

When discussing the signs of the end of the world in a private conversation with His disciples, Jesus warned them four times not to be deceived (see Matthew 24:4, 5, 11, 24). In these verses Jesus warns of false christs and false prophets. This is apparently what Paul later referred to in 2 Corinthians when he warned that Satan and his evil angels would transform themselves into ministers, apostles, and even attempt to personate Christ Himself. Of course, these personations are not really true ministers, the real apostles, or Christ Himself, any more than the witch of Endor was able to produce the real prophet Samuel for the apostate king Saul.

But how will people be able to know the difference if the personations appear so real? The answer is given in Isaiah 8:20. No matter what they look like and how kind they appear to be, "To the law and to the testimony! If they do not speak according to this word, it is because there is no light in them." This sounds pretty simple. But it will be obvious only to those who have been diligent students of the Bible—the very elect.

We are given a description of what the final personation of Christ by Satan will be like. "As the crowning act in the great drama of deception, Satan himself will personate Christ. The church has long professed to look to the Saviour's advent as the consummation of her hopes. Now the great deceiver will make it appear that Christ has come. In different parts of the earth, Satan will manifest himself among men as a majestic being of dazzling brightness, resembling the description of the Son of God given by John in the Revelation. Revelation 1:13-15. The glory that surrounds him is unsurpassed by anything that mortal eyes have yet beheld. The shout of triumph rings out upon the air: 'Christ has come! Christ has come!' The people prostrate themselves in adoration before him, while he lifts up his hands and pronounces a blessing upon them, as Christ blessed His disciples when He was upon the earth. His voice is soft and subdued, yet full of melody. In gentle, compassionate tones he presents some of the same gracious, heavenly truths which the Saviour uttered; he heals the diseases of the people, and then, in his assumed character of Christ, he claims to have changed the Sabbath to Sunday, and commands all to hallow the day which he has blessed. He declares that those who persist in keeping holy the seventh day are blaspheming his name by refusing to listen to his angels sent to them with light and truth. This is the strong, almost overmastering delusion. Like the Samaritans who were deceived by Simon Magus, the multitudes, from the least to the greatest, give heed to these sorceries, saying: This is 'the great power of God.' Acts 8:10" (*The Great Controversy,* pp. 624, 625).

There are only two ways in which the faithful are able to detect the counterfeit. The unscriptural teachings and the manner of Satan's coming or appearance. "But the people of God will not be misled. The teachings of this false christ are not in accordance with the Scriptures. His blessing is pronounced upon the worshipers of the beast and his image, the very class upon whom the Bible declares that God's unmingled wrath shall be poured out.

"And, furthermore, Satan is not permitted to counterfeit the manner of Christ's advent. The Saviour has warned His people against deception upon this point, and has clearly foretold the manner of His second coming. 'There shall arise false christs, and false prophets, and shall show great signs and wonders; insomuch that, if it were possible, they shall deceive the very elect. . . . Wherefore if they shall say unto you, Behold, He is in the desert; go not forth: behold, He is in the secret chambers; believe it not. For as the lightning cometh out of the east, and shineth even unto the west; so shall also the coming of the Son of man be.' Matthew 24:24-27, 31; 25:31; Revelation 1:7; 1 Thessalonians 4:16, 17. This coming there is no possibility of counterfeiting. It will be universally known— witnessed by the whole world.

"Only those who have been diligent students of the Scriptures and who have received the love of the truth will be shielded from the powerful delusion that takes the world captive. By the Bible testimony these will detect the deceiver in his disguise. To all the testing time will come. By the sifting of temptation the genuine Christian will be revealed. Are the people of God now so firmly established upon His word that they would not yield to the evidence of their senses? Would they, in such a crisis, cling to the Bible and the Bible only? Satan will, if possible, prevent them from obtaining a preparation to stand in that day. He will so arrange affairs as to hedge up their way, entangle them with earthly treasures, cause them to carry a heavy, wearisome burden, that their hearts may be overcharged with the cares of this life and the day of trial may come upon them as a thief" (*ibid.,* p. 625).

Yes, the Bible says that there will be false christs and false prophets. But many of these false christs will look like men. "Satan and his angels will appear on this earth as men, and will mingle with those of whom God's Word says, 'Some shall depart from the faith, giving heed to seducing spirits and doctrines of devils'" (*The Truth About Angels,* p. 266).

Satan Redoubles His Efforts Near the End

We are nearing the end of the great prophetic time line. The end of the time of the end is almost upon us. "The great controversy between Christ and Satan, that has been carried forward for nearly six thousand years, is soon to close; and the wicked one redoubles his efforts to defeat the work of Christ in man's behalf and to fasten souls in his snares. To hold the people in darkness and impenitence till the Saviour's mediation is ended, and there is no longer a sacrifice for sin, is the object which he seeks to accomplish" (*The Great Controversy,* p. 518).

Satan knows that if he can get us to neglect prayer and Bible study, we will be overcome by his attacks. Therefore he invents all sorts of things to keep us "too busy" to spend time developing our characters and a knowledge of his deceptions. He gets people focused on moneymaking, hobbies, personal problems, general cares of this life, and, yes, problems in the church.

Satan Brings People Into the Church

Among his other skills, Satan is quite the "evangelist." "Satan is 'the accuser of the brethren,' and it is his spirit that inspires men to watch for the errors and defects of the Lord's people, and to hold them up to notice, while their good deeds are passed by without a mention. He is always active when God is at work for the salvation of souls. When the sons of God come to present themselves before the Lord, Satan comes also among them. In every revival he is ready to bring in those who are unsanctified in heart and unbalanced in mind. When these have accepted some points of truth, and gained a place with believers, he works through them to introduce theories that will deceive the unwary. No man is proved to be a true Christian because he is found in company with the children of God, even in the house of worship and around the table of the Lord. Satan is frequently there upon the most solemn occasions in the form of those whom he can use as his agents" (*ibid.,* p. 395).

In the Bible Satan is referred to as the enemy that sows tares in the field of the Lord. When the servants of the owner asked about the tares among the wheat, which being interpreted is "bad guys in the church," the owner said, "An enemy has done this" (Matthew 13:28). "The great deceiver has many agents ready to present any and every kind of error to ensnare souls—heresies prepared to suit the varied tastes and capacities of those whom he would ruin. It is his plan to bring into the church insincere, unregenerate elements that will encourage doubt and unbelief, and hinder all who desire to see the work of God advance and to advance with it. Many who have no real faith in God or in His word assent to some principles of truth and pass as Christians, and thus they are enabled to introduce their errors as Scriptural doctrines" (*ibid.*, p. 520).

The more we understand the working of Satan the more we realize that it is he who brings in compromise, criticism, lack of faith in the Bible and the Spirit of Prophecy. Our enemies are not those of another race, other church members, those of another political party, or even those of another church—because God still has faithful people in other churches. He calls them "my people" in the message of Revelation 18. Our enemy is Satan and his evil angels and those through whom they are working. "There are multitudes today as truly under the power of evil spirits as was the demoniac of Capernaum. All who willfully depart from God's commandments are placing themselves under the control of Satan. Many a man tampers with evil, thinking that he can break away at pleasure; but he is lured on and on, until he finds himself controlled by a will stronger than his own. He cannot escape its mysterious power. Secret sin or master passion may hold him a captive as helpless as was the demoniac of Capernaum" (*The Faith I Live By,* p. 312).

"Therefore submit to God. Resist the devil and he will flee from you. Draw near to God and He will draw near to you. Cleanse your hands, you sinners; and purify your hearts, you double-minded" (James 4:7, 8). Our minds need to be opened to the leading of God's Spirit and submitted to His molding influence.

CHAPTER 2

World War III

Our universe is a battleground. And it is total war.
    Christians who study the biblical record and the prophetic outline of history call this war "the great controversy." This understanding sharpens our worldview, clarifies what we think about God and Satan, deepens our understanding of history, and determines our eschatological perspective.

The great controversy theme—this overall view of salvation history—is one of the most distinctive points of Adventism. It gives us a perspective that provides a "theory of everything." Everything fits within the great controversy theme. The origin of evil, the fall of man, the plan for the salvation and restoration of man, the first advent, the Second Coming, the great Sabbath of rest for the earth during the millennium, the new earth, eternity future—it's all there!

So why write a book about something we already know? This book will put issues into sharper focus and reveal the battle strategy for both sides in this great controversy. This book will help ensure that you will be on the winning side.

The end-time church has a tendency to be sleepy (see Matthew 25:5)—just when believers need the most diligence and perception. We are nearing the very end of earthly history, and the devil is cranking up his wrath to its full force because he knows that he has just a very short time (Revelation 12:12). "He has set all his agencies at work that men may be deceived, deluded, occupied, and entranced until the day of probation shall be ended, and the door of mercy forever shut" (*Christian Service,* p. 51).

But we know that God has big plans for this time period as well. We must understand what has been revealed about this time. We must be aware of satanic deceptions and the danger that we could become sincerely wrong in our religious commitment.

The War Is Almost Over

After some 6,000 years of fighting, the war is almost over! We can be part of the last church, the remnant church, taking the gospel to all the world—the church that will hold high the banner of Christ—a church that is "awesome as an army with banners."

This last great conflict between truth and error is but the final struggle of the long-standing controversy over the law of God. This battle we are now entering is between the laws of men and the laws of God, between the religion of the Bible and the religion of fable and tradition (GC 582; COL 415; PP 33).

We are definitely involved in the war, but the bottom line is that we are as much the prey and the object of the controversy as we are players in it. We are involved in a spiritual battle—a conflict that is way beyond guns, martial arts, trained military, and gangs. As Paul counseled the Ephesian believers in the conclusion of his letter to them, "Finally, my brethren, be strong in the Lord and in the power of His might. Put on the whole armor of God, that you may be able to stand against the wiles of the devil. For we do not wrestle against flesh and blood, but against principalities, against powers, against the rulers of the darkness of this age, against spiritual hosts of wickedness in the heavenly places. Therefore take up the whole armor of God, that you may be able to withstand in the evil day, and having done all, to stand" (Ephesians 6:10-13).

How It All Began

"And war broke out in heaven: Michael and his angels fought with the dragon; and the dragon and his angels fought, but they did not prevail, nor was a place found for them in heaven any longer. So the great dragon was cast out, that serpent of old, called the Devil and Satan, who deceives the whole world; he was cast to the earth, and his angels were cast out with him" (Revelation 12:7-9). And so began this cosmic war known to many as the great controversy—a battle between good and evil that is being played out on the earth for the souls of men and women. And we now know that it will end in the same manner that it began—in the great battle of Armageddon—the final battle ever between the forces of evil and the armies of heaven led by Jesus Himself.

The deliverance of God's people from this earth is described in the Bible as a battle that involves the whole world. In fact it is the sixth of the seven last plagues which commence at the close of human probation. The scope of the battle is described as follows: "Then the sixth angel poured out his bowl on the great river Euphrates, and its water was dried up, so that the way of the kings of the east might be prepared. And I saw three unclean spirits like frogs coming out of the mouth of the dragon [paganism and spiritualism], out of the mouth of the beast [the Papacy], and out of the mouth of the false prophet [apostate Protestantism]. For they are the spirits of demons, performing signs, which go out to the kings of the earth and of the whole world, to gather them to the battle of the great day of God Almighty. . . . And they gathered them together to the place called in Hebrew, Armageddon" (Revelation 16:12-14, 16).

An Overview of the War

Satan, as contrasted with Jesus the life-giver, has shown himself a life-taker and a life-ruiner. He exalts in violence and death. Ever since he incited Cain to kill his brother Abel he has brought upon the earth strife that has killed untold millions. He has amassed formidable armies against God's people down through the ages. But in spite of the terrible odds against them, when God's people have trusted in Him He has always defended them.

An example of God's power and protection is given in 2 Kings 19:35. At that time a single angel of the Lord destroyed the Assyrian army of King Sennacherib. "And it came to pass on a certain night that the angel of the Lord went out, and killed in the camp of the Assyrians one hundred and eighty-five thousand (185,000); and when they arose in the morning, there were the corpses—all dead."

Throughout this great controversy champions of faith have fought for truth and refused to compromise with the enemy. One example would be the struggles of the Hussites with the Roman Church/State during the Middle Ages. John Huss, you might remember, was executed in 1415 by the Roman Catholic Church/State. Huss, a professor of theology at the University of Prague, was a Bohemian Reformer and a defender of the writings of Wycliff. Huss was summoned by Sigismund, king of Hungary and emperor of the Holy Roman Empire, to the Council of Constance (1414-1418) to give answers to charges of heresy. The council had been called initially to deal with the Great Schism of the West—three separate popes (John XXII, Benedict XIII, and Gregory XII) all claimed to be the legitimate vicar of the Son of God.

John Huss, on being cited to appear before this council, was granted a "safe-conduct," which meant that his safety and freedom were guaranteed by the emperor. He was also told that he would be given a fair hearing. He was nevertheless arrested—in direct violation of the imperial safe-conduct—shortly after his arrival in Constance. Charged with heresy, he was committed to prison. He was never to be a free man again. After months of ill treatment he was condemned and degraded and then turned over to the secular authorities to be burned at the stake.

The historical record notes that "Huss was placed on a platform and clad by seven bishops in full ecclesiastical vestments; then the vestments were one by one stripped from him. The chalice and paten were put into his hand, and then taken away. His tonsure was defaced. They put a high conical paper cap on his head, painted with devils 'clawing his soul with their nails,' and bearing the word 'heresiarch' (a leader in heresy). This done, and his soul having been delivered over to the devil, his body was surrendered to the secular arm.

"Accompanied by a guard of a thousand armed men and a vast crowd of spectators, he was led out of the council precincts. As he passed through the churchyard, Huss saw a bonfire of his books in the public square. Reaching the execution ground, called the 'Devil's Place,' Huss knelt and prayed. His hands were tied behind him, and he was bound to the stake, facing the west. A rusty chain was wound round his neck. Straw and wood were piled around him, and rosin sprinkled upon them. The offer of life was renewed if he would recant, but he refused. Then the lighted fagots were applied. Huss began to sing, but the wind swept the flames into his face and silenced his words. Only his lips moved—until they too were stilled in death for his stand against the Antichrist of Bible prophecy. Then his persecutors stirred his bones with a stick, split open his skull, and flung it back into the flames, with the unconsumed portions of his garments. Thus his body was reduced to ashes, which were gathered up and cast into the Rhine" (L. E. Froom, *The Prophetic Faith of Our Fathers*, Vol. II, pp. 115, 116).

The historical postlude to the death of Huss should teach us a never-to-be-forgotten lesson. *The Great Controversy*, by Ellen White, recounts the historic aftermath of John Huss's sacrifice: "The murderers of Huss did not stand quietly by and witness the triumph of his cause. The pope and the emperor united to crush out the movement, and the armies of Sigismund were hurled upon Bohemia.

"But a deliverer was raised up. Ziska, who soon after the opening of the war became totally blind, yet who was one of the ablest generals of his age, was the leader of the Bohemians. Trusting in the help of God and the righteousness of their cause, that people withstood the mightiest armies that could be brought against them. Again and again the emperor, raising fresh armies, invaded Bohemia, only to be ignominiously repulsed. The Hussites were raised above the fear of death, and nothing could stand against them. A few years after the opening of the war, the brave Ziska died; but his place was filled by Procopius, who was an equally brave and skillful general, and in some respects a more able leader.

"The enemies of the Bohemians, knowing that the blind warrior was dead, deemed the opportunity favorable for recovering all that they had lost. The pope now proclaimed a crusade against the Hussites, and again an immense force was precipitated upon Bohemia, but only to suffer terrible defeat. Another crusade was proclaimed. In all the papal countries of Europe, men, money, and munitions of war were raised. Multitudes flocked to the papal standard, assured that at last an end would be made of the Hussite heretics. Confident of victory, the vast force entered Bohemia. The people rallied to repel them. The two armies approached each other until only a river lay between them. 'The crusaders were in greatly superior force, but instead of dashing across the stream, and closing in battle with the Hussites whom they had come so far to meet, they stood gazing in silence at those warriors.'—Wylie, b. 3, ch. 17. Then suddenly a mysterious terror fell upon the host. Without striking a blow, that mighty force broke and scattered as if dispelled by an unseen power. Great numbers were slaughtered by the Hussite army, which pursued the fugitives, and an immense booty fell into the hands of the victors, so that the war, instead of impoverishing, enriched the Bohemians.

"A few years later, under a new pope, still another crusade was set on foot. As before, men and means were drawn from all the papal countries of Europe. Great were the inducements held out to those who should engage in this perilous enterprise. Full forgiveness of the most heinous crimes was ensured to every crusader. All who died in the war were promised a rich reward in heaven, and those who survived were to reap honor and riches on the field of battle. Again a vast army was collected, and, crossing the frontier they entered Bohemia. The Hussite forces fell back before them, thus drawing the invaders farther and farther into the country, and leading them to count the victory already won. At last the army of Procopius made a stand, and turning upon the foe, advanced to give them battle. The crusaders, now discovering their mistake, lay in their encampment awaiting the onset. As the sound of the approaching force was heard, even before the Hussites were in sight, a panic again fell upon the crusaders. Princes, generals, and common soldiers, casting away their armor, fled in all directions. In vain the papal legate, who was the leader of the invasion, endeavored to rally his terrified and disorganized forces. Despite his utmost endeavors, he himself was swept along in the tide of fugitives. The rout was complete, and again an immense booty fell into the hands of the victors.

"Thus the second time a vast army, sent forth by the most powerful nations of Europe, a host of brave, warlike men, trained and equipped for battle, fled without a blow before the defenders of a small and hitherto feeble nation. Here was a manifestation of divine power. The invaders were smitten with a supernatural terror. He who overthrew the hosts of Pharaoh in the Red Sea, who put to flight the armies of Midian before Gideon and his three hundred, who in one night laid low the forces of the proud Assyrian, had again stretched out His hand to wither the power of the oppressor. 'There were they in great fear, where no fear was: for God hath scattered the bones of him that encampeth against thee: thou hast put them to shame, because God hath despised them.' Psalm 53:5.

"The papal leaders, despairing of conquering by force, at last resorted to diplomacy. A compromise was entered into, that while professing to grant to the Bohemians freedom of conscience, really betrayed them into the power of Rome. The Bohemians had specified four points as the condition of peace with Rome: the free preaching of the Bible; the right of the whole church to both the bread and the wine in the communion, and the use of the mother tongue in divine worship; the exclusion of the clergy from all secular offices and authority; and, in cases of crime, the jurisdiction of the civil courts over clergy and laity alike. The papal authorities at last 'agreed that the four articles of the Hussites should be accepted, but that the right of explaining them, that is, of determining their precise import, should belong to the council—in other words, to the pope and the emperor.'—Wylie, b. 3, ch. 18. On this basis a treaty was entered into, and Rome gained by dissimulation and fraud what she had failed to gain by conflict; for, placing her own interpretation upon the Hussite articles, as upon the Bible, she could pervert their meaning to suit her own purposes.

"A large class in Bohemia, seeing that it betrayed their liberties, could not consent to the compact. Dissensions and divisions arose, leading to strife and bloodshed among themselves. In this strife the noble Procopius fell, and the liberties of Bohemia perished.

"Sigismund, the betrayer of Huss and Jerome, now became king of Bohemia, and regardless of his oath to support the rights of the Bohemians, he proceeded to establish popery. But he had gained little by his subservience to Rome. For twenty years his life had been filled with labors and perils. His armies had been wasted and his treasuries drained by a long and fruitless struggle; and now, after reigning one year, he died, leaving his kingdom on the brink of civil war, and bequeathing to posterity a name branded with infamy" (*The Great Controversy,* pp. 115-118).

The point here should be evident to all. As long as they trusted God and upheld their standards the Hussites prevailed in battle in ways that only God could provide. They even won with a blind general! But when they compromised they lost it all. This is a lesson for us in the great battle that is facing God's faithful people on the earth. God will fight for us if we trust Him, but compromise with the forces of evil will only bring disaster.

God destroyed the army of Egypt in the Red Sea. He routed the Philistines with hornets and with a choir. He destroyed the Midianites with Gideon's small band of unarmed men.

In 2 Chronicles 14 we read the story of the victory of Asa, king of Judah, over Zerah, king of Ethiopia, who came to fight against God's people with an army of 1,000,000 men. When Asa called upon God for help, "the Lord struck the Ethiopians before Asa and Judah. . . . So the Ethiopians were overthrown, and they could not recover, for they were broken before the Lord and His army" (verses 12, 13). Suffice it to say that God is able to deliver His people as He promised He would. We have the evidence.

But here at the end of time we are facing a much more formidable army. Wars and rumors of wars is one of the signs of the end that Jesus told us about (Matthew 24:6). Oh, yes, some have asked how wars could ever be a sign of the end when there have been wars from the beginning. It seems only logical to conclude that in order for wars to be a sign they would have to be bigger and more deadly than anything the earth has ever seen before.

World War I

Shortly before noon on Sunday, June 28, 1914, crowds gathered in Sarajevo, the capital of the Austrian province of Bosnia. The people wanted to see Archduke Francis Ferdinand, who was the heir to the Austria-Hungary throne, and his wife, Sophie. Suddenly a man jumped on the running board of the royal touring car and fired a pistol. Two shots struck Ferdinand and one hit Sophie, who was apparently trying to shield him. They both died almost immediately. The lone assassin was Gavrilo Princip, a young Bosnian student who had lived in Serbia.

Austria-Hungary suspected that its small neighbor Serbia had approved the plot to kill Ferdinand. Accordingly, it declared war on Serbia on July 28, 1914. The war lasted for four years and involved 28 nations of the world. Millions lost their lives. For example, Germany, one of the Central powers, suffered nearly 2 million fatalities, and over 4 million men were wounded. On the Allied side Russia suffered very similar losses.

Recently published information about the political situation in Europe just before World War I has been provided by the Roman Catholic historian John Cornwell, of Cambridge University in England. He states: "At precisely 11:30 on the morning of June 24, 1914, just four days before Archduke Franz Ferdinand of Austria was assassinated at Sarajevo, representatives of the Holy See and the government of Serbia sat down in the *salone* of the Secretariat of State to put their signatures to a treaty known as the Serbian Concordat. Present at the meeting were the principal Serbian negotiators, led by Milenko Vesnitch, Serbian ambassador in Paris, and Luigi Bakotic of the Serbian foreign ministry. For the Vatican was Cardinal Merry del Val and next to him the tall, sleek figure of the thirty-eight-year-old Monsignor Eugenio Pacelli. Pacelli had negotiated and drafted the document over the previous eighteen months. [Pacelli was later to become Pope Pius XII, who was pope during World War II and was also very instrumental in drafting and negotiating the Reich Concordat with Hitler.]

"Within the terms of the treaty, Serbia guaranteed that the Holy See had the right to impose the new Code of Canon Law on its country's Catholic clergy and subjects; that Catholics would have freedom of religion, worship, and education within its territories. Serbia also committed itself to paying stipends to the archbishop of Belgrade, the bishop of Uskub (now Skopje), and clergy serving the Catholic communities. At the same time, the treaty implied the abrogation of the ancient protectorate rights of the Austro-Hungarian Empire over the Catholic enclaves in Serbia's territories" (John Cornwell, *Hitler's Pope—The Secret History of Pius XII* (1999), pp. 48, 49).

Cornwell goes on to say: "When Archduke Franz Ferdinand and his wife were gunned down by a pan-Serbian agitator in Sarajevo on June 28, the emotions prompted by the Serbian Concordat became part of the general groundswell of anti-Serbian anger. . . . The Holy See, it is apparent, was no mere spiritual onlooker concerned exclusively with the spiritual welfare of Catholics in Serbia, but a player on the world scene with its own long-term ambitions and goals" (*ibid.,* pp. 57, 58). There is obviously a lot happening in the play and counterplay of nations that most people know nothing or very little about.

World War II

Most historians date the war from September 1, 1939, when German aircraft, tanks, and motorized troops attacked Poland. By early 1942 all major countries of the world were involved in the most destructive war in history.

World War II killed more persons, cost more money, damaged more property, affected more people, and probably caused more far-reaching changes than any other war in history.

The number of people killed, wounded, or missing between September 1939 and September 1945 can probably never be accurately calculated. We know that more than 10 million Allied servicemen and nearly 6 million servicemen from the Axis countries died in the war. This does not include all the civilians that were destroyed in the bombings or the millions of Jews executed in the death camps. More than 50 countries took part in the war, and the entire world felt its effects. Modern estimates place the number of deaths from both the world wars at around 69 million military and civilian personnel.

The Bombing of Hiroshima

In April 1945 Allied carrier-based planes operating in the East China Sea sank the Japanese battleship *Yamato*. The *Yamato* and the *Musashi,* which had been sunk in 1944, were the largest battleships ever built. With the Japanese navy thus crippled, the U.S. Third Fleet, joined by the British Pacific Fleet, moved to within a short distance of Japan to bombard its cities.

Following the fierce and bloody battles to take the islands of Iwo Jima and Okinawa, which took the lives of nearly 200,000 soldiers in the spring and summer of 1945, the Allies planned to invade the Japanese home island of Kyushu in November.

This invasion, code-named *Operation Olympic,* was to be followed in March 1946 by an invasion of Honshu, the main Japanese home island, in the area near Tokyo. In order to make plans for this invasion, the leaders of Britain, Russia, and the United States met in Potsdam, Germany, in July 1945. And so Harry Truman, Joseph Stalin, and Winston Churchill met in that little suburb of Berlin to figure out a strategy to bring the war to a conclusion. They already knew that while the Japanese people were willing to surrender, the military leaders were not.

The Japanese military, it was reported, were prepared to fight to the last man. In addition, it was determined that the Japanese were prepared to put a million men on the field in the event of an invasion by the Allied powers. It was obvious that an invasion would cause the deaths of hundreds of thousands on both sides. Stalin had reported that he had received a message that the Japanese were willing to negotiate a peace but were not willing to make an unconditional surrender. On July 26 the United States, Britain, and China issued an ultimatum calling for an unconditional surrender and a just peace. When Japan ignored the ultimatum, the United States decided to use the atomic bomb.

Harry Truman kept a diary during this time, and on July 25, 1945, he recorded: "We met at 11:00 a.m. today. That is Stalin, Churchill, and the U.S. president. But I had a most important session with Lord Mountbatten and General Marshall before that. We have discovered the most terrible bomb in the history of the world." He went on to write: "It may be the fire destruction prophesied in the Euphrates Valley era [apparently referring to the battle of Armageddon]. . . . Anyway we think we have found the way to cause the disintegration of the atom. An experiment in the New Mexican desert was startling—to put it mildly. [A military testing lab in Alamagordo had test-fired an atomic bomb just the week before.] . . . This weapon is to be used against Japan between now and August 10. I have told the Secretary of War, Mr. Stimson, to use it so that military objectives and soldiers are the targets and not women and children."

And so at 2:45 on the morning of August 6, 1945, an especially equipped B-29 bomber took off from Tinian Island in the central Pacific. General Leslie Groves, the head of the Manhatten Project, was on hand to see her off. The night before the mission, pilot Paul Tibbets named the aircraft *Enola Gay* after his mother.

Five and a half hours later the *Enola Gay* and her two escort planes were approaching the coast of Japan. The bombardier trained the sights on the bridge between the two sides of the city, and precisely at 8:15 a.m. the first atomic bomb ever used in warfare was dropped on the city of Hiroshima. The bomb was designed to detonate 1,000 feet above the city. When it exploded nearly 100,000 people were killed within a few seconds! The pilots felt the tremendous explosion and saw the awesome mushroom cloud of superheated gas, flames, and smoke rise to a height of 40,000 feet in just a few minutes. Pilot Tibbets commented to his copilot, Bob Lewis, "I think this is the end of the war."

Three days later another atomic bomb dropped on Nagasaki killed more than 40,000. Injured persons from the two bombings nearly equaled the number killed. Many others would die later from radiation sickness. The Japanese people realized that they were helpless if one atomic bomb could cause so much damage.

Just a few days later, on August 14, the Allies received a message from Japan accepting the Potsdam terms. On September 2, aboard the battleship *Missouri* in Tokyo Bay, the Allies and Japan signed the surrender agreement. MacArthur signed for the Allied powers, Nimitz for the United States, and Foreign Minister Mamoru Shigemitsu for Japan. And so ended the costliest, the deadliest, and the most devastating war in world history.

World War III

It is unlikely that there will be an all-out nuclear World War III because man now has the capability with his war machine of destroying every person on the earth—many times over. Many countries of the world now have nuclear weapons. Even more significant is the fact that these nuclear weapons each have a destructive capacity that is many times greater than the atomic bombs dropped on Japan in 1945.

The Bible does not describe the earth as a bombed-out wasteland when the final events take place. In fact, it says that men will be buying and selling, planting and harvesting, marrying and building—many totally oblivious to the events about to happen.

Armageddon

The last great war on the earth—the final battle in the great controversy between good and evil—is called in the Bible "Armageddon." Suffice it to say that most Bible scholars today do not believe that this battle will be fought between the nations of earth on some battlefield in the Middle East. It is now generally understood that Armageddon is the final battle between the forces of evil worldwide and the faithful remnant of God's people. And as He did so mightily in the past, God Himself will intervene to save His people, destroy the wicked, and rescue His people by taking them all to heaven. When the battle is over there will not be a living person on the earth!

Peter describes the destruction on that great day as follows: "But the day of the Lord will come as a thief in the night, in which the heavens will pass away with a great noise, and the elements will melt with fervent heat [sounds like a nuclear reaction], both the earth and the works that are in it will be burned up" (2 Peter 3:10).

Jeremiah describes the devastating effect of Armageddon in terms of the destruction of human life: "And at that day the slain of the Lord shall be from one end of the earth even to the other end of the earth. They shall not be lamented, or gathered, or buried; they shall become refuse on the ground" (Jeremiah 25:33). The entire earth will be littered with the dead bodies of the wicked. And no one will be around—"left behind"—to cry over them or dispose of them. When Jesus comes the second time there will not be "another chance" to get things right with God. That "second chance" concept is one of Satan's master deceptions!

The good news is that those who are faithful to God will be taken to meet the Lord in the air, and He will take them to be with Him in heaven. "For the Lord Himself will descend from heaven with a shout, with the voice of an archangel, and with the trumpet of God [no secret event]. And the dead in Christ will rise first. Then we who are alive and remain shall be caught up together with them in the clouds to meet the Lord in the air. And thus we shall always be with the Lord" (1 Thessalonians 4:16, 17). And in the words of Jesus Himself: "And if I go and prepare a place for you, I will come again and receive you to Myself; that where I am, there you may be also" (John 14:3).

When all is said and done, those living on the earth at the time of the second coming of Christ will be divided into two distinct groups. They are described in many ways in the Bible, but there are always just two groups. One a relatively small group—likely a few million at most; the other a very large group—likely in the billions. The Bible describes these groups as the righteous and the wicked; the saved and the lost; the wheat and the tares; the sheep and the goats; the narrow road travelers and the broad road travelers; the wise and the foolish; the faithful and the unfaithful; obedient and disobedient; doers of the word and hearers only; honest stewards and robbers of God. They can be described as those who have been transformed by the Spirit of God and those who have been deceived by the spirits of Satan.

The sole purpose of this book is to help guide you into the group who are faithful, saved, and alive at the end! "Transgression has almost reached its limit. Confusion fills the world, and a great terror is soon to come upon human beings. The end is very near. <u>We who know the truth should be preparing for what is soon to break upon the world as an overwhelming surprise</u>" (*Testimonies for the Church,* vol. 8, p. 28).

CHAPTER 3

The Spirit of God at Work

Ever since "the Spirit of God hovered over the face of the waters" at Creation, the Holy Spirit has been at work in the great plan for mankind and his restoration to the image of God. "Then God said, 'Let us make man in our image, according to our likeness'" (Genesis 1:26; emphasis supplied). The Holy Spirit has been an active agent of the Godhead in all of salvation history. Christ promised a "Comforter" to His disciples, and the Spirit's active role has been greatly increased in the Christian Era.

Just before the close of His earthly ministry Jesus gave the disciples the assurance of His return. "Let not your heart be troubled; you believe in God, believe also in Me. In My Father's house are many mansions; if it were not so, I would have told you. I go to prepare a place for you. And if I go and prepare a place for you, I will come again and receive you to Myself; that where I am, there you may be also" (John 14:1-3). Though the disciples were happy to hear about the "second coming of Jesus," they were more concerned at the time of losing His presence with them.

Jesus made it clear that He cared deeply for His disciples and would make provision for their needs. He assured them, "If you ask anything in My name, I will do it" (John 14:14). Then He gave them the offer of the highest gift that heaven could offer them. But the gift was promised upon conditions. It was one of those "If you do this, I will do that" promises. "If you love Me, keep My commandments. And I will pray the Father, and He will give you another Helper ["Comforter" in KJV], that He may abide with you forever—the Spirit of truth, whom the world cannot receive, because it neither sees Him nor knows Him; but you know Him, for He dwells with you and will be in you" (John 14:15-17; emphasis supplied).

One of the divine attributes that Christ put aside in the Incarnation was His omnipresence—the ability to be everywhere at once. But Jesus can still be in and with each of us at the same time through the Holy Spirit. "The Holy Spirit is Christ's representative, but divested of the personality of humanity, and independent thereof. Cumbered with humanity, Christ could not be in every place personally. Therefore it was for their interest that He should go to the Father, and send the Spirit to be His successor on earth. No one could then have any advantage because of his location or his personal contact with Christ. By the Spirit the Saviour would be accessible to all. In this sense He would be nearer to them than if He had not ascended on high" (*Review and Herald,* November 19, 1908). In this same Week of Prayer article Ellen White adds: "<u>The Holy Spirit was the highest of all gifts that He could solicit from His Father</u> for the exaltation of His people. The Spirit was to be given as a regenerating agent, and without this the sacrifice of Christ would have been of no avail. The power of evil had been strengthening for centuries, and the submission of men to this satanic captivity was amazing. <u>Sin could be resisted and overcome only through the mighty agency of the third person of the Godhead,</u> who would come with no modified energy, but <u>in the fulness of divine power.</u> It is the Spirit that makes effectual what has been wrought out by the world's Redeemer. It is by the Spirit that the heart is made pure. Through the Spirit the believer becomes a partaker of the divine nature. <u>Christ has given His Spirit as a divine power to overcome all hereditary and cultivated tendencies to evil, and to impress His own character on His church</u>" *(ibid.).*

Our Parallel Need

We have the same need as the disciples. We face the same challenge—taking the gospel to all the world. We are at a crisis hour in the church. Satan is working at high intensity because he knows that he has but a short time. The crisis hour of the church is also a crisis hour for each individual member of the church. And the greatest crisis of all is the battle against sin and unrighteousness fought out in each individual heart and life. This is the real test for every person. We have far less to fear from the gathering crisis we see unfolding in the world around us, and far less to fear from persecution. The real test is the great battle we must fight individually: conquering sin in our hearts and meeting the assaults of Satan upon our own characters.

Daniel 12:1 speaks of a "time of trouble such as never was," which is to come upon the world just before the second coming of Christ. That time of trouble appears to be on the very horizon. We should be preparing for what is soon to break upon the world as an overwhelming surprise. In order to meet this crisis we will need an unwavering faith in God. We can know Him by experience and through the transforming power of the Holy Spirit—the indwelling Christ. "It is often the case that trouble is greater in anticipation than in reality; but this is not true of the crisis before us. The most vivid presentation cannot reach the magnitude of the ordeal. In that time of trial, every soul must stand for himself before God" (*The Great Controversy,* p. 622).

If we are not able to gain victory today over the temptations and trials that beset us, what can we expect in the future? If we don't trust God enough to return our tithe and offerings to Him in times of relative prosperity, how can we ever expect to remain faithful when we can't buy or sell? The prophet Jeremiah asks, "If you have run with the footmen, and they have wearied you, then how can you contend with horses? And if in the land of peace, in which you trusted, they wearied you, then how will you do in the floodplain of the Jordan?" (Jeremiah 12:5).

Struggling Christians who have their hopes fixed on a place in God's soon-coming kingdom need hope. This is no time for filling our hearts with fear for those things that are coming on the earth. God loves us and the great gift that He gave to the disciples is available to us for the same purposes—to perfect our characters and equip us to finish the work.

Faithful Generations

Hebrews 11—the faith chapter—is a divine commentary on the fortitude, the faithfulness, and even the heroism, of many of the great men of God. But in reading the chapter you will note that they did not have an unstable relationship with God—weak one day and strong the next. They did not have a vacillating, fitful experience which, in a sudden crisis, turned into strength and fortitude. In each case, before the crucial times of test they had built a solid relationship with God through explicit and timely obedience and faith in His promises. They had gained the victory over their besetments. They had learned to walk with God. They had learned to communicate with God as with a friend and were conscious of the presence of the Holy Spirit in their lives and ministry. We must continue that heritage in this final generation.

The Purpose of the Holy Spirit

John 14:15-17 contains the promise of the gift of the Spirit of God. Then in verse 26 John mentions two of the purposes of the Spirit: "But the Helper, the Holy Spirit, whom the Father will send in My name, He will [1] teach you all things, and [2] bring to your remembrance all things that I said to you." Jesus made this even plainer later in this explanation with the disciples: "I still have many things to say to you, but you cannot bear them now. However, when He, the Spirit of truth, has come, He will [1] guide you into all truth; for He will [2] not speak on His own authority, but whatever He hears He will speak; and He will [3] tell you things to come" (John 16:12, 13).

Here are just a few of the purposes of the Holy Spirit.

1. Jesus promises that the Holy Spirit will guide us to all truth. We may not be able to take it all at once, but He will guide us to all truth. That is a demonstration of God's merciful character.

2. Jesus assures us that the Holy Spirit will not speak on His own authority. In other words, He doesn't speak independently of the Father and the Son. He doesn't speak contrary to the revealed will of God in the Scriptures. In fact, the Holy Spirit who inspired the men who wrote the Bible (2 Peter 1:21) will not contradict Himself. This important fact directly opposes those who claim to be led by the Spirit beyond the scope of Scripture and even contrary to it.

3. Jesus also tells us that the Spirit "will tell you things to come." This point is perhaps the most incredible and most significant for end times. Those who are filled with the Holy Spirit will be given wisdom to understand the Bible prophecies relating to the future—end times! God wants us to know where we are in time and that His coming is near: "The wise will understand" (Daniel 12:8-10) and "You, brethren, are not in darkness, so that this Day should overtake you as a thief" (1 Thessalonians 5:4). A companion passage to this one is 1 Corinthians 2:9, 10: "Eye has not seen, nor ear heard, nor have entered into the heart of man the things which God has prepared for those who love Him. But God has revealed them to us through His Spirit. For the Spirit searches all things, yes, the deep things of God." It is hard for us to imagine the joy and beauties of heaven, but through inspiration the Holy Spirit has given us a glimpse of these things.

God's Agent in Sanctification

The Holy Spirit is God's agent in the work of sanctification—character transformation. This is also called regeneration in the Bible. It is God's work in us to prepare us to live in the company of holy beings in heaven.

It is to bring us back to the perfection in which man was made originally—before the Fall. Without the life-changing experience of the indwelling Christ by the Holy Spirit, the heart of man is wicked and desperately evil. In Galatians 5 Paul describes what man is like without the indwelling Spirit and with the Spirit. It is quite a contrast.

"Now the works of the flesh are evident, which are: adultery, fornication, uncleanness, licentiousness, idolatry, sorcery, hatred, contentions, jealousies, outbursts of wrath, selfish ambitions, dissensions, heresies, envy, murders, drunkenness, revelries, and the like; of which I tell you beforehand, just as I also told you in time past, that those who practice such things will not inherit the kingdom of God" (verses 19-21).

When the Holy Spirit transforms the heart the fruit of the Spirit become evident in the life of the believer. And what a contrast to the works of the flesh! "But the fruit of the Spirit is love, joy, peace, longsuffering, kindness, goodness, faithfulness, gentleness, self-control. Against such there is no law. And those who are Christ's have crucified the flesh with its passions and desires. If we live in the Spirit, let us also walk in the Spirit" (verses 22-25).

It is interesting to note that the works of the flesh are listed in the Bible as if any one of them could evidence a sinful, unsanctified heart. The fruit of the Spirit, on the other hand, are listed with a singular noun and a singular verb. The "works are" contrasted with the "fruit is." In other words, the fruit of the Spirit includes all of the positive traits!

Jesus explained this experience of the spiritual transformation to Nicodemus. "While the wind is itself invisible, it produces effects that are seen and felt. So the work of the Spirit upon the soul will reveal itself in every act of him who has felt its saving power. When the Spirit of God takes possession of the heart, it transforms the life. Sinful thoughts are put away, evil deeds are renounced; love, humility, and peace take the place of anger, envy, and strife. Joy takes the place of sadness, and the countenance reflects the light of heaven. No one sees the hand that lifts the burden, or beholds the light descend from the courts above. The blessing comes when by faith the soul surrenders itself to God. Then that power which no human eye can see creates a new being in the image of God" (*The Desire of Ages,* p. 173).

So far we have seen from the Bible that the role of the Holy Spirit is to guide us to truth, to help us understand the prophecies, and to do the work of regeneration in our hearts. It is not the work of the Holy Spirit to make us act silly or irrationally—to speak jibberish, to fall down in church, to bark like a dog, and so on. God's purposes for the gift of His Holy Spirit are much higher and holier than that.

What Is the Holy Spirit?

We frequently describe the Holy Spirit as the third person of the Godhead or the trinity. A number of places in the Bible we are given the picture of a triune God. For example, at the baptism of Jesus by John the Father spoke from heaven, saying, "This is my beloved Son," and the Holy Spirit descended in the form of a dove. And when Jesus gave what we call the Great Commission to the disciples He spoke of three persons: "Go therefore and make disciples of all the nations, baptizing them in the name of the Father and of the Son and of the Holy Spirit" (Matthew 28:19). There are many things about God that we can't really comprehend. We call this the mystery of Godliness. We also can't explain the Incarnation, but we believe by faith that it happened.

In a special chapter of *The Acts of the Apostles* titled "The Gift of the Spirit" we are told: "It is not essential for us to be able to define just what the Holy Spirit is. Christ tells us that the Spirit is the Comforter, 'the Spirit of truth, which proceedeth from the Father.' It is plainly declared regarding the Holy Spirit that, in His work of guiding men into all truth, 'He shall not speak of Himself.' John 15:26; 16:13. The nature of the Holy Spirit is a mystery. Men cannot explain it, because the Lord has not revealed it to them. Men having fanciful views may bring together passages of Scripture and put a human construction on them, but the acceptance of these views will not strengthen the church. Regarding such mysteries, which are too deep for human understanding, silence is golden" (pp. 51, 52).

Though we cannot comprehend the Holy Spirit, we can observe His working. We all know people who have definitely been transformed by the Spirit. Jesus told Nicodemus that though the Spirit was invisible one could observe His effects like the power of the wind. Whatever the case, without the work of the Spirit there is no hope of eternal life. Jesus said, "Most assuredly, I say to you, unless one is born of water and the Spirit, he cannot enter the kingdom of God" (John 3:5). It is the Holy Spirit that places the seal of God on all who are saved (see Ephesians 4:30). Those at the time of the end who do not have the seal of God will get the mark of the beast by default.

Receiving the Holy Spirit

We will discuss the prerequisites for receiving the Holy Spirit in much more detail later, but there are two basic steps. They are: ask and obey. Jesus said, "If you then, being evil, know how to give good gifts to your children, how much more will your heavenly Father give the Holy Spirit to those who ask Him!" (Luke 11:13). And when testifying before the Jerusalem Council, Peter stated regarding Jesus: "And we are His witnesses to these things, and so also is the Holy Spirit whom God has given to those who obey Him" (Acts 5:32).

Trying the Spirits

We know that in the great controversy—the battle of the spirits—evil spirits, lying spirits, and the spirits of demons are part of the end-time scenario. And we know that it is by this means that the devil will try to deceive, if possible, even the very elect. This being the case, how are we to distinguish between the spirits? If someone says the spirit is leading him in a certain way, how can we know what spirit it is?

Both the Old and New Testaments give the same advice. We should try the spirits or put them on trial—examine them. "To the law and to the testimony! If they do not speak according to this word, it is because there is no light in them" (Isaiah 8:20). And John warns, "Beloved, do not believe every spirit, but test the spirits, whether they are of God; because many false prophets have gone out into the world" (1 John 4:1). Of course, as these verses indicate, the testing standard is the Word of God.

End-Time Role of the Spirit

The Bible indicates that God's people will be persecuted and cross-examined as part of the final events before the Second Coming. This possibility should not cause us anxiety, because God has promised that the Holy Spirit will tell us what to say. "But when they arrest you and deliver you up, do not worry beforehand, or premeditate what you will speak. But whatsoever is given you in that hour, speak that; for it is not what you speak, but the Holy Spirit" (Mark 13:11). A similar statement in Luke is also very encouraging: "Now when they bring you to the synagogues and magistrates and authorities, do not worry about how or what you should answer, or what you should say. For the Holy Spirit will teach you in that very hour what you ought to say" (verses 11, 12).

But the Holy Spirit is our guide not just in the time of trial. As we make our way through the minefields of life and encounter the devil, roaming around seeking whom he may devour, we need guidance. And God has promised, "Your ears shall hear a word behind you, saying, 'This is the way, walk in it'" (Isaiah 30:21). "I will put My Spirit within you and cause you to walk in My statutes, and you will keep My judgments and do them" (Ezekiel 36:27).

Though these promises were made long ago, "the lapse of time has wrought no change in Christ's parting promise to send the Holy Spirit as His representative. It is not because of any restriction on the part of God that the riches of His grace do not flow earthward to men. If the fulfillment of the promise is not seen as it might be, it is because the promise is not appreciated as it should be. If all were willing, all would be filled with the Spirit. Wherever the need of the Holy Spirit is a matter little thought of, there is seen spiritual drought, spiritual darkness, spiritual declension and death. Whenever minor matters occupy the attention, the divine power which is necessary for the growth and prosperity of the church, and which would bring all other blessings in its train, is lacking, though offered in infinite plenitude" (*The Acts of the Apostles,* p. 50).

And so when Jesus returned to heaven to prepare the mansions that He promised to His disciples He gave that special gift of the Holy Spirit. "It is through the Spirit that Christ dwells in us; and the Spirit of God, received into the heart by faith, is the beginning of the life eternal" (*The Desire of Ages,* p. 388).

CHAPTER 4

The Early Rain

In the Middle East during Old Testament times and the time of Christ the weather was usually quite predictable. Farmers depended on the rains for the germination of the seed after planting. This spring rain was known to all as the "early rain." Then in the fall, or harvesttime, another rainy time came to bring the harvest to full ripeness. This final rainy time was known as the "latter rain."

God inspired the Bible writers to use this very familiar weather pattern to illustrate the work of the Holy Spirit in the establishment of the early church and the ripening of the harvest at the end of the world. This same metaphor is also used in connection with the new birth and the settling into the truth by the individual Christian. "Therefore be patient, brethren, until the coming of the Lord. See how the farmer waits for the precious fruit of the earth, waiting patiently for it until it receives the early and latter rain" (James 5:7). Old Testament passages convey the same message. "Let us know, let us pursue the knowledge of the Lord. His going forth is established as the morning; He will come to us like the rain, like the latter and former rain to the earth" (Hosea 6:3). Four chapters later the prophet again makes an appeal for spiritual growth: "Sow for yourselves righteousness; reap in mercy; break up your fallow ground, for it is time to seek the Lord, till He comes and rains righteousness on you" (Hosea 10:12).

Early Rain Indispensable

It is both logically and explicitly stated in the inspired writings that those who receive the latter rain and are ultimately saved must first receive the early rain. Jesus said, "Most assuredly, I say to you, unless one is born of water and the Spirit, he cannot enter the kingdom of God" (John

3:5). This verse has three very important elements. First, Jesus used the words "most assuredly," indicating the importance of the statement. In the King James Version the words "verily, verily" are used. Second, this reception of the Spirit is in connection with spiritual birth and baptism. And finally, Jesus said that one who has not been born (or baptized) of the Spirit "cannot" enter the kingdom of God. He doesn't say that it is difficult. He says that it is impossible!

Ellen White emphasizes the same points. "The latter rain, ripening earth's harvest, represents the spiritual grace that prepares the church for the coming of the Son of man. But unless the former rain has fallen, there will be no life; the green blade will not spring up. Unless the early showers have done their work, the latter rain can bring no seed to perfection. There must be a constant development of Christian virtue, a constant advancement in Christian experience.

"Every individual must realize his own necessity. The heart must be emptied of every defilement, and cleansed for the indwelling of the Spirit. It was by the confession and forsaking of sin, by earnest prayer and consecration of themselves to God, that the early disciples prepared for the outpouring of the Holy Spirit on the day of Pentecost. The same work, only in greater degree, must be done now.

"There must be no neglect of the grace represented by the former rain. Only those who are living up to the light they have, will receive greater light. Unless we are daily advancing in the exemplification of the active Christian virtues, we shall not recognize the manifestations of the Holy Spirit in the latter rain. It may be falling on hearts all around us, but we shall not discern or receive it" (*The Faith I Live By,* p. 333).

Apparently, the latter rain is sent only to those who have already germinated the seeds of truth in their hearts. The final rain, then, is given to bring the grain to maturity.

"While we cherish the blessing of the early rain, we must not, on the other hand, lose sight of the fact that without the latter rain, to fill out the ears and ripen the grain, the harvest will not be ready for the sickle, and the labor of the sower will have been in vain. Divine grace is needed at the beginning, divine grace at every step of advance, and divine grace alone can complete the work.

"Do not rest satisfied that in the ordinary course of the season, rain will fall. Ask for it. . . . We must seek His favors with the whole heart if the showers of grace are to come to us. We should improve every opportunity of placing ourselves in the channel of blessing. Christ has said, 'Where two or three are gathered together in my name, there am I in the midst.' Matt. 18:20. <u>The convocations of the church, as in camp meetings, the assemblies of the home church, and all occasions where there is personal labor for souls, are God's appointed opportunities for giving the early and the latter rain.</u>

"At every meeting we attend our prayers should ascend that at this very time, God will impart warmth and moisture to our souls. As we seek God for the Holy Spirit, it will work in us meekness, humbleness of mind, a conscious dependence upon God for the perfecting latter rain. If we pray for the blessing in faith, we shall receive it as God has promised.

"The Holy Spirit will come to all who are begging for the bread of life to give to their neighbors" (*ibid.,* p. 334).

Pentecost

Just as there is a new birth experience and a spiritual maturing process—the early and latter rain, so there is a corporate early and latter rain. This means that in addition to the experience of individual members God blesses His corporate church with special outpourings of the power of His Spirit at the beginning of the church and at the very end as well. The corporate early rain was given during the feast of Pentecost in A.D. 31. The final, special outpouring of God's Spirit, will come after the Sunday agitation begins and the consequent shaking of the church. We will study this is some detail in another chapter.

After the Resurrection Jesus met with the disciples and gave them instruction regarding His sending of the Comforter that He had promised before the Crucifixion. "And being assembled together with them, He commanded them not to depart from Jerusalem, but to wait for the Promise of the Father, 'which,' He said, 'you have heard from Me; for John truly baptized with water, but you shall be baptized with the Holy Spirit not many days from now. . . . But you shall receive power when the Holy Spirit has come upon you; and you shall be witnesses to Me in Jerusalem, and in all Judea and Samaria, and to the end of the earth'" (Acts 1:4, 5, 8).

We can learn about how to prepare for the latter rain by observing how the disciples prepared for the early rain. In obedience to Christ's command, they (the disciples) waited in Jerusalem for the promise of the Father—the outpouring of the Spirit. They did not wait in idleness. The record says that they were "continually in the temple praising and blessing God" (Luke 24:53).

"As the disciples waited for the fulfillment of the promise, they humbled their hearts in true repentance and confessed their unbelief. . . . The disciples prayed with intense earnestness for a fitness to meet men and in their daily intercourse to speak words that would lead sinners to Christ. Putting away all differences, all desire for the supremacy, they came close together in Christian fellowship.

"It was after the disciples had come into perfect unity, when they were no longer striving for the highest place, that the Spirit was poured out.

"The outpouring of the Spirit in the days of the apostles was the beginning of the early, or former, rain, and glorious was the result. To the end of time the presence of the Spirit is to abide with the true church" (*Last Day Events,* p. 184).

Early Rain Review
In response to Jesus' instructions for the outpouring of the Holy Spirit the disciples—

obeyed,
waited,
spent time at church,
praised God,
humbled their hearts,
repented of their sins,
confessed their unbelief,
prayed earnestly for witnessing skills,
put away all differences,
had no desire for supremacy over each other,
came into close fellowship,
came into perfect unity,
were no longer striving for the highest place,

THEN THE SPIRIT WAS POURED OUT. And this was the early rain! And what a combination. Their preparation, combined with the power of the Holy Spirit, allowed them to take the gospel to the whole world in their generation.

Filled With the Holy Spirit
The Bible describes the experience in the first four verses of Acts 2: "When the Day of Pentecost had fully come, they were all with one accord in one place. And suddenly there came a sound from heaven, as of a rush-

ing mighty wind, and it filled the whole house where they were sitting. Then there appeared to them divided tongues, as of fire, and one sat upon each of them. And they were all filled with the Holy Spirit and began to speak with other tongues, as the Spirit gave them utterance" (Acts 2:1-4).

And so God equipped the church to do the work of ministry.

Some Christians have had the view that the "tongues" that the disciples evidenced was some gibberish, with no intrinsic meaning other than being a sign that the Spirit had been received. But a careful reading of the passage will indicate that the tongues were languages, well understood by those visiting Jerusalem. All of God's gifts are given for a purpose, and so is the gift of tongues. They "began to speak with other tongues." They were not just making noise. They were speaking! God used the occasion of the great assembly of Jews gathered from all parts of the world to share the good news of the gospel with them in their own languages.

The Bible account of the Pentecost experience mentions three times that the disciples spoke the languages known by those who lived in many places around the world. "Now there were dwelling in Jerusalem Jews, devout men, from every nation under heaven. And when this sound occurred, [the rushing mighty wind] the multitude came together, and were confused, because everyone heard them speak in his own language. Then they were all amazed and marveled, saying to one another, 'Look, are not all these who speak Galileans? And how is it that we hear, each in our own language in which we were born? Parthians and Medes and Elamites, those dwelling in Mesopotamia, Judea and Cappadocia, Pontus and Asia, Phrygia and Pamphylia, Egypt and the parts of Libya adjoining Cyrene, visitors from Rome, both Jews and proselytes, Cretans and Arabs—we hear them speaking in our own tongues the wonderful works of God'" (Acts 2:5-11).

"During the dispersion the Jews had been scattered to almost every part of the inhabited world, and in their exile they had learned to speak various languages. Many of these Jews were on this occasion in Jerusalem, attending the religious festivals then in progress. Every known tongue was represented by those assembled. This diversity of languages would have been a great hindrance to the proclamation of the gospel; God therefore in a miraculous manner supplied the deficiency of the apostles. The Holy Spirit did for them that which they could not have accomplished for themselves in a lifetime. They could now proclaim the truths of the gospel abroad, speaking with accuracy the languages of those for whom they were laboring. This miraculous gift was a strong evidence to the world that their commission bore the signet of Heaven. From this time forth the language of the disciples was pure, simple, and accurate, whether they spoke in their native tongue or in a foreign language" (*The Acts of the Apostles,* p. 39).

Into All the World

The disciples had been told to go into all the world and preach the gospel to every creature. "The commission that Christ gave to the disciples, they fulfilled. As these messengers of the cross went forth to proclaim the gospel, there was such a revelation of the glory of God as had never before been witnessed by mortal man. By the co-operation of the divine Spirit, the apostles did a work that shook the world. To every nation was the gospel carried in a single generation. [See Colossians 1:6, 23—"Which was preached to every creature under heaven."]

"Glorious were the results that attended the ministry of the chosen apostles of Christ. At the beginning of their ministry some of them were unlearned men, but their consecration to the cause of their Master was unreserved, and under His instruction they gained a preparation for the great work committed to them. Grace and truth reigned in their hearts, inspiring their motives and controlling their actions. Their lives were hid with Christ in God, and self was lost sight of, submerged in the depths of infinite love" (*The Acts of the Apostles,* p. 593).

In the providence of God those who had gathered in Jerusalem for Pentecost, who had heard the gospel in their own languages, also became ambassadors for God's cause. Under the direction of the Holy Spirit the followers of Christ were empowered with wisdom and boldness. Thousands were converted in a day. And that one generation carried the gospel to every known nation.

We have a similar and much more solemn message for the world. It embraces the messages of Revelation 14. The gospel message coupled with the judgment hour message! It is the last message of warning for the inhabitants of earth. Even though we have the manpower and the technology to carry the gospel to the world, it will take the power of the Holy Spirit to animate the workers and convict the hearts of men.

God's Spirit Still Available

"The lapse of time has wrought no change in Christ's parting promise to send the Holy Spirit as His representative. It is not because of any restriction on the part of God that the riches of His grace do not flow earthward to men. If the fulfillment of the promise is not seen as it might be, it is because the promise is not appreciated as it should be. If all were willing, all would be filled with the Spirit. Wherever the need of the Holy Spirit is a matter little thought of, there is seen spiritual drought, spiritual darkness, spiritual declension and death. Whenever minor matters occupy the attention, the divine power which is necessary for the growth and prosperity of the church, and which would bring all other blessings in its train, is lacking, though offered in infinite plenitude.

"Since this is the means by which we are to receive power, why do we not hunger and thirst for the gift of the Spirit? Why do we not talk of it, pray for it, and preach concerning it? The Lord is more willing to give the Holy Spirit to those who serve Him than parents are to give good gifts to their children. For the daily baptism of the Spirit every worker should offer his petition to God" (*The Acts of the Apostles*, p. 50).

The early rain experience for each of us is a growing, daily work on our behalf. It prepares us for our walk with God and our growth in grace. It prepares us for the continuing ministry of the Spirit on our behalf for witness and personal spiritual growth.

"Those only who are constantly receiving fresh supplies of grace, will have power proportionate to their daily need and their ability to use that power. Instead of looking forward to some future time when, through a special endowment of spiritual power, they will receive a miraculous fitting up for soul winning, they are yielding themselves daily to God, that He may make them vessels meet for His use. Daily they are improving the opportunities for service that lie within their reach. Daily they are witnessing for the Master wherever they may be, whether in some humble sphere of labor in the home, or in a public field of usefulness" (*ibid.,* p. 55). Note that the word "daily" is used four times.

Though, as we will see in later chapters, the latter rain does not come in its corporate fullness until after the Sunday agitation begins, we must seek it individually now for our own personal need. We must not wait until some future time when God will supernaturally pour out His Spirit upon us. "The third angel's message is swelling into a loud cry, and you must not feel at liberty to neglect the present duty, and still entertain the idea that at some future time you will be the recipients of great blessing, when without any effort on your part a wonderful revival will take place.

Today you are to give yourselves to God, that He may make you vessels unto honor, and meet for His service. Today you are to give yourself to God, that you may be emptied of self, emptied of envy, jealousy, evil surmising, strife, everything that shall be dishonoring to God. Today you are to have your vessel purified that it may be ready for the heavenly dew, ready for the showers of the latter rain; for the latter rain will come, and the blessing of God will fill every soul that is purified from every defilement. It is our work today to yield our souls to Christ, that we may be fitted for the time of refreshing from the presence of the Lord—fitted for the baptism of the Holy Spirit" (*God's Amazing Grace,* p. 205).

Peter gave the same counsel in his second sermon at the Pentecost gathering. "Repent therefore and be converted that your sins may be blotted out, so that times of refreshing may come from the presence of the Lord" (Acts 3:19).

There is indeed a preparation to be made on our part. "We may have had a measure of the Spirit of God, but by prayer and faith we are continually to seek more of the Spirit. It will never do to cease our efforts. If we do not progress, if we do not place ourselves in an attitude to receive both the former and the latter rain, we shall lose our souls, and the responsibility will lie at our own door" (*Last Day Events,* p. 187).

Our eternal salvation is at stake. Receiving the amazing gift of the Spirit is not optional if we intend to be among those who inherit eternal life. We must be growing in grace right now to be in a position to receive the all-important latter rain. "Many have in a great measure failed to receive the former rain. They have not obtained all the benefits that God has thus provided for them. They expect that the lack will be supplied by the latter rain. When the richest abundance of grace shall be bestowed, they intend to open their hearts to receive it. They are making a terrible mistake. The work that God has begun in the human heart in giving His light and knowledge, must be continually going forward. Every individual must realize his own necessity. The heart must be emptied of every defilement, and cleansed for the indwelling of the Spirit. It was by the confession and forsaking of sin, by earnest prayer and consecration of themselves to God, that the early disciples prepared for the outpouring of the Holy Spirit on the day of Pentecost. The same work, only in greater degree, must be done now. Then the human agent had only to ask for the blessing, and wait for the Lord to perfect the work concerning him. It is God who began the work, and He will finish His work, making man complete in Jesus Christ. But there must be no neglect of the grace represented by the former rain. Only those who are living up to the light they have, will receive greater light. Unless we are daily advancing in the exemplification of the active Christian virtues, we shall not recognize the manifestations of the Holy Spirit in the latter rain. It may be falling on hearts all around us, but we shall not discern or receive it" (*Review and Herald,* March 2, 1897).

The Stewardship Connection

Obedience is one of the prerequisites to receiving the transforming Spirit of God. As the work of the disciples and the work done in them is recalled in *The Acts of the Apostles,* Ellen White, near the end of the book, presents an amazing chapter titled "Transformed by Grace." Near the end of the chapter an appeal is made that puts financial faithfulness in its proper place. "Time is rapidly passing into eternity. Let us not keep back from God that which is His own. Let us not refuse Him that which, though it cannot be given with merit, cannot be denied without ruin. He asks for a whole heart; give it to Him; it is His, both by creation and by redemption. He asks for your intellect; give it to Him; it is His. He asks for your money; give it to Him; it is His. 'Ye are not your own, for ye are bought with a price.' 1 Corinthians 6:19, 20" (p. 566).

Of those with money and possessions who have questions about its use in the cause of God, she states: "We call upon you who have means, to inquire with earnest prayer: What is the extent of the divine claim upon me and my property? There is work to be done now to make ready a people to stand in the day of the Lord. Means must be invested in the work of saving men, who, in turn, shall work for others. Be prompt in rendering to God His own. One reason why there is so great a dearth of the Spirit of God is that so many are robbing God" (*Testimonies for the Church,* vol. 5, p. 734).

As we seek God's guidance through the Holy Spirit we will daily seek time with God in private prayer, the study of His Word, and in careful obedience to His commandments. In this way our lives will be transformed into His likeness. Our desire will be to please Him as did Enoch. We will have a conscious dependence upon God for the perfecting latter rain. This will be our protection against evil because "when the enemy comes in like a flood, the Spirit of the Lord will lift up a standard against him" (Isaiah 59:19).

"The Spirit of God, received into the heart by faith, is the beginning of life eternal" (*The Desire of Ages,* p. 388).

CHAPTER 5

The Voice of Conscience

S piritual forces beyond the field of view of our natural eyesight are seeking to influence the direction of our lives. Their influence and suggestions entice us to compromise our standards, to sidetrack us from our heavenward journey. In short, these influences are temptations to sin. On the other hand there is the voice of conscience—the voice of God, if you please, saying, "This is the way, walk in it."

The dictionary defines conscience as the sense or consciousness of the moral goodness or blameworthiness of one's own conduct, intentions, or character, together with a feeling of obligation to do right or be good. We have all heard the admonition "Let your conscience be your guide." Is that really good counsel? What about the statement some make in connection with a particular act: "It might not be OK for you, but it's OK with me"? We know, however, that right and wrong are not based on the opinions of men.

I have found this subject of conscience far more significant and of greater relevance to end-time Christians than I had expected. Let's look at some of the Bible and Spirit of Prophecy references regarding conscience. Perhaps we can make an application to our lives by looking at the Bible characters who demonstrated the power of conscience.

The Bible has much to say about conscience. The word does not appear in the Old Testament in the King James Version. However, its function and operation are implied in the Old Testament in such verses as Genesis 3:8, 1 Samuel 24:5, and Psalm 51:3. From the biblical perspective, all men are endowed by God with a conscience, but not all consciences are equally enlightened and educated.

The Bible describes different kinds of consciences. Paul mentions a "good conscience" (1 Timothy 1:5). He himself was always very careful to keep his conscience clear before God. In his testimony as part of his defense before Felix, Paul stated, "I myself always strive to have a conscience without offense toward God and men" (Acts 24:16). He taught that a good conscience can remain so only as long as faith and integrity are maintained. Enlightened by the Holy Spirit, Paul's conscience could witness to his truthfulness when he expressed his concern for his fellow Jews (Romans 9:1). He was so confident of his blameless conduct that he could appeal to the consciences of others as witnesses of it (see 2 Corinthians 4:2; 2 Timothy 1:3; and Hebrews 13:18).

When Paul outlined for the Corinthian believers the moral overtones of eating meat offered to idols, he implied that such a practice might not be a sin of itself; however, if one's conscience was disturbed by this practice, or if indulgence became a stumbling block to a brother with a weak conscience, then the practice should be avoided (compare 1 Corinthians 8 with 10:19-33).

The apostle also wrote of a "conscience seared" (1 Timothy 4:20) and a defiled conscience (Titus 1:15), probably referring to a conscience which has become insensitive to guilt because of protracted sinning. This type of person is referred to also in Isaiah 5:20 and Micah 3:2. Peter encouraged the believers in Asia Minor (1 Peter 1) to keep their consciences clear by right living, so that evildoers might find nothing by which to accuse them (3:16).

So What Is Conscience?

"Conscience is the voice of God, heard amid the conflict of human passions; when it is resisted, the Spirit of God is grieved" (*Testimonies for the Church*, vol. 5, p. 120). As we shall see, it is the Word of God expressed through the Bible and the voice of the Holy Spirit that help us to develop our conscience and that allows it to be our guide. Now let's put the above statement in its context. When discussing the hardness of Pharaoh's heart when he kept refusing to let the Israelites depart from Egypt, Ellen White explains what conscience is and how it works: "Just what took place in Pharaoh's heart will take place in every soul that neglects to cherish the light and walk promptly in its rays. God destroys no one. The sinner destroys himself by his own impenitence. When a person once neglects to heed the invitations, reproofs, and warnings of the Spirit of God, his conscience becomes seared, and the next time he is admonished, it will be more difficult to yield obedience than before. And thus with every repetition. Conscience is the voice of God, heard amid the conflict of human passions; when it is resisted, the Spirit of God is grieved.

"We want all to understand how the soul is destroyed. It is not that God sends out a decree that man shall not be saved. He does not throw a darkness before our eyes which cannot be penetrated. But man at first resists a motion of the Spirit of God, and, having once resisted, it is less difficult to do so the second time, less the third, and far less the fourth. Then comes the harvest to be reaped from the seed of unbelief and resistance" *(ibid.)*.

The "voice of God" is also explained as the work of the Holy Spirit and as the voice of duty. "The Holy Spirit strives with every man. It is the voice of God speaking to the soul. No human reasoning of the most learned man can define the operations of the Holy Spirit upon human minds and characters, yet they can see the effects upon the life and actions. . . .

"Though we cannot see the Spirit of God, we know that men who have been dead in trespasses and sins become convicted and converted under its operations. The thoughtless and wayward become serious. The hardened repent of their sins, and the faithless believe. The gambler, the drunkard, the licentious, become steady, sober, and pure. The rebellious and obstinate become meek and Christlike. When we see these changes in the character, we may be assured that the converting power of God has transformed the entire man" (*In Heavenly Places,* p. 22).

As we continue to define conscience and see its working in the lives of individual Bible characters who either obeyed their conscience or defiled it, we will see that all who are lost started down the road to destruction by a violation of conscience and all who are saved followed their conscience faithfully, or at some point in their lives heeded the voice of God and asked for restoration by His Spirit.

Conscience is also defined as the voice of duty. The "I know I should . . ." experience. "God claims every power, every capability of action to be invested in the doing of His work. Talents, possessions, everything that is great and noble in man He calls to be exercised in His work. Duty admits no rival, enters into no compromise with any opposing powers. The most precious friends and relatives must not step in between your duty and your God. The voice of duty is the voice of God in our souls. Obedience to its claims brings us into living personal agreement with the highest law in the universe—brings man into alliance with God" (*Review and Herald,* June 7, 1887).

"The voice of duty" and its identification as the conscience is explained more fully in this important statement: "The Lord requires us to obey the voice of duty, when there are other voices all around us urging us to pursue an opposite course. It requires earnest attention from us to distinguish the voice which speaks from God. We must resist and conquer inclination, and obey the voice of conscience without parleying or compromise, lest its promptings cease and will and impulse control. The word of the Lord comes to us all who have not resisted His Spirit by determining not to hear and obey. His voice is heard in warnings, in counsels, in reproof. It is the Lord's message of light to His people. If we wait for louder or better opportunities, the light may be withdrawn, and we left in darkness" (*God's Amazing Grace,* p. 202).

More Than an Animal

"God has given men more than a mere animal life. . . . He has given them a conscience, and He forbids that this gift be in any way misused; it is, rather, to be exalted to the place of authority to which He has assigned it" (*Mind, Character, and Personality,* vol. 1, p. 319).

God has given us "a conscience to convict of sin" (*Counsels on Stewardship,* p. 114). So as we have asked above. Can we then just live by our conscience? Can our conscience be our guide? Note this interesting answer: "The idea is entertained by many that a man may practice anything that he conscientiously believes to be right. But the question is, Has the man a well-instructed, good conscience, or is it biased and warped by his own preconceived opinions? Conscience is not to take the place of 'Thus saith the Lord.' Consciences do not all harmonize and are not all inspired alike. Some consciences are dead, seared as with a hot iron. Men may be conscientiously wrong as well as conscientiously right. Paul did not believe in Jesus of Nazareth, and he hunted the Christians from city to city, verily believing that he was doing service to God" (*ibid.,* p. 322).

So belief that one is right—even sincerely believing one is right—is not necessarily a safe position. Our conscience must be educated by the study of the Word of God and the influence of the Holy Spirit. "The conscience is the regulative faculty, and if a man allows his conscience to become perverted, he cannot serve God aright" (*Manuscript Releases,* vol. 13, p. 155).

Conscience a Sure Guide

"He whose conscience is a sure guide will not stop to reason [i.e., rationalize away] when light shines upon him out of God's Word. He will not be guided by human counsel. He will not allow worldly business to stand in the way of obedience. He will lay every selfish interest at the door of investigation, and will approach the Word of God as one whose eternal interest is hanging in the balance.

"There is a right side—the side of Him who declared, 'I have kept my Father's commandments' (John 15:10). 'The law of the Lord is perfect, converting the soul' (Ps. 19:7). There is a wrong side—the side of the one who in heaven rebelled against God. With his sympathizers he was expelled from the heavenly courts, and from his action we may understand that no matter how high a position a man may occupy in the church or in the world, if he is disloyal to God, if he accepts human laws instead of the laws of Jehovah, he can never enter heaven, for he is living in direct opposition to God" (*The Upward Look,* p. 140).

Conscience, Conviction, Confession, and Conversion

Conscience plays a major role in spiritual transformation. An awakened conscience leads men, women, and young people to Christ and places within them a desire to follow Him. "As your conscience has been quickened by the Holy Spirit, you have seen something of the evil of sin, of its power, its guilt, its woe; and you look upon it with abhorrence. You feel that sin has separated you from God, that you are in bondage to the power of evil. The more you struggle to escape, the more you realize your helplessness. Your motives are impure; your heart is unclean. You see that your life has been filled with selfishness and sin. You long to be forgiven, to be cleansed, to be set free. Harmony with God, likeness to Him—what can you do to obtain it?

"It is peace that you need—Heaven's forgiveness and peace and love in the soul. Money cannot buy it, intellect cannot procure it, wisdom cannot attain to it; you can never hope, by your own efforts, to secure it. But God offers it to you as a gift, 'without money and without price.' Isaiah 55:1. It is yours if you will but reach out your hand and grasp it. The Lord says, 'Though your sins be as scarlet, they shall be as white as snow; though they be red like crimson, they shall be as wool.' Isaiah 1:18. 'A new heart also will I give you, and a new spirit will I put within you.' Ezekiel 36:26.

"You have confessed your sins, and in heart put them away. You have resolved to give yourself to God. Now go to Him, and ask that He will wash away your sins and give you a new heart. Then believe that He does this because He has promised. This is the lesson which Jesus taught while He was on earth, that the gift which God promises us, we must believe we do receive, and it is ours" (*Steps to Christ,* pp. 49, 50).

The Word of God awakens the conscience and leads us to salvation and peace in Christ. "As the sinner looks to the law, his guilt is made plain to him and pressed home to his conscience, and he is condemned. His only comfort and hope is found in looking to the cross of Calvary. As he ventures upon the promises, taking God at His word, relief and peace come to his soul. He cries, 'Lord, Thou hast promised to save all who come unto Thee in the name of Thy Son. I am a lost, helpless, hopeless soul. Lord, save, or I perish.' His faith lays hold on Christ, and he is justified before God" (*Faith and Works,* pp. 99, 100).

Knowing the truth of God is important but not enough to save us. When I attend an evangelistic meeting, my conscience may tell me "This is truth." But if I fail to respond to the promptings of God's Spirit I have not benefitted. "When the truth is held as truth only by the conscience, when the heart is not stimulated and made receptive, the truth only agitates the mind. But when the truth is received as truth by the heart, it has passed through the conscience and captivated the soul by its pure principles. It is placed in the heart by the Holy Spirit, who molds its beauty to the mind that its transforming power may be seen in the character" (*Mind, Character, and Personality,* vol. 1, p. 324).

It is very dangerous for one to trifle with the demands of conscience. Such action only leads away from God and sets a wrong example to others. This is illustrated in the area of healthful living. "The light which God has given upon health reform cannot be trifled with without injury to those who attempt it; and no man can hope to succeed in the work of God while, by precept and example, he acts in opposition to the light which God has sent. The voice of duty is the voice of God,—an inborn, heaven-sent guide,—and the Lord will not be trifled with upon these subjects. He who disregards the light which God has given in regard to the preservation of health, revolts against his own good and refuses to obey the One who is working for his best good" (*Counsels on Health,* p. 562).

Conscience Responds to the Law and the Gospel

"The law and the gospel are in perfect harmony. Each upholds the other. In all its majesty the law confronts the conscience, causing the sinner to feel his need of Christ as the propitiation for sin. The gospel recognizes the power and immutability of the law. 'I had not known sin, but by the law' (Rom. 7:7), Paul declares. The sense of sin, urged home by the law, drives the sinner to the Saviour. In his need man may present the mighty arguments furnished by the cross of Calvary. He may claim the righteousness of Christ; for it is imparted to every repentant sinner" (*God's Amazing Grace,* p. 15).

A sensitive and educated conscience seeks to know the will of God and is eager to do it. A person with such a conscience understands and appreciates the wisdom of God. They know that it is God's desire for each of us to enjoy an abundant life in obedience. "God has made known His will, and it is folly for man to question that which has gone out of His lips. After Infinite Wisdom has spoken, there can be no doubtful questions for man to settle, no wavering possibilities for him to adjust. All that is required of him is a frank, earnest concurrence in the expressed will of God. Obedience is the highest dictate of reason as well as of conscience" (*The Acts of the Apostles,* p. 506).

Just One Compromise

Satan, ever the sly one, seeks only to start men and women down the path to destruction with a simple compromise with conscience. And such a step can lead to destruction. "Our great adversary has agents that are constantly hunting for an opportunity to destroy souls, as a lion hunts his prey. . . . One safeguard removed from conscience, the indulgence of one evil habit, a single neglect of the high claims of duty, may be the beginning of a course of deception that will pass you into the ranks of those who are serving Satan, while you are all the time professing to love God and His cause. A moment of thoughtlessness, a single misstep, may turn the whole current of your lives in the wrong direction. And you may never know what caused your ruin until the sentence is pronounced, 'Depart from Me, ye that work iniquity'" (*Evangelism,* p. 681).

Sometimes our old sinful, selfish nature takes a step away from God that weakens conscience. "He who deliberately stifles his convictions of duty because it interferes with his inclinations will finally lose the power to distinguish between truth and error. The understanding becomes darkened, the conscience callous, the heart hardened, and the soul is separated from God. Where the message of divine truth is spurned or slighted, there the church will be enshrouded in darkness; faith and love grow cold, and estrangement and dissension enter. Church members center their interests and energies in worldly pursuits, and sinners become hardened in their impenitence" (*The Great Controversy,* p. 378).

Lessons From the Garden of Eden

The Bible says, "The wages of sin is death" (Romans 6:23). "Sin, however small it may be esteemed, can be persisted in only at the cost of eternal life. Adam and Eve persuaded themselves that in so small a matter as eating of the forbidden fruit there could not result such terrible consequences as God declared. But this small matter was sin, the transgression of God's immutable and holy law, and it opened the floodgates of death and untold woe upon our world" (*That I May Know Him,* p. 255). That "little" sin, that little compromise with conscience, ultimately cost the life of the Son of God!

Once the conscience has been weakened by compromise, several serious problems occur. It is much easier to violate it a second, third, and fourth time. But in addition, a compromised conscience becomes weakened and unreliable as a guide. "A conscience once violated is greatly weakened. It needs the strength of constant watchfulness and unceasing prayer. He who after hearing the truth turns from it because to accept it would retard his success in business lines turns from God and the light. He sells his soul in a cheap market. His conscience will ever be unreliable. He has made a bargain with Satan, violating his conscience, which if kept pure and upright, would have been of more value to him than the whole world. He who refuses light partakes of the fruit of disobedience, as did Adam and Eve in Eden. When you lose your conscious integrity, your soul becomes a battlefield for Satan; you have doubts and fears enough to paralyze your energies and drive you to discouragement" (*Mind, Character, and Personality,* vol. 1, p. 321).

So how does the "battlefield for Satan" created by a violated conscience manifest itself? Have you ever been rebuffed when you seriously, and after much prayer, tried to talk with someone who was involved in an obvious problem—say a bad habit or a harmful relationship? What kind of response do you typically get from such a person. Is it "Oh, thanks for being concerned for me. Would you pray with me"? Or is it more likely "Quit harassing me. This is none of your business. Stop preaching at me. I don't need any sermons. Quit judging me. What I am doing is no worse that what many others in the church are doing"? Why is this a frequent response? This statement gives an answer: "The same spirit that prompted rebellion in heaven still inspires rebellion on earth. Satan has continued with men the same policy which he pursued with the angels. His spirit now reigns in the children of disobedience. Like him they seek to break down the restraints of the law of God and promise men liberty through transgression of its precepts. Reproof of sin still arouses the spirit of hatred and resistance. When God's messages of warning are brought home to the conscience, Satan leads men to justify themselves and to seek the sympathy of others in their course of sin. Instead of correcting their errors, they excite indignation against the reprover, as if he were the sole cause of difficulty. From the days of righteous Abel to our own time such is the spirit which has been displayed toward those who dare to condemn sin" (*The Great Controversy,* p. 500).

The Power and Influence of One Sin

When commenting on Matthew 6:24, "No man can serve two masters," Ellen White gave this interesting analysis: "The strongest bulwark of vice in our world is not iniquitous life of the abandoned sinner or the degraded outcast; it is that life which otherwise appears virtuous, honorable, and noble, but in which one sin is fostered, one vice indulged. To the soul that is struggling in secret against some giant temptation, trembling upon the very verge of the precipice, such an example is one of the most powerful enticements to sin. He who, endowed with high conceptions of life and truth and honor, does yet willfully transgress one precept of God's holy law, has perverted his noble gifts into a lure to sin. Genius, talent, sympathy, even generous and kindly deeds, may become decoys of Satan to entice other souls over the precipice of ruin for this life and the life to come" (*Thoughts From the Mount of Blessing,* pp. 94, 95).

Satan knows that time is short, and he intensifies his work of deception. If he can get us to rationalize that a single "little" sin is not going to hurt us, he can start us down a road that is really the wrong direction—the broad road that leads to destruction. "One safeguard removed from conscience, the indulgence of one evil habit, a single neglect of the high claims of duty, may be the beginning of a course of deception that will pass you into the ranks of those who are serving Satan, while you are all the time professing to love God and His cause. A moment of thoughtlessness, a single misstep, may turn the whole current of your lives in the wrong direction. And you may never know what caused your ruin until the sentence is pronounced: 'Depart from Me, ye that work iniquity'" (*Testimonies for the Church,* vol. 5, p. 397).

Conscience and Christian Lifestyle

Ellen White uses two areas of Christian lifestyle to illustrate the effects of a weakened conscience. They are the areas of healthful living and stewardship. Let's be honest, most of us know much more about the benefits of a healthful lifestyle and the biblical principles of stewardship than we practice. For example, only about half of Adventist Christians are faithful in returning the tithe to God. Why don't those nontithers feel convicted to return their tithe? It seems that they can just go on year after year and apparently have no qualms about shirking this "obvious duty." The bottom line is simple. They have violated conscience to the point that it no longer bothers them. Ellen White once described a man whose "conscience has been seared, blackened, and crisped with selfishness and sin" (*Testimonies for the Church,* vol. 2, p. 305). It is like the progressive degeneration of toast kept too long in the toaster. It goes from bread to warm bread, to light toast, to dark toast, to burned toast, to charcoal! It is quite likely that at the charcoal stage a person is no longer susceptible to the voice of God through the Holy Spirit.

The Stewardship Connection

We are told, "There must be an awakening among us as a people upon this matter. There are but few men who feel conscience stricken if they neglect their duty in beneficence. But few feel remorseful of soul because they are daily robbing God. If a Christian deliberately or accidentally underpays his neighbor, or refuses to cancel an honest debt, his conscience, unless seared, will trouble him; he cannot rest although no one may know but himself. There are many neglected vows and unpaid pledges, and yet how few trouble their minds over the matter; how few feel the guilt of this violation of duty.

"We must have new and deeper convictions on this subject. The conscience must be aroused, and the matter receive earnest attention; for an account must be rendered to God in the last day, and His claims must be settled" (*Counsels on Stewardship,* p. 319).

The fact that my conscience doesn't bother me when I rob God doesn't lessen the robbery. In fact, in actual, measurable ways, it can be demonstrated that the more God blesses—the better the economy—the more selfish people become. "The world is robbing God upon the wholesale plan. The more He imparts of wealth, the more thoroughly do men claim it as their own, to be used as they shall please. But shall the professed followers of Christ follow the customs of the world? <u>Shall we forfeit peace of conscience, communion with God, and fellowship with our brethren, because we fail to devote to His cause the portion He has claimed as His own?"</u> (*ibid.,* p. 78). It is not just the above statement that proves the point. Actual studies done regarding our own church shows a 53 percent drop in the percentage of income given to the church over the past 15 years! This is in spite of the fact that we have enjoyed major economic growth and have much more discretionary income than at any time in our history.

So what should we do about this lapse of duty and searing of conscience? We are told, "All should regard this matter in the right light. Let no one, when brought into a strait place, take money consecrated to religious purposes, and use it for his advantage, soothing his conscience by saying that he will repay it at some future time. Far better cut down the expenses to correspond with the income, to restrict the wants, and live within the means, than to use the Lord's money for secular purposes" (*ibid.,* p. 79).

The Conscience and Healthful Living

Many today live as if we had never been given a health message. Why? And why is the health message so important? We are told that we should guard well the avenues of the soul (see *The Adventist Home,* p. 401). These avenues are our senses, that are served by our mental and physical capacities. It stands to reason that if these powers are preserved in the best possible condition, we can more effectively ward off the devil's attacks. "Satan sees that he cannot have so great power over minds when the appetite is kept under control as when it is indulged, and he is constantly working to lead men to indulgence. <u>Under the influence of unhealthful food, the conscience becomes stupefied,</u> the mind is darkened, and its susceptibility to impressions is impaired. <u>But the guilt of the transgressor is not lessened because the conscience has been violated till it has become insensible"</u> (*Counsels on Diet and Foods,* p. 247).

Health, Conscience, and End Times

The readers of my previous books know that I believe and teach that we are indeed living in end times. In fact, I believe that every day that passes confirms the validity of the Adventist interpretation of prophecy. Jesus is coming soon! The end of all things is at hand! This being the case, leaders and individual Christians should recognize the value of following God's counsel.

"Our ministers should become intelligent upon this question. They should not ignore it, nor be turned aside by those who call them extremists. Let them find out what constitutes true health reform, and teach its principles, both by precept and by a quiet, consistent example. At our large gatherings, instruction should be given upon health and temperance. Seek to arouse the intellect and the conscience. Bring into service all the talent at command, and follow up the work with publications upon the subject. "Educate, educate, educate," is the message that has been impressed upon me. As we near the close of time, we must rise higher and still higher upon the question of health reform and Christian temperance, presenting it in a more positive and decided manner. We must strive continually to educate the people, not only by our words, but by our practice. Precept and practice combined have a telling influence" (*ibid.*, p. 451).

In sharing our message with others the topic of healthful living should be a part of the education of the conscience. "The matter of presenting true principles of health and temperance must not be passed over as unessential; for nearly every family needs to be instructed on this point. Nearly every person needs to have his conscience aroused to become a doer of the Word of God, practicing self-denial, and abstaining from the unlawful indulgence of appetite. When you make the people intelligent concerning the principles of health reform you do much to prepare the way for the introduction of present truth. Said my Guide, 'Educate, educate, educate.' The mind must be enlightened, for the understanding of the people is darkened. Satan can find access to the soul through perverted appetite, to debase and destroy it.

"The principles of health reform are found in the Word of God. The gospel of health is to be firmly linked with the ministry of the Word. It is the Lord's design that the restoring influence of health reform shall be a part of the last great effort to proclaim the gospel message" (*Evangelism,* p. 515).

Hope for Weakened Conscience

Unless the conscience is actually "fried to a crisp," there is hope that right action can restore it to its rightful place as a sensitive guide. Note these words of hope: "Your conscience has been abused, and has become hardened, but if you will follow the right course, renewed sensitiveness will come to it" (*Mind, Character, and Personality,* vol. 1, p. 323). We are counseled to restore conscience by study of the Word of God and by praying for the guidance of the Holy Spirit. "It is not enough for a man to think himself safe in following the dictates of his conscience. . . . The question to be settled is, Is the conscience in harmony with the Word of God? If not, it cannot safely be followed, for it will deceive. <u>The conscience must be enlightened by God. Time must be given to a study of the Scriptures and to prayer.</u> Thus the mind will be established, strengthened, and settled" (*ibid.,* p. 324).

Not sure what condition your conscience is in? Try this test. "Take your conscience to the Word of God and see if your life and character are in accordance with the standard of righteousness which God has there revealed. You can then determine whether or not you have an intelligent faith and what manner of conscience is yours. The conscience of man cannot be trusted unless it is under the influence of divine grace. Satan takes advantage of an unenlightened conscience, and thereby leads men into all manner of delusions, because they have not made the Word of God their counselor. Many have invented a gospel of their own in the same manner as they have substituted a law of their own for God's law" (*ibid.,* p. 323).

The results of studying the Word of God go way beyond any expectations. This interesting statement shares the consequences:

"The Holy Spirit has been given us as an aid in the study of the Bible. Jesus promised, 'The Comforter, which is the Holy Ghost, whom the Father will send in My name, He shall teach you all things, and bring all things to your remembrance, whatsoever I have said unto you.' John 14:26. <u>When the Bible is made the study book, with earnest supplication for the Spirit's guidance, and with a full surrender of the heart to be sanctified through the truth, all that Christ has promised will be accomplished.</u> The result of such Bible study will be

- well-balanced minds.
- The understanding will be quickened,
- the sensibilities aroused.
- The conscience will become sensitive;
- the sympathies and sentiments will be purified;
- a better moral atmosphere will be created;
- and new power to resist temptation will be imparted.
- Teachers and students will become active and earnest in the work of God"

(*Counsels to Parents, Teachers, and Students,* p. 357).

What an awesome transformation! When we study God's Word with the aid of the Holy Spirit, in addition to our consciences becoming more sensitive seven other major changes will occur in our lives! This is good news!

Another very positive statement proclaims, "Yield yourself to Christ without delay; He alone, by the power of His grace, can redeem you from ruin. He alone can bring your moral and mental powers into a state of health. Your heart may be warm with the love of God; your understanding, clear and mature; your conscience, illuminated, quick, and pure; your will, upright and sanctified, subject to the control of the Spirit of God. You can make yourself what you choose. If you will now face rightabout, cease to do evil and learn to do well, then you will be happy indeed; you will be successful in the battles of life, and rise to glory and honor in the better life than this" (*The Faith I Live By,* p. 133).

The Value of the Word

King David explains how to come back to God and how to stay with God.

"How can a young man cleanse his way?
By taking heed according to Your word.
"Your word I have hidden in my heart,
That I might not sin against You" (Psalm 119:9, 11).

When we do the work of evangelism people are impressed by our example of kindness, integrity, and love as well as the fact that we uphold the Bible as our standard of faith and practice. "Our work is to win men to belief of the truth, win by preaching and by example also, by living godly lives. The truth in all its bearings is to be acted, showing the consistency of faith with practice. The value of our faith will be shown by its fruit. The Lord can and will impress men by our intense earnestness. Our dress, our deportment, our conversation and the depth of a growing experience in spiritual lines, all are to show that the great principles of truth we are handling are a reality to us. Thus the truth is to be made impressive as a great whole and command the intellect. Truth, Bible truth, is to become the authority for the conscience and the love and life of the soul" (*Evangelism,* p. 542).

In addressing young people, Ellen White made this appeal: "Youth, in the name of Jesus I appeal to you whom I shall soon meet around the throne of God, Study your Bible. It will prove to you not only the pillar of cloud by day but the pillar of fire by night. It opens before you a path leading up and still upward, bidding you go forward. The Bible—you do not know its worth! It is a book for the mind, for the heart, for the conscience, the will, and the life. It is the message of God to you, in such simple style that it meets the comprehension of a little child. The Bible—precious Book!" (*The Faith I Live By,* p. 20).

A Wounded Conscience

Trying to be a Christian and still live like the world causes untold grief to many. A major change in life will come when we understand the value of a clear conscience and the many rewards of accepting the promises of God. "There are many whose hearts are aching under a load of care because they seek to reach the world's standard. They have chosen its service, accepted its perplexities, adopted its customs. Thus their character is marred, and their life made a weariness. In order to gratify ambition and worldly desires, they wound the conscience, and bring upon themselves an additional burden of remorse. The continual worry is wearing out the life forces. Our Lord desires them to lay aside this yoke of bondage. He invites them to accept His yoke; He says, 'My yoke is easy, and My burden is light.' He bids them seek first the kingdom of God and His righteousness, and His promise is that all things needful to them for this life shall be added. Worry is blind, and cannot discern the future; but Jesus sees the end from the beginning. In every difficulty He has His way prepared to bring relief. Our heavenly Father has a thousand ways to provide for us, of which we know nothing. Those who accept the one principle of making the service and honor of God supreme will find perplexities vanish, and a plain path before their feet" (*The Desire of Ages,* p. 330).

Just as a disregard of the laws of health can lead to a weakened conscience, following the health laws strengthens the conscience. "Health is an inestimable blessing and one more closely related to conscience and religion than many realize" (*Counsels to Parents, Teachers, and Students,* p. 294). "That time is well spent which is directed to the establishment and preservation of sound physical and mental health. Firm, quiet nerves and a healthy circulation help men to follow right principles and to listen to the promptings of conscience" (*ibid.,* p. 298).

"We should educate ourselves, not only to live in harmony with the laws of health, but to teach others the better way. . . . The conscience must be aroused to the duty of practicing the principles of true reform. God requires that His people shall be temperate in all things. Unless they practice true temperance, they will not, they cannot, be susceptible to the sanctifying influence of the truth" (*Counsels on Diet and Foods,* p. 451).

Transforming Power

It is important to teach the truth and to understand the truth, but real transformation comes only when we allow the Holy Spirit to make application to the life. "The preaching of the word will be of no avail without the continual presence and aid of the Holy Spirit. This is the only effectual teacher of divine truth. Only when the truth is accompanied to the heart by the Spirit will it quicken the conscience or transform the life. One might be able to present the letter of the word of God, he might be familiar with all its commands and promises; but unless the Holy Spirit sets home the truth, no souls will fall on the Rock and be broken. No amount of education, no advantages, however great, can make one a channel of light without the co-operation of the Spirit of God. The sowing of the gospel seed will not be a success unless the seed is quickened into life by the dew of heaven. Before one book of the New Testament was written, before one gospel sermon had been preached after Christ's ascension, the Holy Spirit came upon the praying apostles. Then the testimony of their enemies was, 'Ye have filled Jerusalem with your doctrine.' Acts 5:28" (*The Desire of Ages,* p. 671).

And when the Spirit is urging truth during the study of God's Word there is a desire to be obedient. "Whenever one renounces sin, which is the transgression of the law, his life will be brought into conformity to the law, into perfect obedience. This is the work of the Holy Spirit. The light of the Word carefully studied, the voice of conscience, the strivings of the Spirit, produce in the heart genuine love for Christ, who gave Himself a whole sacrifice to redeem the whole person, body, soul, and spirit. And love is manifested in obedience" (*Evangelism,* p. 308).

CHAPTER 6

The Violation of Conscience

In the battle of the spirits—the great controversy—nothing is of more value, from a human perspective, and calculated to bring more protection to the soul than an educated conscience. And there is no greater detriment to soul salvation than a violated conscience.

Many of our favorite Bible characters were men of conscience. Christian consistency marked the actions of Daniel and Joseph. Daniel would have sacrificed his position in the court of the king and maybe even life itself in order to uphold principles of health and maintain his body temple. He was so committed to his relationship with God that he was willing to be thrown to the lions rather than compromise his religious practices and violate his conscience.

Joseph's answer to the enticements of a beautiful woman reveals the power of religious principle. He would not betray the confidence of his earthly master and, whatever the consequences, he would be true to his Master in heaven. Under the inspecting eye of God and holy angels many do what they would not dare in the presence of their fellow men, but Joseph's first thought was of God. "How can I do this great wickedness, and sin against God?" he said.

What made these men such faithful followers? They had decided (Daniel "purposed" in his heart) that they would not violate conscience. Understanding and following the will of God was their top priority. They had accepted God's promise to direct them. "Your ears shall hear a word behind you, saying, 'This is the way, walk in it.' Whenever you turn to the right hand or whenever you turn to the left" (Isaiah 30:21).

"Daniel and his companions had a conscience void of offense toward God. But this is not preserved without a struggle. What a test was brought on the three associates of Daniel when they were required to worship the great image set up by King Nebuchadnezzar in the plains of Dura! Their principles forbade them to pay homage to the idol, for it was a rival to the God of heaven. They knew that they owed to God every faculty they possessed, and while their hearts were full of generous sympathy toward all men, they had a lofty aspiration to prove themselves entirely loyal to their God" (*In Heavenly Places*, p. 149).

Conscience and the Crucifixion

The events surrounding the crucifixion of Christ demonstrate the actions of conscience and the consequences in the lives of men.

Peter, the disciple who had promised to go with Jesus to prison and to death had a bout with conscience. Peter denied Jesus. Then he saw the Saviour. Their eyes met, and all was revealed. Jesus' face was pale and revealed His suffering, yet He looked on Peter with compassion and forgiveness. This pierced Peter's heart like an arrow. His conscience was aroused. He rushed from the scene and out into the darkness. Confused and bewildered, he at last found himself in the Garden of Gethsemane. In bitter remorse he remembered how Jesus had suffered there just a few hours before, while he and the other disciples had slept. Peter had declared in the judgment hall that he didn't know Jesus, but now he realized how well Jesus knew him. He remembered the words of Jesus: "But I have prayed for thee, that thy faith fail not" (Luke 22:32). Peter then sought forgiveness.

What a contrast with the story of Judas! When Jesus saw Judas leading the crowd into the garden that night, "Jesus said to him, 'Friend, wherefore art thou come?' His voice trembled with sorrow as He added, 'Judas, betrayest thou the Son of man with a kiss?' This appeal should have aroused the conscience of the betrayer, and touched his stubborn heart; but honor, fidelity, and human tenderness had forsaken him. He stood bold and defiant, showing no disposition to relent. He had given himself up to Satan, and he had no power to resist him" (*The Desire of Ages*, p. 696).

The devil encourages us to violate our conscience, but when that road leads to despair, he abandons us to our shame and guilt. Ellen White describes this in the final words of Judas. "As the trial drew to a close, Judas could endure the torture of his guilty conscience no longer. Suddenly a hoarse voice rang through the hall, sending a thrill of terror to all hearts: 'He is innocent; spare Him, O Caiaphas!' The tall form of Judas was now seen pressing through the startled throng. His face was pale and haggard, and great drops of sweat stood on his forehead. Rushing to the throne of judgment, he threw down before the high priest the pieces of silver that had been the price of his Lord's betrayal. Eagerly grasping the robe of Caiaphas, he implored him to release Jesus, declaring that He had done nothing worthy of death. Caiaphas angrily shook him off, but was confused, and knew not what to say. The perfidy of the priests was revealed. It was evident that they had bribed the disciple to betray his Master.

"'I have sinned,' again cried Judas, 'in that I have betrayed the innocent blood.' But the high priest, regaining his self-possession, answered with scorn, 'What is that to us? see thou to that.' Matt. 27:4. The priests had been willing to make Judas their tool; but they despised his baseness. When he turned to them with confession, they spurned him.

"Judas now cast himself at the feet of Jesus, acknowledging Him to be the Son of God, and entreating Him to deliver Himself. The Saviour did not reproach His betrayer. He knew that Judas did not repent; his confession was forced from his guilty soul by an awful sense of condemnation and a looking for of judgment, but he felt no deep, heartbreaking grief that he had betrayed the spotless Son of God, and denied the Holy One of Israel. Yet Jesus spoke no word of condemnation. He looked pityingly upon Judas, and said, For this hour came I into the world.

"A murmur of surprise ran through the assembly. With amazement they beheld the forbearance of Christ toward His betrayer. Again there swept over them the conviction that this Man was more than mortal. But if He was the Son of God, they questioned, why did He not free Himself from His bonds and triumph over His accusers?

"Judas saw that his entreaties were in vain, and he rushed from the hall exclaiming, It is too late! It is too late! He felt that he could not live to see Jesus crucified, and in despair went out and hanged himself" (*ibid.,* p. 722).

The lives of the disciples John and Judas are contrasted in *The Acts of the Apostles:* "In striking contrast to the sanctification worked out in the life of John is the experience of his fellow disciple, Judas. Like his associate, Judas professed to be a disciple of Christ, but he possessed only a form of godliness. He was not insensible to the beauty of the character of Christ; and often, as he listened to the Saviour's words, conviction came to him, but he would not humble his heart or confess his sins. By resisting the divine influence he dishonored the Master whom he professed to love. John warred earnestly against his faults; but Judas violated his conscience and yielded to temptation, fastening upon himself more securely his habits of evil. The practice of the truths that Christ taught was at variance with his desires and purposes, and he could not bring himself to yield his ideas in order to receive wisdom from heaven. Instead of walking in the light, he chose to walk in darkness. Evil desires, covetousness, revengeful passions, dark and sullen thoughts, were cherished until Satan gained full control of him.

"John and Judas are representatives of those who profess to be Christ's followers. Both these disciples had the same opportunities to study and follow the divine Pattern. Both were closely associated with Jesus and were privileged to listen to His teaching. Each possessed serious defects of character; and each had access to the divine grace that transforms character. But while one in humility was learning of Jesus, the other revealed that he was not a doer of the word, but a hearer only. One, daily dying to self and overcoming sin, was sanctified through the truth; the other, resisting the transforming power of grace and indulging selfish desires, was brought into bondage to Satan.

"Such transformation of character as is seen in the life of John is ever the result of communion with Christ. There may be marked defects in the character of an individual, yet when he becomes a true disciple of Christ, the power of divine grace transforms and sanctifies him. Beholding as in a glass the glory of the Lord, he is changed from glory to glory, until he is like Him whom he adores" (*The Acts of the Apostles,* pp. 558, 559).

Four paragraphs of the amazing chapter "Transformed by Grace" explain what it means to follow the dictates of an enlightened conscience and become transformed by the grace of God. "True sanctification comes through the working out of the principle of love. 'God is love; and he that dwelleth in love dwelleth in God, and God in him.' 1 John 4:16. The life of him in whose heart Christ abides, will reveal practical godliness. The character will be purified, elevated, ennobled, and glorified. Pure doctrine will blend with works of righteousness; heavenly precepts will mingle with holy practices.

"Those who would gain the blessing of sanctification must first learn the meaning of self-sacrifice. The cross of Christ is the central pillar on which hangs the 'far more exceeding and eternal weight of glory.' 'If any man will come after Me,' Christ says, 'let him deny himself, and take up his cross, and follow Me.' 2 Corinthians 4:17; Matthew 16:24. It is the fragrance of our love for our fellow men that reveals our love for God. It is patience in service that brings rest to the soul. It is through humble, diligent, faithful toil that the welfare of Israel is promoted. God upholds and strengthens the one who is willing to follow in Christ's way.

"Sanctification is not the work of a moment, an hour, a day, but of a lifetime. It is not gained by a happy flight of feeling, but is the result of constantly dying to sin, and constantly living for Christ. Wrongs cannot be righted nor reformations wrought in the character by feeble, intermittent efforts. It is only by long, persevering effort, sore discipline, and stern conflict, that we shall overcome. We know not one day how strong will be our conflict the next. So long as Satan reigns, we shall have self to subdue, besetting sins to overcome; so long as life shall last, there will be no stopping place, no point which we can reach and say, I have fully attained. Sanctification is the result of lifelong obedience.

"None of the apostles and prophets ever claimed to be without sin. Men who have lived the nearest to God, men who would sacrifice life itself rather than knowingly commit a wrong act, men whom God has honored with divine light and power, have confessed the sinfulness of their nature. They have put no confidence in the flesh, have claimed no righteousness of their own, but have trusted wholly in the righteousness of Christ" (*ibid.,* pp. 560, 561).

Governor Pilate

During the trial of Jesus, Pilate, the Roman governor, declared, "I find no fault in Him at all" (see John 18, 19). "If at the first Pilate had stood firm, refusing to condemn a man whom he found guiltless, he would have broken the fatal chain that was to bind him in remorse and guilt as long as he lived. Had he carried out his convictions of right, the Jews would not have presumed to dictate to him. Christ would have been put to death, but the guilt would not have rested upon Pilate. But Pilate had taken step after step in the violation of his conscience. He had excused himself from judging with justice and equity, and he now found himself almost helpless in the hands of the priests and rulers. His wavering and indecision proved his ruin" (*The Desire of Ages,* p. 731).

"Pilate longed to deliver Jesus. But he saw that he could not do this, and yet retain his own position and honor. Rather than lose his worldly power, he chose to sacrifice an innocent life. How many, to escape loss or suffering, in like manner sacrifice principle. Conscience and duty point one way, and self-interest points another. The current sets strongly in the wrong direction, and he who compromises with evil is swept away into the thick darkness of guilt" (*ibid.*, p. 738).

Herod

We are told that intemperance had led Herod down the road of compromised conscience. He actually admired John the Baptist, and was convinced that he was a man of God. Because of John's influence he began to make changes in his life. We are told, "In many things Herod had reformed his dissolute life. But the use of luxurious food and stimulating drinks was constantly enervating and deadening the moral as well as the physical powers, and warring against the earnest appeals of the Spirit of God, which had struck conviction to the heart of Herod, arousing his conscience to put away his sins. Herodias was acquainted with the weak points in the character of Herod. She knew that under ordinary circumstances, while his intelligence controlled him, she could not obtain the death of John" (*Temperance*, p. 49). So she prepared a great birthday celebration for Herod. It was an occasion of gluttony and intoxication. Then she arranged for her beautiful daughter, Salome, to dance before the king and his friends. With Herod's resistence down, she was able to order the head of John on a platter.

There can be no pain like that of a guilty conscience—Judas discovered that. And so Herod could find no rest after the death of John. He was oppressed with the fear that a curse was upon him. Many of the things that he had heard from the lips of John now spoke to his conscience. When Herod later heard of the works of Christ he thought that John was raised from the dead and sent forth to condemn him. "Herod was reaping that which God had declared to be the result of a course of sin,—'a trembling heart, and failing of eyes, and sorrow of mind: and thy life shall hang in doubt before thee; and thou shalt fear day and night, and shalt have none assurance of thy life: in the morning thou shalt say, Would God it were even! and at even thou shalt say, Would God it were morning! for the fear of thine heart wherewith thou shalt fear, and for the sight of thine eyes which thou shalt see.' Deut. 28:65-67. The sinner's own thoughts are his accusers; and there can be no torture keener than the stings of a guilty conscience, which give him no rest day nor night" (*The Desire of Ages*, p. 223).

But wait, we are not through with Herod. His downward spiral took him even lower. About three years later when Jesus was brought before him his conscience was gone—not just seared—it was crisp like charcoal!

We have this report of that occasion: "Herod's conscience was now far less sensitive than when he had trembled with horror at the request of Herodias for the head of John the Baptist. For a time he had felt the keen stings of remorse for his terrible act; but his moral perceptions had become more and more degraded by his licentious life. Now his heart had become so hardened that he could even boast of the punishment he had inflicted upon John for daring to reprove him. And he now threatened Jesus, declaring repeatedly that he had power to release or to condemn Him. But no sign from Jesus gave evidence that He heard a word" (*ibid.*, p. 730).

Herod was angry that Jesus would not speak to him. He asked for Jesus to work a miracle. But since he had rejected the greatest of the prophets, Jesus had no further words for him. For as Jesus had earlier told the Pharisees, some would not believe though one was raised from the dead (see Luke 16:30, 31). Herod had committed the unpardonable sin. There was no hope for him!

John Huss

John Huss suffered a martyr's death. His mock trial, the violation of his "safe conduct," and his mistreatment and murder contrasted with his steadfastness and integrity. His last appearance before the council is remembered this way: "For the last time, Huss was brought before the council. It was a vast and brilliant assembly—the emperor, the princes of the empire, the royal deputies, the cardinals, bishops, and priests, and an immense crowd who had come as spectators of the events of the day. From all parts of Christendom had been gathered the witnesses of this first great sacrifice in the long struggle by which liberty of conscience was to be secured.

"Being called upon for his final decision, Huss declared his refusal to abjure, and, fixing his penetrating glance upon the monarch whose plighted word had been so shamelessly violated, he declared: 'I determined, of my own free will, to appear before this council, under the public protection and faith of the emperor here present.'—Bonnechose, vol. 2, p. 84. A deep flush crimsoned the face of Sigismund as the eyes of all in the assembly turned upon him" (*The Great Controversy*, p. 108). Then followed terrible humiliation and ignominious death. The world was not worthy of this remarkable man.

Martin Luther

Over a century later, as the Reformation began, Martin Luther was called before the "Diet at Worms." He was asked to retract his written documents and recant his statements about righteousness by faith. His response was indicative of an enlightened conscience. "Luther had spoken in German; he was now requested to repeat the same words in Latin. Though exhausted by the previous effort, he complied, and again delivered his speech, with the same clearness and energy as at the first. God's providence directed in this matter. The minds of many of the princes were so blinded by error and superstition that at the first delivery they did not see the force of Luther's reasoning; but the repetition enabled them to perceive clearly the points presented.

"Those who stubbornly closed their eyes to the light, and determined not to be convinced of the truth, were enraged at the power of Luther's words. As he ceased speaking, the spokesman of the Diet said angrily: 'You have not answered the question put to you. . . . You are required to give a clear and precise answer. . . . Will you, or will you not, retract?'

"The Reformer answered: 'Since your most serene majesty and your high mightinesses require from me a clear, simple, and precise answer, I will give you one, and it is this: I cannot submit my faith either to the pope or to the councils, because it is clear as the day that they have frequently erred and contradicted each other. Unless therefore I am convinced by the testimony of Scripture or by the clearest reasoning, unless I am persuaded by means of the passages I have quoted, and unless they thus render my conscience bound by the word of God, I cannot and I will not retract, for it is unsafe for a Christian to speak against his conscience. Here I stand, I can do no other; may God help me. Amen'" (*The Great Controversy,* pp. 159, 160).

When Luther spoke the entire assembly was speechless with amazement. He was later visited in his room by princes, counts, barons, and other dignitaries. "The people gazed upon him as if he were more than human. Even those who had no faith in his doctrines could not but admire that lofty integrity which led him to brave death rather than violate his conscience" (*ibid.,* p. 165). What a giant of commitment and conscience! One wonders how many today would be willing to die for the dictates of conscience.

Luther Not Martyred

"God had provided a way of escape for His servant in this hour of peril. A vigilant eye had followed Luther's movements, and a true and noble heart had resolved upon his rescue. It was plain that Rome would be satisfied with nothing short of his death; only by concealment could he be preserved from the jaws of the lion. God gave wisdom to Frederick of Saxony to devise a plan for the Reformer's preservation. With the co-operation of true friends the elector's purpose was carried out, and Luther was effectually hidden from friends and foes. Upon his homeward journey he was seized, separated from his attendants, and hurriedly conveyed through the forest to the castle of Wartburg, an isolated mountain fortress. Both his seizure and his concealment were so involved in mystery that even Frederick himself for a long time knew not whither he had been conducted. This ignorance was not without design; so long as the elector knew nothing of Luther's whereabouts, he could reveal nothing. He satisfied himself that the Reformer was safe, and with this knowledge he was content" (*ibid.,* p. 168).

Luther spent nearly a year in a friendly exile in the Wartburg castle/fortress. During that time he wrote many tracts and translated the New Testament into the German language.

Easy to Rationalize

When we are brought to a choice between duty and inclination, it is all too easy to rationalize and attempt to minimize the danger of violating conscience. Do any of these thought processes sound familiar?

"I know I should be tithing, but . . ." (I can't afford to. I am in debt. The church misuses the money. The church has apostatized. I am supporting what I believe is best, etc., etc.).

"I know I shouldn't be watching this, but . . ." (I'm an adult and it won't hurt me. I can handle a little cursing and nudity. I am in the privacy of my home and not a bad influence on anyone, etc., etc.).

"I know I shouldn't be eating this, but . . ." (A little bit won't hurt me. God knows my heart is right. It's hard to eat right when you are traveling, etc., etc.).

Such rationalization is really an attempt to quiet conscience. We are arguing with the Holy Spirit. This is starting down the road to the unpardonable sin!

Accordingly, we are told, "Do not excuse yourself in any error. If you have one objectionable trait, which you find it difficult to subdue, do not talk of your weakness as something that others must bear with. Do not soothe your conscience with the thought that you cannot overcome the peculiarities that deform your character, nor listen to Satan's suggestion that they are not very grievous. There is no way by which you may be saved in sin. Every soul that gains eternal life must be like Christ, 'holy, harmless, undefiled, separate from sinners.' [HEB. 7:26.] The followers of Christ must shine as lights in the midst of a crooked and perverse generation" (*Gospel Workers,* 1892, p. 445).

A Conscience of Your Own

We can share information with people, but unless they are willing to study for themselves and submit to the working of the Holy Spirit, we are just wasting our time. Take the area of modesty in dress, for example. "If we are Christians, we shall follow Christ, even though the path in which we are to walk cuts right across our natural inclinations. There is no use in telling you that you must not wear this or that, for if the love of these vain things is in your heart, your laying off your adornments will only be like cutting the foliage off a tree. The inclinations of the natural heart would again assert themselves. You must have a conscience of your own" (*Child Guidance,* p. 429).

"The fear of the Lord is the beginning of wisdom. Those who overcome as Christ overcame will need to constantly guard themselves against the temptations of Satan. The appetite and passions should be restricted and under the control of enlightened conscience, that the intellect may be unimpaired, the perceptive powers clear, so that the workings of Satan and his snares may not be interpreted to be the providence of God. Many desire the final reward and victory which are to be given to overcomers, but are not willing to endure toil, privation, and denial of self, as did their Redeemer. It is only through obedience and continual effort that we shall overcome as Christ overcame.

"The controlling power of appetite will prove the ruin of thousands, when, if they had conquered on this point, they would have had moral power to gain the victory over every other temptation of Satan. But those who are slaves to appetite will fail in perfecting Christian character. The continual transgression of man for six thousand years has brought sickness, pain, and death as its fruits. And as we near the close of time, Satan's temptation to indulge appetite will be more powerful and more difficult to overcome" (*Counsels on Health,* p. 574).

Resisting the Spirit's pleading prepares the way for a second resistance. The heart becomes hardened and the conscience seared. "On the other hand, every resistance of temptation makes resistance more easy. Every denial of self makes self-denial easier. Every victory gained prepares the way for a fresh victory. Each resistance of temptation, each self-denial, each triumph over sin, is a seed sown unto eternal life. Every unselfish action gives new strength to spirituality. No one can try to be like Christ without growing more noble and more true" (*Lift Him Up,* p. 299).

Getting Things Right Someday

I've heard people say that it is premature to get excited about the second coming of Christ. They say that we are a long way from the Second Coming. When the Sunday Law comes, they say, then we will really be at the end—then they will become more involved and, in essence, "get right with God." But will they? History clearly indicates that it just won't happen that way. In Matthew 24 and Luke 17 we are told that as it was in the days of Noah, so it will be in the days when the Son of Man comes. "The period of their probation was about to expire. Noah had faithfully followed the instructions which he had received from God. The ark was finished in every part as the Lord had directed, and was stored with food for man and beast. And now the servant of God made his last solemn appeal to the people. With an agony of desire that words cannot express, he entreated them to seek a refuge while it might be found. Again they rejected his words, and raised their voices in jest and scoffing. Suddenly a silence fell upon the mocking throng. Beasts of every description, the fiercest as well as the most gentle, were seen coming from mountain and forest and quietly making their way toward the ark. A noise as of a rushing wind was heard, and lo, birds were flocking from all directions, their numbers darkening the heavens, and in perfect order they passed to the ark. Animals obeyed the command of God, while men were disobedient. Guided by holy angels, they 'went in two and two unto Noah into the ark,' and the clean beasts by sevens. The world looked on in wonder, some in fear. Philosophers were called upon to account for the singular occurrence, but in vain. It was a mystery which they could not fathom. But men had become so hardened by their persistent rejection of light that even this scene produced but a momentary impression. As the doomed race beheld the sun shining in its glory, and the earth clad in almost Eden beauty, they banished their rising fears by boisterous merriment, and by their deeds of violence they seemed to invite upon themselves the visitation of the already awakened wrath of God" (*Patriarchs and Prophets,* p. 97).

In spite of this obviously supernatural event <u>not even one person changed his mind and joined Noah in the ark.</u> If we have put off making a decision to follow God we might not be able to make it later, even in the presence of supernatural events. Now is the time to be counted on God's side.

"The greatest want of the world is the want of men—men who will not be bought or sold, men who in their inmost souls are true and honest, men who do not fear to call sin by its right name, men whose conscience is as true to duty as the needle to the pole, men who will stand for the right though the heavens fall.

"But such a character is not the result of accident; it is not due to special favors or endowments of Providence. A noble character is the result of self-discipline, of the subjection of the lower to the higher nature—the surrender of self for the service of love to God and man" (*Education,* p. 57).

Conscience is indispensable to our salvation. Pray for an enlightened conscience and the power from God to follow its promptings.

CHAPTER 7

The Unpardonable Sin

God's gracious act of forgiveness is our only hope for eternal life. We are totally dependent on Christ for our salvation and the forgiveness of our sins. And yet there is a sin that God will not, cannot, forgive. It has been called the unpardonable sin. If there is indeed a sin that God will not forgive, then it is the most serious sin and should be avoided all cost.

Just what is this sin that God will not forgive? We are living in a time of great evil. We hear daily of such atrocities as gang rapes, multiple murders, parents killing their children, children killing their parents—the list could go on and on. Just how gross does sin have to be for God to refuse to forgive it? We know, for example, that God will forgive murder. King David was forgiven as he repented of murdering Uriah. But would God forgive a multiple murderer? What if he killed 168 people, as in the case of Timothy McVeigh? And what about Hitler murdering 6 million Jews?

The Bible says, "Therefore He is also able to save to the uttermost those who come to God through Him, since He ever lives to make intercession for them" (Hebrews 7:25). God says that He will forgive "to the uttermost" if we come to Him through Jesus, because Jesus lives to make intercession for us. But perhaps part of the answer to our questions about the unpardonable sin is answered in this verse. If God is able to forgive any sin that we bring through Jesus, maybe the sin He can't forgive is one we fail to bring to Him through Jesus.

The Biblical Description
When God told Noah of His plan to destroy the earth, He said, "My Spirit will not always strive with man." Genesis 6:3. In appealing to Israel in the time of King David, God said, "Harden not your heart, as in the

provocation, [and] as [in] the day of temptation in the wilderness: When your fathers tempted me, proved me, and saw my work. Forty years long was I grieved with [this] generation, and said, It [is] a people that do err in their heart, and they have not known my ways: Unto whom I sware in my wrath that they should not enter into my rest." Psalm 95:8-11. Notwithstanding this urgent appeal God later reported, "Yet they hearkened not unto me, nor inclined their ear, but hardened their neck: they did worse than their fathers." Jeremiah 7:26.

This "hardening of the heart" or "neck" as some Old Testament verses describe it is a persistent refusal to follow God's leading. It was Israel's ultimate downfall. It was their unpardonable sin as a nation. They never got over it.

The New Testament is much more specific regarding the sin God will not forgive. In Matthew 12:31, 32 Jesus said,

"Therefore I say to you, every sin and blasphemy will be forgiven men, but the blasphemy against the Spirit will not be forgiven men.

"Anyone who speaks a word against the Son of Man, it will be forgiven him; but whoever speaks against the Holy Spirit, it will not be forgiven him, either in this age or in the age to come."

The synoptic passage in Mark 3:28, 29 expresses the thought this way:

"Assuredly, I say to you, all sins will be forgiven the sons of men, and whatever blasphemies they may utter;

"But he who blasphemes against the Holy Spirit never has forgiveness, but is subject to eternal condemnation."

And Luke's account puts it this way:

"And anyone who speaks a word against the Son of Man, it will be forgiven him; but to him who blasphemes against the Holy Spirit, it will not be forgiven" (Luke 12:10).

When Stephen, one of the seven deacons, spoke before the Jerusalem Council, he concluded by saying:

> "You stiff-necked and uncircumcised in heart and ears! You always resist the Holy Spirit; as your fathers did, so do you" (Acts 7:51).

Persistent resistence to the Holy Spirit caused God to reject the Jews as a nation and turn to the Christian church as "His chosen people." The Pharisees actually accused Jesus of working His miracles by the power of Satan. "By rejecting the light that was shining upon them, by refusing to examine the evidence to see whether the messages were from heaven, the Pharisees sinned against the Holy Ghost. . . . The Jews pursued their course of rejecting Christ until, in their self-deceived, deluded state, they thought that in crucifying Him they were doing God a service. Thus it will be with all who resist the entreaties of the Spirit of God, and persist in doing what they know to be wrong. The Spirit once resisted, there will be less difficulty in resisting it a second time. If we maintain the independence of the natural heart, and refuse the correction of God, we shall, as did the Jews, stubbornly carry out our own purposes and ideas in the face of the plainest evidence, and shall be in danger of as great deception as came on them. In our blind infatuation we may go to as great lengths as they did, and yet flatter ourselves that we are doing work for God. Those who continue in this course will reap what they have sown. They were afforded a shelter, but they refused it. The plagues of God will fall, and He will prevent them not" (*Review and Herald,* July 27, 1897).

The leaders of God's people had become so self-centered, so absorbed in the rounds of religious ritual that they committed the unpardonable sin and killed the Son of God. There is a modern application for us. "In this our day the sin of the Pharisees is being repeated. Many are turning from light, refusing to listen to the warning of God's Spirit. But by closing the heart to divine impressions, we put away the forgiveness which our Redeemer is so graciously offering to us. By rejecting mercy and truth, we prepare for a course of resistance which, if followed, will continue till we have no power to do otherwise. A point is reached where the most pointed appeals are without effect. The desire to submit to God and to do His will is no longer felt. The spiritual senses become dulled. Darkness is the result, and how great is that darkness!" *(ibid.)*. By rejecting Christ the Jewish people committed the unpardonable sin; and by refusing our invitations of mercy, we commit the same error.

It Is a Condition

"The sin of blasphemy against the Holy Spirit does not lie in any sudden word or deed; it is the firm, determined resistance of truth and evidence.

"God destroys no one. The sinner destroys himself by his own impenitence. No one need look upon the sin against the Holy Ghost as something mysterious and indefinable. <u>The sin against the Holy Ghost is the sin of persistent refusal to respond to the invitation to repent</u>" (*The Faith I Live By,* p. 58).

The unpardonable sin is not a specific act. It is rather a condition. It is the rejection of God's last call of mercy. In a sense it could involve a specific sin. It could be a secret sin that one will just not give up, though impressed repeatedly by the Holy Spirit. It could be smoking, drinking, lustful thoughts, viewing pornography, etc. It could even be a more open sin such as a critical spirit. Whatever the case, the one committing the sin either refuses to give it up or has rationalized it away by saying to himself, "It's such a little thing. It doesn't hurt anyone else. There is really no fault in it," etc., etc.

And so God finally is left to say, "Ephraim is joined to idols, let him alone" (Hosea 4:17).

The Great Controversy Becomes Real

In battling for the souls of men the devil comes with evil thoughts, suggestions to compromise, and other temptations. The Holy Spirit comes with the voice of conscience, the providential leadings of God, and the Word of God—the Bible.

"Conscience is the voice of God, heard amid the conflict of human passions; when it is resisted, the Spirit of God is grieved" (*The Faith I Live By,* p. 58).

What Is the Unpardonable Sin?

Ellen White describes the unpardonable sin this way: "No one need look upon the sin against the Holy Ghost as something mysterious and indefinable. The sin against the Holy Ghost is the sin of persistent refusal to respond to the invitation to repent" (*Review and Herald,* June 29, 1897).

Early Adventist leader W. W. Prescott stated, "The unpardonable sin is the sin that refuses to be pardoned; it is the refusal to hear Him concerning a sin, and to turn from that sin; it is the sin of refusing His instruction; it is the sin of unbelief concerning His warnings; it is the stubbornness of the heart that will not turn from sin, which seals the fate of any people or any individual" (*Review and Herald,* May 19, 1903).

Of the billions who will be lost at the end, are there just a few here and there with hardened hearts that have committed the unpardonable sin? No, since the Spirit has worked with the heart of every person, at least to some degree, everyone who is lost has committed the unpardonable sin. They have chosen their own way—ultimately Satan's way—rather than the way of the Lord—the way that leads to life.

The Trap of the Unpardonable Sin
Just one small delay in responding to the call of God through His Holy Spirit can start a person down the road to the unpardonable sin. The example of Felix, the Roman governor at Caesarea, describes why it is so important to respond immediately when the Spirit calls us. Apparently Felix had just two opportunities to respond to the call of God. The first opportunity came when the Jews came down from Jerusalem to accuse Paul. They gave their false accusations and then Felix heard Paul. Following Paul's defense Felix now had a more accurate account of the way of the Lord, but he failed to make a decision. He was, however, favorably impressed by Paul because he commanded the centurion guarding Paul to let him have liberty—i.e., he was just under house arrest—and to let his friends visit and provide for him.

The Bible describes the second opportunity this way: "And after some days, when Felix came with His wife Drusilla, who was Jewish, he sent for Paul and heard him concerning the faith in Christ. Now as he reasoned about righteousness, self-control, and the judgment to come, Felix was afraid and answered, 'Go away for now, when I have a convenient time I will call for you'" (Acts 24:24, 25).

Ellen White draws an interesting picture of this experience when Felix and Drusilla heard Paul. "The Jewish princess well understood the sacred character of that law which she had so shamelessly transgressed, but her prejudice against the Man of Calvary steeled her heart against the word of life. But Felix had never before listened to the truth, and as the Spirit of

God sent conviction to his soul, he became deeply agitated. Conscience, now aroused, made her voice heard, and Felix felt that Paul's words were true. Memory went back over the guilty past. With terrible distinctness there came up before him the secrets of his early life of profligacy and bloodshed, and the black record of his later years. He saw himself licentious, cruel, rapacious. Never before had the truth been thus brought home to his heart. Never before had his soul been so filled with terror. The thought that all the secrets of his career of crime were open before the eye of God, and that he must be judged according to his deeds, caused him to tremble with dread.

"But instead of permitting his convictions to lead him to repentance, he sought to dismiss these unwelcome reflections. The interview with Paul was cut short. 'Go thy way for this time,' he said; 'when I have a convenient season, I will call for thee.'

"How wide the contrast between the course of Felix and that of the jailer of Philippi! The servants of the Lord were brought in bonds to the jailer, as was Paul to Felix. The evidence they gave of being sustained by a divine power, their rejoicing under suffering and disgrace, their fearlessness when the earth was reeling with the earthquake shock, and their spirit of Christlike forgiveness, sent conviction to the jailer's heart, and with trembling he confessed his sins and found pardon. Felix trembled, but he did not repent. The jailer joyfully welcomed the Spirit of God to his heart and to his home; Felix bade the divine Messenger depart. The one chose to become a child of God and an heir of heaven; the other cast his lot with the workers of iniquity.

"A ray of light from heaven had been permitted to shine upon Felix, when Paul reasoned with him concerning righteousness, temperance, and a judgment to come. That was his heaven-sent opportunity to see and to forsake his sins. But he said to the messenger of God, 'Go thy way for this time; when I have a convenient season, I will call for thee.' He had slighted his last offer of mercy. Never was he to receive another call from God" (*The Acts of the Apostles*, pp. 425-427). If we are honest with ourselves, it is likely that most of us have had hundreds of calls from God, "This is the way, walk in it." But how many calls will God offer us? Felix had only two!

Redeem the Time
God's counsel through the Holy Spirit is to respond today—now!

"Therefore, as the Holy Spirit says: 'Today, if you will hear His voice, do not harden your hearts as in the rebellion, in the day of the trial in the wilderness, where your fathers tested Me, tried Me, and saw my works forty years. Therefore I was angry with that generation, and said, "They always go astray in their heart, and they have not known My ways." So I swore in My wrath, "They shall not enter My rest." '

"Beware, brethren, lest there be in any of you an evil heart of unbelief in departing from the living God; but exhort one another daily, while it is called 'Today,' lest any of you be hardened through the deceitfulness of sin. For we have become partakers of Christ if we hold the beginning of our confidence steadfast to the end, while it is said:

" 'Today, if you will hear His voice, do not harden your hearts as in the rebellion' " (Hebrews 3:7-15).

Here we see the pleadings of God through the Holy Spirit. He is urging, "Don't put it off. Do it TODAY!" We must respond in a positive way to the voice of God.

God has chosen the agency of the Holy Spirit to communicate with us. Accordingly, when we fail to respond to the urgings of the Holy Spirit we cut off the channel of communication between ourselves and heaven. God doesn't just want to talk with us, He wants to change us, to transform us, to fit us to live with Him in heaven—in the company of holy beings. This is why the work of the Holy Spirit was explained so carefully to Nicodemus by Jesus. Commenting on this, Ellen White stated: <u>"When the Spirit of God takes possession of the heart, it transforms the life.</u> Sinful thoughts are put away, evil deeds are renounced; love, humility, and peace take the place of anger, envy, and strife. Joy takes the place of sadness, and the countenance reflects the light of heaven. No one sees the hand that lifts the burden, or beholds the light descend from the courts above. The blessing comes when by faith the soul surrenders itself to God. Then that power which no human eye can see creates a new being in the image of God" (*The Desire of Ages,* p. 173).

Someday
The trite expression "The road to hell is paved with good intentions"

is actually very true when human nature is observed in the Bible and everyday life. Preoccupation with pleasure seeking, moneymaking, or just the cares of this life, keeps many people from taking the time to plan for the future life. But more troubling even than busyness is the person who does take time to take inventory of his life, and then decides to put off making any necessary changes. In the chapter on repentance in *Steps to Christ* this thought process and its final end is described.

"Many are quieting a troubled conscience with the thought that they can change a course of evil when they choose; that they can trifle with the invitations of mercy, and yet be again and again impressed. They think that after doing despite to the Spirit of grace, after casting their influence on the side of Satan, in a moment of terrible extremity they can change their course. But this is not so easily done. The experience, the education, of a lifetime, has so thoroughly molded the character that few then desire to receive the image of Jesus.

"Even one wrong trait of character, one sinful desire, persistently cherished, will eventually neutralize all the power of the gospel. Every sinful indulgence strengthens the soul's aversion to God. The man who manifests an infidel hardihood, or a stolid indifference to divine truth, is but reaping the harvest of that which he has himself sown. In all the Bible there is not a more fearful warning against trifling with evil than the words of the wise man that the sinner 'shall be holden with the cords of his sins.' Proverbs 5:22" (pp. 33, 34).

The process of rejecting the Holy Spirit is rarely an open and outright cursing of God. It is usually a gradual process. Suppression of the Spirit's urging. A small compromise made. The voice of God becomes weaker—actually our spiritual perceptions are muted. And so spiritual darkness closes in until it is night in the soul. When the Spirit is finally rejected, there is no more that God can do for the soul.

The Holy Spirit is clearly essential to salvation; in fact, all those saved from among those living on the earth at the Second Coming will have received the latter rain—the final outpouring of the Holy Spirit's power. On the other hand, the lost—by far the largest number—will have all committed the unpardonable sin!

Perhaps one of the most startling realities of the unpardonable sin is that many who have committed it are still active in Christian churches! All three of the stories in Matthew 25 tell of Christians—even Adventists (see *Christ's Object Lessons,* p. 406)—living in the last days who are eventually lost because they fail to be transformed by the Holy Spirit. "For a time, persons who have committed this sin may appear to be children of God; but when circumstances arise to develop character and show what manner of spirit they are of, it will be found that they are on the enemy's ground, standing under his black banner" (*Testimonies for the Church*, vol. 5, p. 634).

What Should We Do?

We cannot truly have any realistic idea of what God has done for us or what He is preparing for us. If we did, nothing on this earth would be appealing to us. Our entire energies would be spent preparing for the coming kingdom.

When the prodigal son "came to himself" he realized that any house on this earth would be substandard to those that his "Father" is preparing for those that love Him. In the June 29, 1897, issue of *The Review and Herald* Ellen White made this strong appeal to the readers: "As one who loves your soul, I would warn you not to delay, waiting for a time when you will be more inclined to serve God than at the present time. Every hour that you delay, you bind yourself away from God, erect barriers against Him in your habits and practises, and make more difficult your repentance and return to the paths of righteousness. May God help the backslider and the sinner no longer to remain in the entanglement which the evil one is strengthening around them. Wait not to reason, wait not to measure possibilities and probabilities. Break with the deceiver at once. Insult no longer the Spirit of God. Press your way to the throne of grace through the opposing powers of hell. You are standing on the brink of the eternal world. Make a rush for the kingdom of God. It will require every energy of mind and purpose of soul. Delay not, saying, "I am not religiously inclined." This very fact should make you fear lest the Spirit of God is being grieved away for the last time. Dare you run the risk?"

She continued to plead, "I would warn you to fear lest you sin against the Holy Ghost, and be left to your own course, sunk in moral lethargy, and never obtain forgiveness. Why allow yourselves to be longer educated in the school of Satan, and pursue a course of action that will make repentance and reformation impossible? Why resist the overtures of mercy? Why say, 'Let me alone,' until God shall be compelled to give you your desire, since you will have it so? Those who resist the Spirit of God think that they will repent at some future day, when they get ready to take a decided step toward reformation; but repentance will then be beyond their power.

"Never, never, feel at liberty to trifle with the opportunities granted to you. Study the will of God; do not study how you can avoid keeping the commandments of God, but study rather how you may keep them in sincerity and truth, and truly serve Him whose property you are. Do not be satisfied with meeting a low standard, but consult the Spirit of God, obey its dictates, serve God in the beauty of holiness, and render glory to His name."

We sometimes have a tendency to downplay the sinfulness of sin and compromise in this age of extreme tolerance—i.e., I'm OK, You're OK. Some actually praise people who openly compromise church standards. Seeing someone flaunting their jewelry at church or violating the health principles we say, "Well, at least they are not a hypocrite." But "the fact that a man is not a hypocrite does not make him any the less really a sinner. When the appeals of the Holy Spirit come to the heart, our only safety lies in responding to them without delay. When the call comes, 'Go work today in My vineyard,' do not refuse the invitation. 'Today if ye will hear His voice, harden not your hearts.' Heb. 4:7. It is unsafe to delay obedience. You may never hear the invitation again" (*Christ's Object Lessons,* p. 280).

Help Available

The Bible and the Spirit of Prophecy give us assurance that God wants to forgive us and transform us. He will do this if we will allow Him. Let's review just a few of the promises:

"If we confess our sins, He is faithful and just to forgive us our sins and to cleanse us from all unrighteousness" (1 John 1:9).

"When the enemy comes in like a flood, the Spirit of the Lord will lift up a standard against him" (Isaiah 59:19).

"The one who comes to me I will by no means cast out" (John 6:37).

"Come to Me, all you who labor and are heavy laden, and I will give you rest" (Matthew 11:28).

"For God so loved the world that He gave His only begotten

Son, that whoever believes in Him should not perish but have everlasting life" (John 3:16).

"Therefore he is also able to save to the uttermost those who come to God through Him, since He ever lives to make intercession for them" (Hebrews 7:25).

And, of course, there are many more—dozens more! They are underscored by Spirit of Prophecy passages like the following:

"Satan is watching every opportunity in order that he may destroy both soul and body; but Jesus is ready to pardon all your sins, and to make you a child of God, an heir of heaven" (*The Youth's Instructor,* August 8, 1895).

"It is not necessary that anyone should yield to the temptations of Satan and thus violate his conscience and grieve the Holy Spirit. Every provision has been made in the Word of God whereby all may have divine help in their endeavors to overcome" (*God's Amazing Grace,* p. 81).

"It is our privilege to go to Jesus and be cleansed, and to stand before the law without shame or remorse" (*The Faith I Live By,* p. 103).

"The Scriptures are the great agency in this transformation of character. Christ prayed, 'Sanctify them through thy truth: thy word is truth' (John 17:17). If studied and obeyed, the Word of God works in the heart, subduing every unholy attribute. The Holy Spirit comes to convict of sin, and the faith that springs up in the heart works by love to Christ, conforming us, body, soul, and spirit, to His will" (*In Heavenly Places,* p. 21).

"No matter how sinful a person has been, no matter what his position may be, if he will repent and believe, coming unto Christ and trusting Him as his personal Saviour, he may be saved unto the uttermost" (*That I May Know Him,* p. 243).

The Spirit and the Sealing

Those living at the time of the second coming of Christ will be divided into two groups. They are the saved and the lost: the faithful and the unfaithful, etc. And everyone will receive either the mark of the beast or the seal of God. Those who are sealed are protected during the seven last plagues. We dare not grieve or turn off the Holy Spirit who is charged with sealing us for eternity! "And do not grieve the Holy Spirit of God, by whom you were sealed for the day of redemption" (Ephesians 4:30).

"It is a serious thing to grieve the Holy Spirit; and it is grieved when the human agent seeks to work himself, and refuses to enter the service of the Lord because the cross is too heavy, or the self-denial too great. The Holy Spirit seeks to abide in each soul. If it is welcomed as an honored guest, those who receive it will be made complete in Christ.

"Are we striving with all our power to attain to the stature of men and women in Christ? Are we seeking for His fullness, ever pressing toward the mark set before us—the perfection of His character? When the Lord's people reach this mark, they will be sealed in their foreheads. Filled with the Spirit, they will be complete in Christ, and the recording angel will declare, 'It is finished'" (*God's Amazing Grace*, p. 216).

The awful judgments of God are soon to fall on the world. By every account—the prophetic time line, the end-time signs in the natural world, the distress in civil governments, the changes in religious entities, and the moral condition of earth's inhabitants—we are nearing the end of all things. All who desire to go to heaven should be reviewing God's great plan of salvation and meeting the conditions for salvation. Our highest aim in life should be to prepare for heaven. Let's not put off until tomorrow what we must do today. It is time to awake and act like men and women who are on the borders of the eternal world. Time is too short to dwell on matters of no eternal consequence.

CHAPTER 8

The Great False Revival

In the great controversy between good and evil, the devil will use his most powerful deceptions at the end of time. His final strategy of deception is to pretend to be Christian in his activities. This should not surprise us because the antichrist power is itself the largest Christian organization in the world. And Satan's final and most deceptive act is to personate Christ's coming. To many Christians he will seem to be Jesus. Not until the plagues begin to fall will they realize that they have been duped. But just before this final desperate act, Satan will seek to bring about a counterfeit revival—a false latter rain, if you please. And because everyone knows that nominal Christianity needs a revival, thousands, even millions, will be deceived by the emotional counterfeit latter rain.

"Revivals" in the Churches

What I will share next is not intended to be critical or judgmental but to factually recount what is happening in the so-called "Holy Spirit Revivals" current in the Christian scene. The Bible warns that in the last days there will be Christians "having the form of godliness but denying its power. And from such people turn away" (2 Timothy 3:5). This "form" doesn't mean that there won't be excitement and enthusiasm. It is that there will not be the accompanying reformation and transformation. True revival brings about reformation and regeneration—even our sanctification. If we have a genuine experience with God, we will not only love God but we will also love His law and seek to obey Him. Our lives will change. The things we once loved we will not hate and the things we once hated we will now love. Let's take a look at some of the better known modern revival movements.

Brownsville Revival

"Nearly 2 million visitors have thronged to evening services at Brownsville Assembly of God in Pensacola, Florida, since revival erupted on Father's Day in 1995.

" 'It's just as fresh to me today as it was two and a half years ago,' says evangelist Steve Hill, who has been guest preaching at the church since then. During that span, 122,000 have signed 'decision cards' indicating conversion or rededication.

"A year ago, the Brownsville Revival School of Ministry opened with 120 full-time students, split evenly between revival converts and those who experienced renewal, according to Michael L. Brown, the school's dean. Brown says that by the fall 1997 semester, the school, which offers a two-year theology degree emphasizing missions and evangelism, had 511 students from 46 countries.

"Revival leaders also have taken their messages on the road leading two-night rallies in Dallas, Saint Louis, Toledo, Memphis, Birmingham, and Anaheim. 'Our goal is to bring this revival to key cities in the U.S.,' says Hill, 'and these meetings are a divine opportunity for people who have been revived to bring their unsaved family members to church without going inside a church.'

"In the 2.4 million-member Assemblies of God (AG), revival has broken out in dozens of congregations around the country. 'The impact has been powerful,' says Thomas Trask, the denomination's general superintendent. 'Many, many of the pastors have gone [to Brownsville] searching, looking, and believing, and they have witnessed the power of God. It has done something for their hearts and lives' " (*Christianity Today,* February 9, 1998).

Christian Research Institute's Hank Hanegraaff attended the meetings to observe the phenomenon. After four visits he said, "I don't see it as a revival at all." He ends up calling it a "counterfeit revival." He criticized the Brownsville church for "serious distortions of biblical Christianity . . . an overemphasis on subjective experience . . . nonbiblical spiritual practices, Scripture twisting, and false and exaggerated claims" *(ibid.).*

Bonnke's Great Millennial Crusade

German evangelist Reinhard Bonnke is conducting mass healings and evangelistic crusades all over the continent of Africa. The February 5, 2001, issue of *Christianity Today* gave a nine-page report of his work. The following information was taken from that report, which focused primarily on the country of Nigeria.

"On a sweltering afternoon in the Nigerian city of Lagos last November [2000], amid heavy traffic and polluted air, a large banner hung from an overpass for all to see. It pictured the gleaming face of a white European man. With one hand, he pointed a Bible toward the sky. With the other, he held a microphone to his mouth. COME AND RECEIVE YOUR MIRACLE, the banner proclaimed.

"That evening, 550,000 people gathered on 80 acres of bare ground to listen to Bonnke. Spiritually hungry Nigerians—whose lives are bounded by poverty, violence, and an unforgiving climate—could hardly wait to feast on the good news the preacher promised to bring. Many Nigerians walked hours, traveling through the giant, slum-like city to arrive at the spare crusade site. Neither chairs nor portable toilets were on hand.

"As the pulsating drums and opening music subsided, Bonnke looked out into a sea of humanity and began his message, using simple words in a vibrant, heavily accented English: 'Jesus is the Savior of Nigeria!' he shouted. 'All of Nigeria is going to heaven!'

"'Paralyzed people are going to walk,' he told them. 'The blind will see!' Hundreds surged to the central platform, hoping to proclaim publicly that they had been healed. 'Come back tomorrow night,' Bonnke told them afterward. 'Don't miss your miracle!' The crusade crowd grew larger each subsequent evening. Bonnke, embracing his role as preacher, prophet, and storyteller, held an audience averaging 1 million with his arresting gaze and boundless energy. They listened to him in eager anticipation of a divine deliverance from their poverty-stricken, disease-invested world. This was Bonnke's Great Millennial Crusade."

Bonnke has held such crusades in 46 of the 53 countries on the African continent. The crowd of 1.6 million for a single night in Lagos stands as one of the largest Christian gatherings in modern times. But veteran missionaries say that there is very little change in the lives of the people when the "blessing and prosperity gospel" preachers leave. One missionary in Lagos said, "I don't see God at work. Honestly, I see a lot of performance. Church is the center of their social life." Another reported, "There is apathy about the Word of God in our society. The Bible says we should study to show ourselves approved unto God. But people run around for what they can gain for the present time, and because of it, you hardly see people taking the time to study the Word of God, to search the Scripture."

Again, as the Bible predicted, having a form of godliness, but denying its power.

Benny Hinn Ministries

Another modern revival and healing phenomenon is the Benny Hinn Ministry. From his official Web site we learn: "Benny Hinn is a recognized and respected teacher, healing evangelist, and best-selling author. His teaching ministry effectively touches millions each week through his daily half-hour television program, *This Is Your Day!* [It] can be seen internationally in over 190 countries. Tens of thousands gather to experience God's saving and healing power at his monthly Miracle Crusades held throughout the United States and around the world.

"Hinn was born in 1952 in Jaffa, Israel, into a Palestinian family of Greek and Armenian heritage. He was raised in the Greek Orthodox Church and attended French [Roman] Catholic schools in Israel. The family emigrated to Toronto, Canada, in 1968.

"He became a charismatic Christian in 1972 and was greatly influenced by the ministry of the late evangelist Kathryn Kuhlman. Hinn's public ministry began in December 1974 in Oshawa, Ontario. He was soon holding weekly healing meetings in Toronto that attracted thousands.

"In the early 1980's, he moved to Orlando, Florida, where he became pastor of the World Outreach Center. His international crusade and daily television ministry began in 1990 and has continued to expand. Crowds of over a million have attended services at his international crusades." This is what he says about himself!

Other outside observers have a different view. Christian Witness Ministries states on their Web site: "Benny Hinn is a Roman Catholic mystic, who is taking the Pentecostal and Charismatic Church down the ecumenical road towards Rome."

When people see him on TV or read about him on the Internet, many see right away that he is not following biblical principles. The Bible says that when people preach misleading things, "Go not forth." Yet many ignore this counsel, and continue to watch or go in person to his meetings. This way they are deceived and soon become supporters and followers of Hinn. For example, a few years ago an Adventist minister and his family went to one of the Hinn healing crusades with a sick granddaughter, and today he has left the church and become a healer himself. He tells his story on a Web site and says that now he feels the electrifying power of the Holy Spirit and has healed all types of disease.

Though this pastor may not have known of this at the time, Benny Hinn now says that he communicates with the dead and talks in person with Elijah and Jesus. He visits the graves of Kathryn Kuhlman—a deceased faith healer and spiritist—and Aimee McPherson—founder of the Foursquare Gospel church, at the Forest Lawn Cemetery in California. He now claims to have talked with Kuhlman, who introduced him to the Holy Spirit.

Hinn claimed recently that Jesus, God's Son, will soon appear with him on the platform at one of his crusades. On April 2, 2000, Hinn appeared with Paul Crouch on the TBN Praise-a-thon. On that program Hinn stated, "Ladies and gentlemen, Jesus is shaking the world! Now something else is happening that to me is awesome! Absolutely awesome! The Lord is physically appearing in the Muslim world. I'm telling you, Paul, I am hearing it now more and more and more. Since we preachers cannot go there, Jesus is just going there Himself." Later in the same program Hinn reported, "I believe—hear this, hear this! I believe, that Jesus, God's Son, is about to appear physically, in meetings and to believers around the world, to wake us up! He appeared after His resurrection and He is about to appear before His second coming! You know a prophetess sent me a word through my wife, right here, and she said, 'Tell your husband that Jesus is go'n to physically appear in his meetings.' I am expecting to see, I am telling you that—I feel it's going to happen. I, I, I'm careful in how I am saying it now, because I know the people of Kenya are listening. I know deep in my soul, something supernatural is going to happen in Nai—in Nairobi, Kenya. I feel that. I may very well come back, and you and Jan [Paul's wife] are coming to Nairobi with me, but Paul, we may very well come back with footage of Jesus on the platform! You know that the Lord appeared in Romania recently, and there's a video of it? Where the Lord appeared in the back of a church and you see Him on video walking down the aisle? . . . Now hear this, I am prophesying this! Jesus Christ, the Son of God, is about to appear physically in some churches, and some meetings, and to many of His people, for one reason—to tell you He is about to show up! Jesus is coming, saints!"

Genuine Revivals

I have mentioned three of the world's great "revivalists," all of whom, I believe, are part of Satan's counterfeit just before the real thing. As I have stated in other books, the counterfeit will appear genuine in every way—with much music, prayer, preaching, healing, and a spirit of love and enthusiasm. But there is one sure way to determine whether or not they are the genuine article—the biblical test. Do they speak according to God's Word? The false revivalists still believe in the natural immortality of the soul and Sunday sacredness! And all three of the examples that I have mentioned have those two characteristics present. "Through the two great errors, the immortality of the soul and Sunday sacredness, Satan will bring the people under his deceptions. While the former lays the foundation of spiritualism, the latter creates a bond of sympathy with Rome.

"Persons will arise pretending to be Christ Himself, and claiming the title and worship which belong to the world's Redeemer. They will perform wonderful miracles of healing, and will profess to have revelations from heaven contradicting the testimony of the Scriptures.

"But the people of God will not be misled. The teachings of this false christ are not in accordance with the Scriptures. His blessing is pronounced upon the worshipers of the beast and his image, the very class upon whom the Bible declares that God's unmingled wrath shall be poured out" (*Last Day Events,* p. 157).

But, no doubt, focusing on the ingredients of the genuine revival that will come is more important for us now. Chapter 27, "Modern Revivals," in *The Great Controversy,* outlines clearly the intentions of Satan at the end and shows how to identify a genuine revival.

"Many of the revivals of modern times have presented a marked contrast to those manifestations of divine grace which in earlier days followed the labors of God's servants. It is true that a widespread interest is kindled, many profess conversion, and there are large accessions to the churches; nevertheless <u>the results are not such as to warrant the belief that there has been a corresponding increase of real spiritual life. The light which flames up for a time soon dies out, leaving the darkness more dense than before</u>" (*The Great Controversy,* p. 463). For example, what is it like in Lagos, Nigeria, two weeks after Bonnke's Great Millennial Crusade with more than one million average attendance?

Ellen White goes on to say, "Notwithstanding the widespread declension of faith and piety, there are true followers of Christ in these churches. Before the final visitation of God's judgments upon the earth <u>there will be among the people of the Lord such a revival of primitive godliness as has not been witnessed since apostolic times.</u> The Spirit and power of God will be poured out upon His children. At that time many will separate themselves from those churches in which the love of this world has supplanted love for God and His word. Many, both of ministers and people, will gladly accept those great truths which God has caused to be proclaimed at this time to prepare a people for the Lord's second coming. <u>The enemy of souls desires to hinder this work; and before the time for such a movement shall come, he will endeavor to prevent it by introducing a counterfeit.</u> In those churches which he can bring under his deceptive power he will make it appear that God's special blessing is poured out; <u>there will be manifest what is thought to be great religious interest. Multitudes will exult that God is working marvelously for them, when the work is that of another spirit.</u> Under a religious guise, Satan will seek to extend his influence over the Christian world" (*ibid.,* p. 464).

These false revivals are described as follows: "There is an emotional excitement, a mingling of the true with the false, that is well adapted to mislead. Yet none need be deceived. In the light of God's word it is not difficult to determine the nature of these movements. Wherever men neglect the testimony of the Bible, turning away from those plain, soul-testing truths which require self-denial and renunciation of the world, there we may be sure that God's blessing is not bestowed. And by the rule which Christ Himself has given, 'Ye shall know them by their fruits' (Matthew 7:16), it is evident that these movements are not the work of the Spirit of God" *(ibid.).*

The key element missing in the false revivals is an upholding of the law of God. A misunderstanding of the character and perpetuity of God's law has led to errors in understanding conversion and sanctification. This has lowered the standard of piety in the church today. God's law is a transcript of His character—therefore he who does not love the law of God does not love the gospel. When men throw out the law the gospel loses its value and importance in the minds of men.

"The law of God, from its very nature, is unchangeable. It is a revelation of the will and the character of its Author. God is love, and His law is love. Its two great principles are love to God and love to man. 'Love is the fulfilling of the law.' Romans 13:10. The character of God is righteousness and truth; such is the nature of His law. Says the psalmist: 'Thy law is the truth;' 'all Thy commandments are righteousness.' Psalm 119:142, 172. And the apostle Paul declares: 'The law is holy, and the commandment holy, and just, and good.' Romans 7:12. Such a law, being an expression of the mind and will of God, must be as enduring as its Author.

"It is the work of conversion and sanctification to reconcile men to God by bringing them into accord with the principles of His law" (*ibid.*, p. 467).

The Bible says, "The law of the Lord is perfect, converting the soul" (Psalm 19:7). "Without the law, men have no just conception of the purity and holiness of God or of their own guilt and uncleanness. They have no true conviction of sin and feel no need of repentance. Not seeing their lost condition as violators of God's law, they do not realize their need of the atoning blood of Christ. The hope of salvation is accepted without a radical change of heart or reformation of life. Thus superficial conversions abound, and multitudes are joined to the church who have never been united to Christ" (*ibid.*, p. 468).

Modern Revivals Neglect Sanctification

"Erroneous theories of sanctification, also, springing from neglect or rejection of the divine law, have a prominent place in the religious movements of the day. These theories are both false in doctrine and dangerous in practical results; and the fact that they are so generally finding favor, renders it doubly essential that all have a clear understanding of what the Scriptures teach upon this point.

"True sanctification is a Bible doctrine. The apostle Paul, in his letter to the Thessalonian church, declares: 'This is the will of God, even your sanctification.' And he prays: 'The very God of peace sanctify you wholly.' 1 Thessalonians 4:3; 5:23. The Bible clearly teaches what sanctification is and how it is to be attained. The Saviour prayed for His disciples: 'Sanctify them through Thy truth: Thy word is truth.' John 17:17. And Paul teaches that believers are to be 'sanctified by the Holy Ghost.' Romans 15:16. What is the work of the Holy Spirit? Jesus told His disciples: 'When He, the Spirit of truth, is come, He will guide you into all truth.' John 16:13. And the psalmist says: 'Thy law is the truth.' By the word and the Spirit of God are opened to men the great principles of righteousness embodied in His law. And since the law of God is 'holy, and just, and good,' a transcript of the divine perfection, it follows that a character formed by obedience to that law will be holy. Christ is a perfect example of such a character. He says: 'I have kept My Father's commandments.' 'I do always those things that please Him.' John 15:10;

8:29. The followers of Christ are to become like Him—by the grace of God to form characters in harmony with the principles of His holy law. This is Bible sanctification" (*ibid.*, p. 469).

Error in the false revivals all boils down to this: "The sanctification now gaining prominence in the religious world carries with it a spirit of self-exaltation and a disregard for the law of God that mark it as foreign to the religion of the Bible. Its advocates teach that sanctification is an instantaneous work, by which, through faith alone, they attain to perfect holiness. 'Only believe,' say they, 'and the blessing is yours.' No further effort on the part of the receiver is supposed to be required. At the same time they deny the authority of the law of God, urging that they are released from obligation to keep the commandments. But is it possible for men to be holy, in accord with the will and character of God, without coming into harmony with the principles which are an expression of His nature and will, and which show what is well pleasing to Him?" (*ibid.*, p. 471).

Test of Man's Profession

In three short paragraphs Ellen White lays out the folly of a profession without obedience to the laws of God. "The desire for an easy religion that requires no striving, no self-denial, no divorce from the follies of the world, has made the doctrine of faith, and faith only, a popular doctrine; but what saith the word of God? Says the apostle James: 'What doth it profit, my brethren, though a man say he hath faith, and have not works? can faith save him? . . . Wilt thou know, O vain man, that faith without works is dead? Was not Abraham our father justified by works, when he had offered Isaac his son upon the altar? Seest thou how faith wrought with his works, and by works was faith made perfect? . . . Ye see then how that by works a man is justified, and not by faith only.' James 2:14-24.

"The testimony of the word of God is against this ensnaring doctrine of faith without works. **It is not faith** that claims the favor of Heaven without complying with the conditions upon which mercy is to be granted, **it is presumption;** for genuine faith has its foundation in the promises and provisions of the Scriptures.

"Let none deceive themselves with the belief that they can become holy while willfully violating one of God's requirements. The commission of a known sin silences the witnessing voice of the Spirit and separates the soul from God. 'Sin is the transgression of the law.' And 'whosoever sinneth [transgresseth the law] hath not seen Him, neither known Him.' 1 John 3:6. Though John in his epistles dwells so fully upon love, yet he does not hesitate to reveal the true character of that class who claim to be sanctified while living in transgression of the law of God. 'He that saith, I know Him, and keepeth not His commandments, is a liar, and the truth is not in him. But whoso keepeth His word, in him verily is the love of God perfected.' 1 John 2:4, 5. Here is the test of every man's profession. We cannot accord holiness to any man without bringing him to the measurement of God's only standard of holiness in heaven and in earth. If men feel no weight of the moral law, if they belittle and make light of God's precepts, if they break one of the least of these commandments, and teach men so, they shall be of no esteem in the sight of Heaven, and we may know that their claims are without foundation" (*ibid.,* p. 472).

By Their Fruits

There are many factors in identifying counterfeit and true revivals. One, however, seems especially prominent in the New Testament. It is the fact that our bodies are the temple of the Holy Spirit. "Do you not know that your body is the temple of the Holy Spirit who is in you, whom you have from God, and you are not your own? For you were bought at a price; therefore glorify God in your body and in your spirit, which are God's" (1 Corinthians 6:19, 20). When commenting on this verse and topic Ellen White notes, "Slaves of tobacco, claiming the blessing of entire sanctification, talk of their hope of heaven; but God's word plainly declares that 'there shall in no wise enter into it anything that defileth.' Revelation 21:27. . . . He whose body is the temple of the Holy Spirit will not be enslaved by a pernicious habit. His powers belong to Christ, who has bought him with the price of blood. His property is the Lord's. How could he be guiltless in squandering this entrusted capital?" (*ibid.,* pp. 474, 475).

Healthful living, when properly understood, is not a restriction on our freedom. Its principles have been given to us to help us to have clear minds to discern the deceptions of Satan.

Because Satan is a student of the Bible he knows better than we do how the final events will take place. He will anticipate the work of God and try to preempt the acts of God. "I saw that God has honest children among the nominal Adventists and the fallen churches, and before the plagues shall be poured out, ministers and people will be called out from these churches and will gladly receive the truth. Satan knows this; and before the loud cry of the third angel is given, he raises an excitement in these religious bodies, that those who have rejected the truth may think that God is with them" (*Last Day Events,* p. 158).

Even in the Church

Satan knows that time is short and has doubled his efforts to deceive. Years ago when the church had to deal with the Holy Flesh movement in connection with the Indiana camp meeting in 1890, we were told that the loud, wild music they used would come back to the church just before the close of probation (see *Selected Messages,* vol. 2, pp. 31-39). Apparently Ellen White saw the gospel rock and excitement that is beginning to creep into the church today. She warned, "There will be shouting, with drums, music, and dancing. The senses of rational beings will become so confused that they cannot be trusted to make right decisions. . . .

"A bedlam of noise shocks the senses and perverts that which if conducted aright might be a blessing. The powers of satanic agencies blend with the din and noise to have a carnival, and this is termed the Holy Spirit's working. . . . Those things which have been in the past will be in the future. Satan will make music a snare by the way in which it is conducted.

"Let us give no place to strange exercisings, which really take the mind away from the deep movings of the Holy Spirit. God's work is ever characterized by calmness and dignity" (*ibid.,* p. 159).

Deception Almost Universal

The devil is so skillful at deception that even the most educated and intelligent people will be deceived. "Ministers, lawyers, doctors, who have permitted these falsehoods to overmaster their spirit of discernment, will be themselves deceivers, united with the deceived. A spiritual drunkenness will take possession of them" (*ibid.,* p. 171). The spiritualistic miracles of the appearance of dead relatives and Satan's personation of Christ are almost overwhelming to people. Only those who have their minds fortified with the Word of God will stand unmoved.

"The Bible will never be superseded by miraculous manifestations. The truth must be studied, it must be searched for as hidden treasure. Wonderful illuminations will not be given aside from the Word or to take the place of it. Cling to the Word, receive the engrafted Word which will make men wise unto salvation.

"The last great delusion is soon to open before us. Antichrist is to perform his marvelous works in our sight. <u>So closely will the counterfeit resemble the true that it will be impossible to distinguish between them except by the Holy Scriptures. By their testimony every statement and every miracle must be tested</u>" (*ibid.,* p. 170).

We have been warned! Very interesting and unusual things will happen soon. We must prepare by carefully studying the Word of God. We must put on the armor of God. This false revival is beginning now. We see it in the "ministry" of Benny Hinn and even in our own churches at times.

CHAPTER 9

Spirits of the Dead

O ur lives are actually two journeys at the same time. One is our physical journey and the other is our journey toward our eternal destiny. Obviously, we would all like to live to see Jesus come the second time. However, if we die because of illness or accident before that time, we can have the hope of the resurrection. The Bible describes our earthly death as walking through the valley of the shadow of death (see Psalm 23:4). We are not actually "walking" during death. The Bible elsewhere describes death as an unconscious sleep before the resurrection. We need to look at what the Bible teaches about death and see why other non-biblical views about death are dangerous deceptions.

Man Knows Not His Time

As a friend of mine says, we are all born with a harmful condition. We are all old-age positive. No matter what we do to smooth our wrinkles, we all get them. We may prolong our life and enhance its quality by exercise, proper diet, and other helpful practices, but we are still subject to death. Death is no respecter of persons. It is the fate of all—the rich, the poor, the unknown, and the famous. The January 3, 1998, issue of *World* reported on some well-known individuals who had died in 1997. The list was of people who were well known in society:

- William Brennan, retired Supreme Court justice considered one of the most influential judicial activists in America's history. Age 91.
- John Denver, singer and environmental activist. Age 53. Plane crash.
- Diana, Princess of Wales. Age 36. Auto accident.
- Roberto C. Goizueta, who fled Communist Cuba and became a chief of the Coca-Cola Co. Age 65. Lung cancer.
- Bob Jones, Jr., fundamentalist leader and chancellor of Bob Jones

University. Age 86. Cancer.
- James A. Michener, best-selling novelist. Age 90. Kidney failure.
- Robert Mitchum, actor. Age 79. Emphysema, cancer.
- Mother Teresa, the Roman Catholic nun revered for her ministry to the poor. Age 87.
- Rich Mullins, Christian singer. Age 42. Auto accident.
- Pat Paulsen, comedian who ran satirical campaigns for the White House. Age 69. Cancer.
- Mobutu Sese Seko, Zairian strongman overthrown in 1997 after nearly 32 years of rule. Age 66. Prostate cancer.
- Red Skelton, TV and film clown-comedian. Age 84.
- James Stewart, actor. Age 89. Blood clot on his lung.
- Gianni Versace, Italian fashion designer who dressed celebrities. Age 50. Murder.
- John Wimber, founder of the International Association of Vineyard Churches. Age 63. Brain hemorrhage.

In just this short account we see the fate of all mankind. The ages ranged from 36 to 91, and every decade in between. They were religious and nonreligious. The cause of death was either accident, murder, or illness. But they are now all dead. Their journey through life has ended. But what happens when a person dies? Do they know what is going on in the land of the living?

Man's Condition in Death

The Bible tells us that at Creation man had conditional immortality. That is, as long as he was faithful to God's commands he would have access to the tree of life and therefore could live on and on. Since the Fall of man, however, we no longer have access to the tree of life, and therefore are "subject to death." Our hope of eternal life is in Christ. He "died for us"—the second death; therefore though we may die now, it is only a sleep. At the second coming of Christ there will be a general resurrection of the righteous who have lived down through the ages. They will awake to newness of life—immortality—to live with Christ forever.

The book *Bible Readings for the Home* devotes nine sections to Christian anthropology—exactly 50 pages! The book is largely in question-and-answer form—with the answers being given in Bible texts. The following excerpt will help the reader to see that the Bible is clear on this topic and that its teachings should form our belief and understanding of it.

What Death Is Like

"By what figure does the Bible represent death?

'But I would not have you to be ignorant, brethren, concerning them which are asleep, that ye sorrow not, even as others which have no hope.' 1 Thessalonians 4:13. (See also 1 Corinthians 15:18, 20; John 11:11-14.)

Note.—In sound sleep one is wholly lost to consciousness; time goes by unmeasured; and mental activity is suspended for the time being.

"Where do the dead sleep?

'And many of them that sleep in the dust of the earth shall awake.' Daniel 12:2. (See also Ecclesiastes 3:20; 9:10.)

"How long will they sleep there?

'So man lieth down, and riseth not: till the heavens be no more, they shall not awake, nor be raised out of their sleep.' Job 14:12.

Thoughts and Feelings of the Dead

"What does one in this condition know about his family?

'His sons come to honor, and he knoweth it not; and they are brought low, but he perceiveth it not of them.' Job 14:21.

"What becomes of man's thoughts at death?

'His breath goeth forth, he returneth to his earth; in that very day his thoughts perish.' Psalm 146:4.

"Do the dead know anything?

'For the living know that they shall die: but the dead know not any thing. Ecclesiastes 9:5.

"Do they take part in earthly things?

'Also their love, and their hatred, and their envy, is now perished; neither have they any more a portion for ever in any thing that is done under the sun.' Verse 6.
Note.—If one remained conscious after death, he would know of the promotion or dishonor of his sons; but in death one loses all the attributes of mind—love, hatred, envy, etc. Thus it is plain that his thoughts have perished, and that he can have nothing more to do with the things of this world. But if, as taught by some, man's powers of thought continue after death, he lives; and if he lives, he must be somewhere. Where is he? Is he in heaven, or in hell? If he goes to either place at death, what then is the need of a future judgment, or of a resurrection, or of the second coming of Christ? If men go to their rewards at death, before the judgment takes place, then their rewards precede their awards.

"How much does one know of God when dead?

'For in death there is no remembrance of Thee.' Psalm 6:5.
Note.—As already seen, the Bible everywhere represents the dead as asleep, with not even a remembrance of God. If they were in heaven or hell, would Jesus have said, "Our friend Lazarus sleepeth"? John 11:11. If so, calling him to life was really robbing him of the bliss of heaven that rightly belonged to him. The parable of the rich man and Lazarus (Luke 16) teaches not consciousness in death, but that riches will avail nothing in the judgment and that poverty will not keep one out of heaven."
(*Bible Readings for the Home,* current hard cover ed., pp. 469, 470.)

During the year 2000 the people of Israel celebrated the 3,000th-year anniversary of the 40-year reign of King David. Knowing of David's standing among the Jews, Peter mentions him twice in his sermon on the day of Pentecost. He declared, "Men and brethren, let me speak freely to you of the patriarch David, that he is both dead and buried, and his tomb is with us to this day. . . . For David did not ascend into the heavens" (Acts 2:29, 34).

Since the dead, according to the Bible, are asleep and don't know anything, then if someone claims to be speaking with the dead, he is either lying or speaking with the devil! For as Paul warned, "We do not wrestle against flesh and blood, but against principalities, against powers, against the rulers of the darkness of this age, against spiritual hosts of wickedness in heavenly [high] places" (Ephesians 6:12).

The idea that man survives death in a conscious state is based on the first of Satan's lies to the human family—"You will not surely die" (Genesis 3:4). Yet the devil's lie has been believed and perpetuated by mankind, even Christians, down through time. The logical results of this belief can be and often are deadly. Let me illustrate.

On to the Next Level?

They were watching the skies and the Internet for a sign. And they found one. As Comet Hale-Bopp grew bright in the sky, the 39 members of the Heaven's Gate cult descended into true darkness. They did it quietly, in a rich California suburb called Rancho Santa Fe. Orchestrated by a former choir director, their mass suicide was supposed to liberate them. The promise of their leader? He said that by dying they would ascend on a cloud of light to a higher plane.

Astronomical charts may also have helped determine the timing of the Heaven's Gate suicides. They apparently began to kill themselves on the weekend of March 22, 23, 1997, around the time that Hale-Bopp got ready to make its closest approach to Earth. That weekend also witnessed a full moon and, in parts of the United States, a lunar eclipse. In addition, the weekend included Palm Sunday, the beginning of the Christian Holy Week. Shrouds placed on the corpses were purple, the color of Passiontide, or, for New Agers, the color of those who have passed to a higher plane.

The 21 women and 18 men who took their lives engaged in a systematic, well-planned, and orchestrated suicide. Notes and videos they prepared ahead of time show they all apparently took part willingly and cheerfully in what they termed "escaping their containers"—their bodies—so they could go on "to the next level."

The first news reports of the incident stated that the 39 people were all young men because they all had closely cropped hair, wore baggy black pants and shirts and identical black-and-white Nike running shoes. Not till the bodies were examined at the coroner's office was it discovered that 21 of the group were women. In addition, further examination of passports and personal identification showed that their ages ranged from 26 to 72.

The group had suitcases packed with clothes, spiral notebooks, and for some reason, lip balm. For some unknown reason, each person had some quarters and a $5 bill in their pocket.

What really happened in this largest mass suicide in U.S. history? By their self-inflicted death they closed their own probation. But did they go somewhere? Did they get to the spaceship they said was hidden behind the Hale-Bopp comet? Will they be back for a visit? How can we know? Should anyone follow them as they invited others to do? What really happens when one dies? Can we know these things? Yes, indeed!—and we *must* know the truth in order to be prepared against this and other last deceptions of Satan.

Deceptions of Spiritualism

We can answer these questions by looking at the origins of the Heaven's Gate cult and then comparing the beliefs of the cult with the great standard of truth. The tremendously deceptive power of spiritualism can be demonstrated in the activities of the people involved in the cult. The group's beliefs were a strange mixture of biblical expressions, astrological charts, new age, spiritualism, and science fiction television programs such as *Star Trek,* the *X Files,* etc.

Cult leader Marshall Herff Applewhite was the son of a Presbyterian minister who moved around Texas as a church builder. Applewhite was blessed with good looks and a powerful singing voice. At one point in his life he apparently had plans to study for the ministry himself, but gave up these plans to pursue a career in music. He seemed to enjoy life as a family man, with a wife and two children.

Then his struggle with homosexuality unraveled both his marriage and his academic post in a religious school. The Washington *Post* reported that in 1971 he checked into a psychiatric hospital to be cured of his homosexuality. He had been fired as a music professor at Houston's University of St. Thomas, a Roman Catholic school, after an affair with a student. He had been fired from another job for similar reasons in 1964.

"College records show that Applewhite left [the University of St. Thomas] in 1970 for 'health problems of an emotional nature.' Suffering from depression and shame, hearing 'voices,' he checked into a hospital, asking to be 'cured' of his homosexual desires. He told his sister he had suffered a 'near death experience' after a heart attack, but he may actually have suffered from a drug overdose, according to Ray Hill, a radio-show host in Texas who knew Applewhite at the time. 'He was kind of a Timothy Leary type,' said Hill" (*Newsweek,* April 7, 1997).

According to *Time* magazine, "Applewhite spun his own myth: the personal turmoil was the result of his body's coming under the influence of a being from the 'Next level,' part of the discovery that he was one of 'the Two.'" The "Two" he referred to were the two witnesses of Revelation that were to prepare the way for the kingdom of heaven.

It was during his hospitalization that Applewhite met "the other half of the two." She was Bonnie Lu Nettles, then 44. She was a nurse and a wife and mother of four children. Her daughter Terrie, who was interviewed by CNN after the suicide of the Heaven's Gate group, stated that her mother "dabbled in astrology and far-out religions and had been told by a couple of spiritualists that there was going to be this guy coming into her life. Then Herff showed up. They linked together on a spiritual plane." One can easily see the power and deception of spiritualism by the fact that he left his wife and two children and she left her husband and four children to become "the two witnesses of Revelation."

After "the Two linked up on the spiritual plane," "Nettles attended drama classes that Applewhite taught in Houston; she drew up his astrological charts and channeled her spiritual adviser 'Brother Francis' for guidance. In 1972 she helped him start the Christian Arts Center, a protocult that taught astrology and metaphysics. Applewhite had always been intense and charming. Now he became charismatic. Says Terrie Nettles: 'I felt like I was in the presence of an incredible human being. It was like I was being lifted.' She adds, 'I felt privileged to be with my mother and Herff. I was the only one who could talk with them together. Their followers had to talk to them in groups, not individually'" (*Time,* April 7, 1997).

In 1975 Nettles and Applewhite left Houston for California for lecture and recruitment trips in the West. Neither apparently ever saw their families again. Soon after arriving in California and beginning their cult, the "Two" began calling themselves nicknames such as "Guinea" and "Pig," "Bo" and "Peep," a reference to their roles as shepherds. Later they were called "Him" and "Her," and finally the musical "Do" and "Ti."

Powerful Pull of False Christs

The members of the Heaven's Gate cult believed that Applewhite, alias "Do," was "the One, a modern-day Christ." "The Two proclaimed that 'Bo' had been Jesus, Elijah, and Moses in his former lives." But the real Jesus warned His followers, "Then if anyone says to you, 'Look, here is the Christ!' or 'There!' do not believe it. For false christs and false prophets will rise and show great signs and wonders to deceive, if possible, even the elect. See, I have told you beforehand. Therefore if they say to you, 'Look, He is in the desert!' do not go out; or 'Look, He is in the inner rooms!' do not believe it" (Matthew 24:23-26). Now we can see why Jesus said, "Don't go, don't look, don't believe it." Let us learn a lesson from those who were deceived.

"John M. Craig of Durango, Colo., was 41 when he joined Applewhite's cult in 1975. Craig was a successful rancher and businessman, a strapping outdoors man who had bit parts as a cowboy in several movies. He also had six young children. One day in July an old college friend came to visit; two days later Craig drove off with him to hear Applewhite and his partner then, Bonnie Nettles, speak in Denver. The next morning, according to a family friend, Craig's wife woke up and there was a note that said he was gone to meet the spaceship because 'the end of the world was coming.' Craig never returned; his wife divorced him two years later and raised the children herself. Stories in the local papers last week mentioned rumors of financial troubles, but other sources, including his former wife, denied them. 'Nobody,' she said, 'will be able to explain why he did it.' He went to a meeting, and then he was gone" (*Newsweek,* April 7, 1997).

And then there was Yvonne McCurdy-Hill, 39, from Cincinnati, Ohio. "An employee at the U.S. post office, she loved to surf the Web, there entering Heaven's Gate. By August she had sold her BMW, cashed in her post office pension, sold her house and apportioned her five children, including infant twins, among her relatives. Then with her husband Steven, she joined Heaven's Gate in California. Steven didn't last as a cultist, but Yvonne did—to the finish. Her family and friends remain baffled. Said one, 'Yvonne is the last I would have thought would end like this'" (*Time,* April 7, 1997).

There were 37 others! Many with similar stories. They saw a flier, they went to a meeting—and they were gone. The Bible says, "There is a way that seems right to a man, but its end is the way of death" (Proverbs 14:12). This verse is repeated word for word in Proverbs 16:25. It is apparently repeated for emphasis. Paul also gives a very strong warning of this very thing: "The coming of the lawless one is according to the working of Satan, with all power, signs, and lying wonders, and with all unrighteous deception among those who perish, because they did not receive the love of the truth, that they might be saved. And for this reason God will send them strong delusion, that they should believe the lie" (2 Thessalonians 2:9-11). The truth, as we have seen, is God's Word. One cannot have such a hybrid religion and expect to avoid deception. How can we avoid being deceived by this powerful working of Satan? It is only through a knowledge of God's Word and our determination to follow it alone.

Back to the Bible

The Bible should be the full and ultimate authority for the Christian. That's why we need to know what the Bible has to say about death. Apparently, even in Old Testament times men had a fascination with trying to communicate with the dead. The Bible counsel is: "When they say to you, Seek those who are mediums and wizards, who whisper and mutter, should not a people seek their God? Should they seek the dead on behalf of the living? To the law and to the testimony! If they do not speak according to this word, it is because there is no light in them" (Isaiah 8:19, 20).

When I study the Bible topically, I attempt to look up every verse on a given topic. I can then get the big picture and follow up by looking at the details. This gives a true picture of what the Bible says on each topic that it mentions. Then my understanding of the topic becomes my doctrine on that subject.

Some time ago, on a flight from Chicago to Nashville, the young man sitting next to me noted that I was looking at the *Newsweek* coverage of the Heaven's Gate cult. He asked if I had any idea why those people did that. I told him that I thought they had a wrong understanding of Scripture, and in addition they used extrabiblical sources for their understanding of life and death. Then I told him about my study method. I told him that one could more easily determine the truth about any topic by using this method. I told him, for example, that if one really wanted to know what the Bible taught about "baptism" he could simply look up in an exhaustive concordance, like Young's or Strong's, all the words that deal with baptism. There are 51 verses that use the word "baptized," 22 verses use the word "baptism," 7 verses use "baptize," and 4 use the word "baptizing." That is a total of 84 verses that one could study in their context to determine what the Bible teaches about baptism.

One quickly sees that, in the Bible context, one repents before he is baptized. This rules out infants, because they cannot understand the nature of sin and forgiveness. So the baptism the Bible teaches is a baptism of faith. In addition, when the Bible talks about a baptism taking place there are always two people involved. The one baptizing and the one being baptized. They go together down into the water and the one being baptized is dipped or immersed under the water. There are many other things that could be learned about baptism using this method. But you already know one thing for sure. If you were "sprinkled" as an "infant," you weren't "baptized" in the biblical sense.

This explanation seemed to make sense to the man I was talking with, so I told him the same thing could be done on the subject of death. I told him that the great preponderance of the evidence when one studies Christian anthropology indicates that when a person dies his breath returns to God (the breath of the good and the bad returns to God), and his body returns to dust. In his grave man rests in a state of unconsciousness until the resurrection. The great mass of biblical evidence is that when one dies, "he sleeps with his fathers." The young man then said, "But didn't Jesus promise the thief who was hanging beside Him on the cross that he would be with Him in paradise that day?" I told him that many had drawn that conclusion from the reference, but when it is compared to others and studied in detail itself one can see that Jesus was giving the man assurance and not talking about what happens when you die.

But the young man persisted, "How do you know that Jesus wasn't promising the thief that he would be in heaven that day?" "By studying the story," I said. Let's look at the big picture. First, we know that Jesus was crucified on Friday, the preparation day, He rested in the grave on Sabbath, and then on Sunday, He was resurrected.

When Mary came to the tomb on Sunday morning (the first day of the week), she was weeping because she thought Jesus was still in the tomb. But the tomb was empty and an angel told her, "He is not here, for He is risen!" (Matthew 28:6). Then a voice called her name—"Mary!" She immediately recognized the voice of Jesus and was so excited she wanted to embrace Him. But He stopped her by saying, "Do not cling to Me, for I have not yet ascended to My Father" (John 20:17).

In addition, we are told that the Jews didn't want to keep those who had been crucified on the cross over the Sabbath. They broke the legs of the thieves so that they couldn't get away. But since Jesus was already dead, they did not break His legs (see John 19:31-33). So while Jesus died on Friday, the thief didn't. And even on Sunday Jesus had not ascended to heaven. The conclusion is simple and inescapable: neither Jesus nor the thief went to heaven on Friday.

Now here is the point: Either Jesus was lying to the thief about going to heaven that day or He was giving him assurance, that day, and not talking about what happens when one dies. The latter is the only possible conclusion! Any "problem" text that appears to conflict with the preponderance of the evidence can be explained by careful study. It made sense to my seatmate on the plane!

What Is Man?

The Creation account says, "And the Lord God formed man of the dust of the ground, and breathed into his nostrils the breath of life; and man became a living being" (Genesis 2:7). The King James Version says "a living soul." Here we have the basic constituent elements of man: the body (dust or earth) plus breath equals a living being or soul. Man does not *have* a soul. He *is* a soul. So what happens when one dies? The process is simply reversed. The breath returns to God and the body returns to dust. Man is no longer a living being. "Then the dust will return to the earth as it was, and the spirit [breath] will return to God who gave it" (Ecclesiastes 12:7).

This is the bottom line. Only God has immortality (1 Timothy 6:16). The devil's first recorded lie, spoken to Eve in the Garden of Eden, was "You shall not surely die" (Genesis 3:4). So where do people get the idea that the soul escapes the body at death and lives on as a conscious entity? This comes from Greek dualism: from Pythagoras (died 5 B.C.); from Plato (died 350 B.C.); from Aristotle (died 320 B.C.); and from many others who were influenced by Greek philosophy—such as Thomas Aquinas (died A.D. 1274). Aquinas, who was a pagan convert to Christianity, became a leading Roman Catholic theologian. But these ideas did not originate in the Scriptures, which are the standard of truth.

We all know what earth and dust are, but what is the breath of life? It is the spark of life. It is the vital force that enables man to function. It is the breath of God. The English Bible calls the breath "Spirit."

In the Old Testament two words are used to denote spirit or breath. They are *N'shamah* and *Ruach. N'shamah* is used 21 times in the Old Testament. It can mean either the physical act of breathing or the breath itself. Most frequently it refers to respiration.

A typical example of the use of this word is found in Genesis 7 when the Bible describes the results of the Flood: "And all flesh died that moved on the earth: birds and cattle and beasts and every creeping thing that creeps on the earth, and every man. All in whose nostrils was the breath of the spirit of life, all that was on the dry land died" (Genesis 7:21, 22). According to this verse and many others, all living creatures, man and animals, have the same breath or life principle.

If when the breath returns to God some conscious entity "goes to heaven," then both animals and man "go to heaven at death"—and there is no distinction between the righteous and the wicked! This conclusion is obviously absurd. Not one passage of the 21 in the Old Testament that uses *N'shamah* says anything about man being immortal!

Ruach occurs 377 times in the Old Testament. The King James Version translates the word as "spirit" 232 times; as "wind" 91 times; as "breath" 28 times; and the balance is of various other uses. Obviously, the three uses above are the most common as in Genesis 8:1 where God caused a wind to pass over the earth. "It is also used to denote vitality (Judges 15:19), courage (Joshua 2:11), temper or anger (Judges 8:3), disposition (Isaiah 54:6), moral character (Ezekiel 11:19), and the seat of the emotions (1 Samuel 1:15).

"In the sense of breath, the *ruach* of men is identical with the *ruach* of animals (Eccl. 3:19). The *ruach* of man leaves the body at death (Ps. 146:4) and returns to God (Eccl. 12:7; cf. Job 34:14). *Ruach* is used frequently of the Spirit of God, as in Isaiah 63:10. Never in the Old Testament, with respect to man, does *ruach* denote an intelligent entity capable of sentient existence apart from a physical body.

"The New Testament equivalent of *ruach* is *pneuma,* 'spirit,' from *pneo,* 'to blow,' or 'to breathe.' As with *ruach,* there is nothing inherent in the word *pneuma* denoting an entity in man capable of conscious existence apart from the body, nor does the New Testament usage with respect to man in any way imply such a concept" (*Seventh-day Adventists Believe,* p. 83).

The Biblical Meaning of Soul

The word translated "soul" in the English Bible is *nephesh* in the Old Testament and *psuche* in the New Testament. *Nephesh* is used about 750 times in the Old Testament. It can mean breath, life, person, or appetite. The Hebrew *Nephesh chayyah* has been translated "living being" or "living soul." But the Bible also uses the same term to refer to marine animals, insects, reptiles, and beasts (Genesis 1:20, 24; 2:19). So the "breath of life" is not limited to people. Every living creature possesses it. *Psuche* is used in the New Testament 155 times. It also refers to a person, a personal pronoun (as in my soul or simply "me"), life, emotional life, or animals. In total there are over 900 passages where *nephesh* or *psuche* are used, and not one passage mentions immortal in connection with these words. The Old and New Testaments are in complete agreement on this topic. These words are not used as being part of a person, but rather it is the person (see Genesis 14:21; Numbers 5:6; and Deuteronomy 10:22).

"The biblical evidence indicates that sometimes *nephesh* and *psuche* refer to the whole person and at other times to a particular aspect of man, such as the affections, emotions, appetites, and feelings. This usage, however, in no way shows that man is a being made up of two separate and distinct parts. The body and the soul exist together; together they form an indivisible union. The soul has no conscious existence apart from the body. There is no text that indicates that the soul survives the body as a conscious entity" (*ibid.,* pp. 82, 83).

What Difference Does It Make?

So what difference does what a person believes about man's condition in death make anyway? We will all find out eventually, won't we? Yes, but "the doctrine of man's consciousness in death, especially the belief that spirits of the dead return to minister to the living, has prepared the way for modern spiritualism. If the dead are admitted to the presence of God and holy angels, and privileged with knowledge far exceeding what they before possessed, why should they not return to the earth to enlighten and instruct the living? If, as taught by popular theologians, spirits of the dead are hovering about their friends on earth, why should they not be permitted to communicate with them, to warn them against evil, or to comfort them in sorrow? How can those who believe in man's consciousness in death reject what comes to them as divine light communicated by glorified spirits. Here is a channel regarded as sacred, through which Satan works for the accomplishment of his purposes" (*The Great Controversy,* pp. 551, 552).

There is ample evidence that millions of people believe in the unbiblical teaching of the immortality of the soul. Let me share just two illustrations of this. On the back cover of the Catholic weekly, *Our Sunday Visitor,* April 6, 1997, a book was advertised under the heading "Help Those Who

Have Died." The book is titled *Charity for the Suffering Souls.* The advertising text reads as follows: "Father John A. Nageleisen provides proof from Scripture on the existence and torments of Purgatory. Tells what the fire is like. Gives the conditions of the suffering souls as to pain and consolations. Analyzes the credibility of departed souls that have returned to warn those on earth. Covers the means of relieving the poor souls—holy water, mass, alms, fasting, etc. Includes motives for helping the poor souls, and how they assist their benefactors. Contains novenas and prayers. Beautiful illustrations, 408 pp. PB. Imprimatur of several bishops."

This idea of departed souls returning to warn those on earth is pure spiritualism, yet it is openly advertised in *Our Sunday Visitor.* Thankfully, many Catholic believers are beginning to realize that such teachings of their church do not harmonize with the Scriptures. In the "Ask Me a Question" section of the March 9, 1997, edition of *Our Sunday Visitor* a person writes this question:

"Question: The Church teaches that when we die, we are judged and go to heaven or hell. Are we not awaiting the Second Coming, when all will be resurrected and judged?"

Then "Father" Frank Sheedy gives this answer:

"Answer: The Church teaches that there are two judgments, particular and general. The Catechism tells us that each person receives eternal retribution in his or her immortal soul at the very moment of death—either heaven (immediately or through purification) or everlasting damnation. This is the particular judgment.

"After the Second Coming of Christ there will be a general, or Last Judgment, when our souls will be reunited to our bodies and a different judgment will be for all to understand (see Mt. 25)."

Preparing for the Great Deception

We must thoroughly study this topic so that our minds will be fortified against the deceptions of Satan. We need a clear understanding of man's condition in death from the biblical perspective in order to avoid being misled by the doctrines of devils. Unless we make this preparation we are sitting ducks for the devil's deceptions. One can easily see how spiritualism is invading television programming, including movies, serials, and even cartoons! No doubt the most insidious deception regarding spiritualism is that it is being taught right in the churches—places where poor souls should be able to seek a refuge from Satan.

We must remember as the Bible declares, "For the living know that they will die; but the dead know nothing, and they have no more reward, for the memory of them is forgotten. Also their love, their hatred, and their envy have now perished; nevermore will they have a share in anything done under the sun" (Ecclesiastes 9:5, 6).

CHAPTER 10

Spiritualism Invades the Church

S p"""spiritualists believe that the existence and personal identity of the individual continues after the change called death. Life here, they say, and the life hereafter is all one life, whose continuity of consciousness is unbroken by that mere change in form whose process we call death. For them communication with the so-called dead is a fact, proven by the phenomena of spiritualism. From a Christian perspective, we say that spiritualism, in its most narrow terms, is the belief in the immortality of the soul *and* that men who are still living can communicate with the "spirit" of those who are dead.

We, who hold the Bible to be true, believe that death is a state of unconscious sleep and that there is no communication between the living and those who have died. We further believe that the so-called spirits of the dead that seek to communicate with living men are really evil spirits, fallen evil angels—demons, if you please. Spiritualism in its most dramatic form is Satan's final work of deception. We are told that almost the entire world will board this train headed for hell.

In fact, <u>many of the devil's deceptions are precursors that lead to belief in and the practice of spiritualism.</u> In other words, the road to spiritualism is paved with satanic deceptions. Spiritualism is the central factor in the great controversy at its very end.

Modern Spiritualism

Certainly the devil's encounter with Eve in the Garden of Eden and his assertion "Ye shall not surely die" was really the beginning of spiritualism. But for the purposes of this book we will concern ourselves with the discussion of spiritualism's last-day expressions. In the last days it moves from witchcraft, which is hated and despised by Christians, to a new and more deceptive "Christianized" form. This form is accepted and espoused by the majority of Christians around the world and even endorsed and encouraged by Pope John Paul II—the proclaimed moral leader of the Christian church.

Modern spiritualism began in a small wooden house in the village of Hydesville, New York; a small community on the Erie Canal some 250 miles northwest of New York City. There lived John D. Fox, a Methodist farmer, along with his wife and two daughters, Margaretta, age 15, and Catherine (aka Katie) age 12. A third married daughter, Mrs. Fish, lived in nearby Rochester, New York. On March 31, 1848, the two younger daughters had just gone to bed, and were soon to be joined by their parents in the same room, when the girls heard mysterious raps on the wall. For some reason these rappings were attributed to a spirit. An alphabetic code was set upon whereby the girls "communicated" with these entities. When the "spirit" was addressed in that manner, it answered, giving information about local events. It was soon accepted that the raps were made by the spirit of a man who was buried in the cellar. This theory was further enlarged by a story that raps had been heard there by former occupants of the house.

The girls didn't seem at all disturbed about the phenomenon. But, according to the record, their mother's hair turned white in a week. Shortly after the beginning of these experiences, Margaretta went to Rochester to stay with her sister, Mrs. Fish, and Katie visited the community of Auburn. Wherever the girls went the raps were heard. Mrs. Fish and others became mediums also, and the phenomenon spread rapidly. In just three years communication with the spirits through these so-called mediums was a reality up and down the Atlantic Coast. By 1851 there were an estimated 100 mediums in New York alone. Thus began modern spiritualism in America.

From that time to the present spiritualism has spread rapidly around the world. For a more in-depth study of modern spiritualism consult my book *Sunday's Coming,* chapter 10. I do not intend to cover all the details here that I did in the previous book but rather to here give an update to the "Christianized" form of modern spiritualism.

Spiritualism in the "Mother Church"

There was a period of time following Vatican II that Roman Catholicism referred to the Orthodox churches and the Protestant churches as "sister churches." But now following the release by the Catholic Church of *Dominus Iesus (The Lord Jesus)* the church has officially reinstated the notion that full salvation is available only in the Roman Catholic Church and that all other Christian churches will henceforth be referred to not as sister churches but daughter churches. This document was authorized for publication by the pope himself and signed by Joseph Cardinal Ratzinger on August 6, 2000. Ratzinger is the "prefect" or director of the Office of the Congregation for the Doctrine of the Faith—formerly known as the Office of the Inquisition.

I mention this information to point out that the Roman Catholic Church, which now numbers over a billion nominal members worldwide—one in six of all the inhabitants of earth—has now officially and publically accepted the primary tenets of spiritualism. In the government of the United States there are now 150 Catholics in the 107th Congress, and three of the nine justices on the U.S. Supreme Court are also Roman Catholic. These details are significant because this is the church that wants to be the mother church of all Christians. Their acceptance of spiritualism is a major fulfillment of end-time prophecy. It is a direct fulfillment of the predictions of the Bible and the Spirit of Prophecy.

Over the centuries many pagan beliefs and practices have crept into the Roman Catholic Church. Thomas Aquinas—a 12th-century convert to the church from paganism—introduced many errors. He became the church's leading theologian and introduced much of Greek dualism from the philosophies of Plato and Aristotle. This dualism includes the division of the body from the soul; and the idea that the soul lives on in spirit form after death. With this "philosophical/theological" concept in the belief system, those espousing such a view are sitting ducks for spiritualism.

Prayers to the Saints

Over the centuries the Catholic Church encouraged prayers to the saints—that is, praying to a dead person. Historically there were very few if any instances of the saints talking back to those who prayed to them. However, this changed with the doctrine of the Bodily Assumption of Mary. On November 1, 1950, Pope Pius XII made the allegedly infallible *ex cathedra* declaration in his Apostolic Constitution *Munificentissimus Deus* that "the immaculate Mother of God and ever Virgin Mary was at the end of her life assumed into heaven body and soul." In commenting on this, author Dave Hunt explains, "In the Constitution the pope claimed that the dogma of the assumption had been unanimously believed in the Church from the very beginning and that it was fully supported by Scripture. In fact, the dogma was unknown to the early church and is unsupported by Scripture. Such papal declarations simply responded to the popular sentiment of Catholics and contributed to the growing cult of Mary" (Dave Hunt, *A Woman Rides the Beast,* p. 444).

But what about the current pope? "No one is more convinced of the validity of the Fatima visitations than the present pope. Nor is anyone more devoted to Mary. John Paul II, who has 'dedicated himself and is Pontificate to Our Lady,' bears the M for Mary in his coat of arms; his personal motto, embroidered on the side of his robes in Latin, is *totus tuns sum Maria* (Mary, I'm all yours). The pope has unusual personal reasons for this special devotion. The assault upon his life occurred on May 13, 1981, the anniversary day of the Virgin's alleged first appearance on May 13, 1917, at Fatima, Portugal. In a vision during his convalescence she told him that she had spared his life for a special mission he must fulfill in bringing peace.

"Returning to the Vatican after his recovery, John Paul II prayed at the tombs of his immediate predecessors and declared, 'There could have been another tomb, but the blessed Virgin . . . has willed it otherwise.' He added gratefully and reverently, 'For everything that happened to me on that day, I felt that extraordinary Motherly protection and care, which turned out to be stronger than the deadly bullets.' Why, Hunt asks, would you need God when you have Mary's protection?

"The thankful pope made a pilgrimage to Fatima on May 13, 1982 [one year after the assassination attempt], where he 'prayed before the statue of Our Lady of Fatima. Thousands heard him speak and consecrate the world to Mary as she had requested'" (*ibid.,* pp. 458, 459).

It is interesting that nowhere in the Bible is there a prayer to Mary, not one instance of her miraculously helping anyone, nor any promises that she could or would. Yet "more Catholic prayers are offered to Mary and more attention and honor is given to her than to Christ and God combined. There are thousands of shrines to Mary around the world, with tens of millions of visitors annually, but only one small and scarcely known shrine to Christ located in Beauvoir, Quebec" (*ibid.,* p. 435).

Return to Fatima

On May 13, 1917, three Portuguese shepherd children claimed to have seen "a most beautiful lady" while watching sheep on a hillside west of the village of Fatima. She reportedly told the children she had come "from heaven." In subsequent apparitions "Mary" told the children that two of them would die in childhood and come to be with her, and the surviving child would live to see the second coming of Christ. Francisco and Jacinta did die of illness in childhood, and the surviving child, Lucia, is now 93 years of age. Lucia is now a cloistered Carmelite nun.

The Catholic Church has reported, "Jacinta and Francisco Marto, two of the three shepherd children of Fatima, are now Blessed. On May 13, 2000, at 10:50 a.m. in Portugal, John Paul II pronounced the liturgical formula of beatification during a Mass he celebrated in the field in front of the Basilica of Cova de Iria. More than 500,000 people were present. Thus did John Paul think it best, in the Jubilee Year 2000, to celebrate May 13, [the] 83rd anniversary of the first apparitions of Fatima in 1917 and [the] 19th anniversary of the 1981 attempt on his life in St. Peter's Square" (*Inside the Vatican,* January 2001, p. 48).

The pope has visited the Fatima shrine many times and prays to Mary and offers incense to her on a regular basis. Since we know that Mary is dead and resting in her grave until the resurrection, the actions by the pope—who wants to be the religious leader of the world—demonstrate, practically speaking, that he is a spiritualist.

Demons Working Miracles

Those who claim to have seen Marian apparitions are in some cases fabricating what they say they saw. Many admit that when they spend time and money to visit a famous Marian shrine they don't want to go away without seeing something, so they imagine that they saw something. But this is not the case for every apparition. Some have been seen by a number of people at the same time. They in fact do see a supernatural event, but "These persons overlook the testimony of the Scriptures concerning the wonders wrought by Satan and his agents. It was by satanic aid that Pharaoh's magicians were enabled to counterfeit the work of God. Paul testifies that before the second advent of Christ there will be similar manifestations of satanic power. The coming of the Lord is to be preceded by 'the working of Satan with all power and signs and lying wonders, and with all deceivableness of unrighteousness.' 2 Thessalonians 2:9, 10. And the apostle John, describing the miracle-working power that will be manifested in the last days, declares: 'He doeth great wonders, so that he maketh fire come down from heaven on the earth in the sight of men, and deceiveth them that dwell on the earth by the means of those miracles which he had power to do.' Revelation 13:13, 14. <u>No mere impostures are here foretold. Men are deceived by the miracles which Satan's agents have power to do, not which they pretend to do</u>" (*The Great Controversy*, p. 553).

Adapted to All Classes of People

Satan is not putting his deceptive techniques all in one basket. He custom tailors his spiritualistic deceptions to fit each person's specific weakness. "The prince of darkness, who has so long bent the powers of his mastermind to the work of deception, <u>skillfully adapts his temptations to men of all classes and conditions.</u> To persons of culture and refinement he presents spiritualism in its more refined and intellectual aspects, and thus succeeds in drawing many into his snare" (*ibid.*, p. 554).

We are told that near the end—the time in which we are now living—spiritualism will cover some of its most objectionable characteristics such as communication with the dead, spirit manifestations, and open Satan worship with a veneer of respectability. <u>"It is true that spiritualism is now changing its form and, veiling some of its more objectionable features, is assuming a Christian guise.</u> But its utterances from the platform and the press have been before the public for many years, and in these its real character stands revealed. These teachings cannot be denied or hidden.

"Even in its present form, so far from being more worthy of toleration than formerly, <u>it is really a more dangerous, because a more subtle, deception. While it formerly denounced Christ and the Bible, it now professes to accept both.</u> But the Bible is interpreted in a manner that is pleasing to the unrenewed heart, while its solemn and vital truths are made of no effect. Love is dwelt upon as the chief attribute of God, but it is degraded to a weak sentimentalism, making little distinction between good and evil. God's justice, His denunciations of sin, the requirements of His holy law, are all kept out of sight. The people are taught to regard the Decalogue as a dead letter. Pleasing, bewitching fables captivate the senses and lead men to reject the Bible as the foundation of their faith. <u>Christ is as verily denied as before; but Satan has so blinded the eyes of the people that the deception is not discerned</u>" (*ibid.*, p. 558).

Two very popular phenomena that have spiritualistic roots are sweeping the world at present. The foundation for the acceptance of these ideas has been laid carefully by Satan. Ministers have proclaimed unbiblical doctrines in regard to the state of the dead from "Christian" pulpits around the world for many years. Spiritualistic phenomena and paranormal activity are depicted on television and in the movies as a very real part of life. Of course this carries over to all forms of communication—including music and reading material. And now that the foundation has been laid, "Spiritualism is about to take the world captive. There are many who think that Spiritualism is upheld through trickery and imposture, but this is far from the truth. Superhuman power is working in a variety of ways, and few have any idea as to what will be the manifestations of Spiritualism in the future" (*Evangelism,* p. 603).

Satan has a religion; he has a synagogue and devout worshipers. And in order to increase the ranks of his followers, he uses all kinds of deceptions.

The Holistic Health Movement

Everyone recognizes that physical health is one of our most valuable assets. Yet we live in a time where there is much suffering and pain. In an attempt to get away from drugs and from invasive surgery, many people today are turning to Alternative Health Care providers. Through this avenue Satan is entering into the health-care delivery business and is making serious inroads. Many of Satan's health-care deceptions come from heathenism and Eastern mysticism. Note this insightful statement: "There are many who shrink with horror from the thought of consulting spirit mediums, but who are attracted by more pleasing forms of spiritism, such as the Emmanuel movement. Still others are led astray by the teachings of Christian Science, and by the mysticism of theosophy and other Oriental religions.

"The apostles of nearly all forms of spiritism claim to have the power to cure the diseased. They attribute their power to electricity, magnetism, the so-called "sympathetic remedies," or to latent forces within the mind of man. And there are not a few, even in this Christian age, who go to these healers, instead of trusting in the power of the living God and the skill of well-qualified Christian physicians.

"The mother, watching by the sickbed of her child, exclaims, 'I can do no more! Is there no physician who has power to restore my child!' She is told of the wonderful cures performed by some clairvoyant or magnetic healer, and she trusts her dear one to his charge, placing it as verily in the hand of Satan as if he were standing by her side. In many instances the future life of the child is controlled by a satanic power, which it seems impossible to break.—*Review and Herald,* Jan. 15, 1914" (*Evangelism,* p. 606).

Please note carefully the points I have underlined above. Satan's more pleasing forms of spiritualism come from among other things, Oriental religions and health practices. Followers of the new spiritualism claim to be able to cure disease through the power of electricity, etc. A person subjected to that type of "healing" can come under the control of Satan. In place of this counterfeit we are told that we should trust in the power of God and the skill of well-qualified Christian physicians. "God has placed it in our power to obtain a knowledge of the laws of health. He has made it a duty to preserve our physical powers in the best possible condition, that we may render to Him acceptable service. <u>Those who refuse to improve the light and knowledge that have been mercifully placed within their reach are rejecting one of the means which God has granted them to promote spiritual as well as physical life. They are placing themselves where they will be exposed to the delusions of Satan</u>" (*Counsels on Health,* p. 454).

Many are enticed to think that it is all right if there is a scientific explanation or if certain "experts" give their blessing on a particular questionable practice. "The very name of witchcraft is now held in contempt. The claim that men can hold intercourse with evil spirits is regarded as a fable of the Dark Ages. <u>But spiritualism, which numbers its converts by hundreds of thousands, yea, by millions, which has made its way into scientific circles,</u> which has invaded churches, and has found favor in legislative bodies, and even in the courts of kings—<u>this mammoth deception is but a revival, in a new disguise, of the witchcraft condemned and prohibited of old</u>" (*The Great Controversy,* p. 556).

Ellen White points out that the source of these so-called electric currents is really Satan. "While they speak with scorn of the magicians of old, the great deceiver laughs in triumph as <u>they yield to his arts under a different form.</u> His agents still claim to cure disease. They attribute their power to electricity, magnetism, or the so-called "sympathetic remedies." <u>In truth, they are but channels for Satan's electric currents.</u> By this means he casts his spell over the bodies and souls of men" (*Testimonies for the Church,* vol. 5, p. 193).

But we haven't seen his "best" stuff yet. "Wonderful scenes, with which Satan will be closely connected, will soon take place. God's Word declares that Satan will work miracles. He will make people sick, and then will suddenly remove from them his satanic power. They will then be regarded as healed. <u>These works of apparent healing will bring Seventh-day Adventists to the test.</u> Many who have had great light will fail to walk in the light, because they have not become one with Christ.—Letter 57, 1904" (*Selected Messages,* vol. 2, p. 53). Those who look for miracles as a sign of divine intervention are in serious danger of deception. By these "lying wonders" Satan will deceive, if possible, the very elect. Let's not think for a moment that we are not susceptible to spiritualism. That is why Jesus warned, "Go not forth" to see them. "There are strong men, precious in the sight of God, who are under a spell. They do not realize that they are represented by the foolish virgins. Scientific spiritualistic philosophy has taken the minds of some from the message to be proclaimed at this time" (*Manuscript Releases,* vol. 3, p. 361).

And when strong men are sucked in by spiritualism many other poor souls follow their lead. "The time has come when even in the church and in our institutions, some will depart from the faith, giving heed to seducing spirits and doctrines of devils. But God will keep that which is committed to Him. Let us draw near to Him, that He may draw near to us. . . . Through those who depart from the faith, the power of the enemy will be exercised to lead others astray" (*Selected Messages,* vol. 3, p. 411).

A Case in Point—The Eoin Giller Story

Originally from Australia and trained as a Seventh-day Adventist minister at Avondale College, Eoin Giller moved to the United States and worked as a minister in several conferences including Arizona and New York. He has since left the Seventh-day Adventist Church following an association with the "healing ministry of Benny Hinn" and the "Toronto Airport Blessing." Now back in Australia, he considers himself a healer and a prophet. In the interest of accuracy, I will quote directly from Eoin Giller's own words as he posted them on the Internet.

"The importance of what I believe to be a revelation from God for the Seventh-day Adventist Church impels me to write this background account so that seasoned Christian leaders may understand a little about who I am, and the spirit in which I bring my testimony at this critical hour for the Church. . . . I invite you to reserve judgment until the fruit of this work is fully manifested. May God bless you as you ponder a small portion of one man's experience of the supernatural in our time.

"A new experience of God's Spirit entered my life in 1991. I noticed that my hands began to burn with heat sometimes during a regular weekly prayer meeting in the Desert Valley Church in Tucson, Arizona. At first I ignored it, but the sensation gradually increased from week to week, and it came only in prayer meeting! What could it mean? Was it the stealthy advance of arthritis, or some dread malady? It wasn't until three years later, that I discovered from experienced Spirit-baptized Christians that people who experience this radiant burning heat in the nerves of their hands are often the recipients of the biblical gift of healing mentioned in 1 Corinthians 12."

Giller then relates how he healed himself of migraine headaches and also "healed" several church members in Albany, New York, of back problems. He then relates this story of involvement with TV healer Benny Hinn.

"My second granddaughter was born a few days after Christmas. This happy event was marred by the gradual unfolding of Kymber's physical difficulties. Her left hand was twisted and curled back at her side. Her head seemed to be always on its side on her left shoulder. When we lifted her up above our heads, she would 'body surf' as we called it. Instead of curling up with flexed limbs like a normal baby her whole body would stretch out rigid. A crisis developed when Kymber was hospitalized for some days with uncontrollable seizures. Heavy medication eventually controlled the seizures, but by then we were all aware that Kymber had suffered some sort of brain damage, a condition that medical science could not help.

"My daughter Sherryn [Kymber's mother] and her husband Thumper (Don is his first name) were burned out as Adventist young adults. They had stopped regular church attendance, having been exposed to too much legalism and critical attitudes among church people. But Sherryn had not stopped seeking the Lord. In her desperation to have her baby healed, she was watching Benny Hinn on TV. One morning she asked me if I would take her to a Benny Hinn crusade and see if the Lord would heal Kymber. I thought about the implications of attending the Hinn crusade. As an Adventist pastor I would incur potential risk to my employment. But Sherryn's pleading eyes won the day. By then I had become convinced that the days of miracles were not over, and that God could heal Kymber when medical science had no cure. This was Kymber's hope for a normal life and future, and all else fell into a very second place beside the hope for her healing. I decided to take Sherryn and Kymber to a Benny Hinn crusade in Philadelphia the next week. But I did ask Sherryn to keep the two-day trip quiet, for the sake of fragile church members.

"Sherryn, Kymber, and I booked into a motel south of Philadelphia. We stood in line for hours to get into the Thursday evening crusade meeting, and eventually secured seats in the bleachers on the lefthand side of the auditorium. Neither Sherryn nor I had ever experienced such powerful, God-centered worship. It was simply awesome! During the worship, a young woman standing in the row in front of Sherryn turned and asked if she could hold Kymber. Sherryn passed her across. As the young woman played with Kymber she raised her above her head. For the first time ever I saw Kymber lifted up without her body stiffening in the body-surf position. I thought nothing of it at the time.

"Sherryn was amazed at the numbers and qualities of the healings manifested in the meeting. So was I! It was clear that Benny Hinn could not pay enough actors to fake the hundreds of healings. We saw people walk out of wheelchairs, blind eyes and deaf ears opened, oxygen tanks discarded, and healings of almost every kind. The reaction of the people healed and their relatives convinced us that this was genuine healing. Benny Hinn gave all the glory to God. We were convinced that this was not Satan casting out Satan. The creative miracles were stamped with divinity.

"Then Pastor Hinn gave an altar call. My burned-out daughter responded. Years of experiencing traditional Christianity dropped away in a moment. She had seen the hand of God. This was the real thing. Sherryn carried Kymber down to the floor of the auditorium (still unaware of her daughter's healing), and surrendered her life to Christ. She was born again. (This was the greater of the two miracles for us that night, for the miracle of the new birth reaches into eternity.)

"When we arrived back to our hotel, Sherryn took Kymber's temperature. The baby was so hot, Sherryn was concerned Kymber was catching some malady. We were too new to the physical phenomena which accompany divine healings to recognize that heat is often significant in physical healings. The thermometer indicated a normal body temperature. 'Strange!' we thought. 'Strange' is the right word! One doesn't normally take a damaged and sick baby to church and return home to report a wonderful healing, at least not in conservative or evangelical religious circles. Yes, Kymber was healed from neurological damage that had been with her since birth. Her hand has uncurled, her head is upright, and her seizures have completely stopped. She has been taken off phenobarbital and has been given a clean bill of health."

Giller then relates how his "healing ministry" has developed and that in the last three years he has witnessed over 30 verifiable miracles. He goes on to relate:

"Coming now to recent times, a deeper experience awaited me in 1994. On October 22 of that year many Adventist clergy in the New York Conference attended the one hundred and fiftieth anniversary of the Millerite great disappointment. After much heart-searching and prayer, my family chose rather to travel to Worcester, MA, to attend a Benny Hinn crusade on that same day.

"I'll never forget what happened in that crusade. The Lord gave me the baptism in fire! Prior to this experience, I had regarded the words of John the Baptist as largely metaphorical: 'When He comes, He will baptize you in the Spirit and with fire.' During that morning crusade meeting, fire rolled through my body for two and a half hours. I could not focus on the worship, the preaching, or the healings. I was immersed in fire, lost to everything around me. Pastor Hinn even spoke a word of knowledge about the fire on someone in the congregation."

Giller then reports about his trip to the Toronto Airport Vineyard Christian Fellowship and the outpouring of the Holy Spirit. He says it was at this meeting that he received the prophetic gift. And now as a prophet, "the Lord has revealed to me the secrets of people's hearts, and instructed me how to minister to them in ways I would never have thought of on my own."

As a postlude to this remember that at the beginning of his "testimony" Eoin Giller asked the reader to "reserve judgment until the fruit of this work is fully manifest." What has happened since? Now Benny Hinn, who started Giller down this road away from God's remnant church, is confessing publically that he is praying at the graves of and communicating with dead healers of the past—this can only be called spiritualism. And pastors from Australia now report that Giller is praying for people with amalgam dental fillings and they are turning to gold!

The Harry Potter Phenomenon

The Harry Potter novels have swept the globe, bridging cultures, changing the book business, and creating trends. "Three and a half years ago, no one on earth had heard of Harry Potter except J. K. [Joanne Kathleen] Rowling, the writer who dreamed him up, and the publishers' readers who had rejected the manuscript of her first book featuring the bespectacled boy wizard. And now? Four Harry Potter novels later, translations into 42 languages later, 76 million copies sold worldwide later? Strange, strange things are happening wherever on Earth the young fictional hero and his friends can be found" (*Time,* December 25, 2000–January 1, 2001).

The three main characters are Harry Potter and his two best friends at the Hogwarts School of Witchcraft and Wizardry. A wizard is one skilled in magic or a sorcerer. There will be a total of seven Harry Potter novels— three more to go. *Time* goes on to say, "No one can explain the literally unprecedented Harry Potter phenomenon, starting with Rowling, now 35, whose life has been changed utterly by the product of her imagination. Seven years ago, she was the single mother of a small daughter, living in a two-room flat in Edinburgh, listening to mice skittering between the walls. Now she is internationally famous and earning, according to various estimates, somewhere in the range of $30 million to $40 million a year" *(ibid.).*

J. K. Rowling was the cover feature on the December 2000 issue of *Reader's Digest* with the large headline "The Woman Who Bewitched the World." In this article Rowling tells of how her mother died of MS at the age of 45. Then in a moving scene in her first book, *Harry Potter and the Sorcerer's Stone,* "Harry stares into a magic mirror that lets him see what he most craves in his life. In it he sees his dead parents seemingly alive. It is a rare autobiographical insight into Rowling's feelings about her own loss."

No big thing you say? Think of it this way. With the number of books sold, there are at least 76 million young minds out there that have been prepared for the paranormal—for the bewitching influence of Satan. "Spiritualism is the masterpiece of deception. It is Satan's most successful and fascinating delusion" *(Signs of the Times,* August 26, 1889).

We are warned that in the last days we must be careful about what we read so as not to be overcome by the power of Satan. "We have reached the perils of the last days, when some, yes, many, shall depart from the faith, giving heed to seducing spirits and doctrines of devils. Be cautious in regard to what you read and how you hear. Take not a particle of interest in spiritualistic theories. Satan is waiting to steal a march upon everyone who allows himself to be deceived by his hypnotism. He begins to exert his power over them just as soon as they begin to investigate his theories" *(Medical Ministry,* p. 101).

The Powerful Grip of Spiritualism

"There are few who have any just conception of the deceptive power of spiritualism and the danger of coming under its influence. Many tamper with it merely to gratify their curiosity. They have no real faith in it and would be filled with horror at the thought of yielding themselves to the spirits' control. But they venture upon the forbidden ground, and the mighty destroyer exercises his power upon them against their will. Let them once be induced to submit their minds to his direction, and he holds them captive. It is impossible, in their own strength, to break away from the bewitching, alluring spell. Nothing but the power of God, granted in answer to the earnest prayer of faith, can deliver these ensnared souls" (*The Great Controversy,* p. 558).

"All who indulge sinful traits of character, or willfully cherish a known sin, are inviting the temptations of Satan. They separate themselves from God and from the watchcare of His angels; as the evil one presents his deceptions, they are without defense and fall an easy prey. Those who thus place themselves in his power little realize where their course will end. Having achieved their overthrow, the tempter will employ them as his agents to lure others to ruin" *(ibid.).*

If you have ever wondered about what it will be like at the end, then extrapolate from the current spiritualistic phenomenon in its many forms. Satan is building on nearly 6,000 years of experience in this area. "Satan has long been preparing for his final effort to deceive the world. The foundation of his work was laid by the assurance given to Eve in Eden: 'Ye shall not surely die.' 'In the day ye eat thereof, then your eyes shall be opened, and ye shall be as gods, knowing good and evil.' Genesis 3:4, 5. Little by little he has prepared the way for his masterpiece of deception in the development of spiritualism. He has not yet reached the full accomplishment of his designs; but it will be reached in the last remnant of time. Says the prophet: 'I saw three unclean spirits like frogs; . . . they are the spirits of devils, working miracles, which go forth unto the kings of the earth and of the whole world, to gather them to the battle of that great day of God Almighty.' Revelation 16:13, 14. Except those who are kept by the power of God, through faith in His word, the whole world will be swept into the ranks of this delusion. The people are fast being lulled to a fatal security, to be awakened only by the outpouring of the wrath of God" *(ibid.,* p. 561).

Many who are taken in by the deceptions of spiritualism will not realize that they have been deceived. In other words, they are not consciously "working for the devil." But when they are awakened to the deception by the outpouring of the wrath of God in the seven last plagues—they will literally go crazy. "The developments of these last days will soon become decided. <u>When these spiritualistic deceptions are revealed to be what they really are—the secret workings of evil spirits— those who have acted a part in them will become as men who have lost their minds"</u> (*This Day With God,* p. 312).

Battle of the Spirits

Yes, the invisible forces of good and evil are in a fierce battle for the souls of men, women, and young people. In the near future "many will be confronted by the spirits of devils personating beloved relatives or friends and declaring the most dangerous heresies. These visitants will appeal to our tenderest sympathies and will work miracles to sustain their pretensions. We must be prepared to withstand them with the Bible truth that the dead know not anything and that they who thus appear are the spirits of devils. <u>Satanic agencies in human form will take part</u> in this last great conflict to oppose the building up of the kingdom of God. <u>And heavenly angels in human guise will be on the field</u> of action. The two opposing parties will continue to exist till the closing up of the last great chapter in this world's history" (*Maranatha,* p. 167).

God's Promised Protection

We are no match for this invisible, mighty foe, and his evil angels. But God has defeated them before and His angels "excel in strength." So we must stay close to Jesus for protection. Jesus in Revelation 3:10 promises us, "Because you have kept My command to preserve, I also will keep you from the hour of trial which shall come upon the whole world, to test those who dwell on the earth."

"He [Jesus] would sooner send every angel out of heaven to protect His people than leave one soul that trusts in Him to be overcome by Satan" (*The Great Controversy,* p. 560). We have many powerful and reassuring promises. "But if the one in danger perseveres, and in his helplessness casts himself upon the merits of the blood of Christ, <u>our Saviour listens to the earnest prayer of faith, and sends a reinforcement of those angels that excel in strength to deliver him.</u> Satan cannot endure to have his powerful rival appealed to, for he fears and trembles before His strength and majesty. <u>At the sound of fervent prayer, Satan's whole host trembles.</u> He continues to call legions of evil angels to accomplish his object. And when angels, all-powerful, clothed with the armory of heaven, come to the help of the fainting, pursued soul, <u>Satan and his host fall back,</u>

<u>well knowing that their battle is lost</u>" (*Testimonies for the Church,* vol. 1, p. 345).

We have a part to play in our own safety. We are to walk in the path of duty—to be obedient to the commands of God. Accordingly, this last promise is conditional: "Angels of God will preserve His people while they walk in the path of duty; but there is no assurance of such protection for those who deliberately venture upon Satan's ground" (*Evangelism,* p. 607).

An End-Time Phenomenon

We know from Revelation 12:12 that when Satan works with great wrath he knows that he has only a short time left. In the same perspective, "Paul, in his second letter to the Thessalonians, points to the special working of Satan in spiritualism as an event to take place immediately before the second advent of Christ. Speaking of Christ's second coming, he declares that it is "after the working of Satan with all power and signs and lying wonders." 2 Thessalonians 2:9" (*Maranatha,* p. 168). These desperate workings of Satan should awaken us to the realization that we are standing on the threshold of the literal second coming of Christ.

CHAPTER 11

Weighing the Evidence

Sometimes the evidence of God's leading is almost overwhelming and undeniable. At other times the evidence while it is available, must be diligently searched for. From the biblical perspective it was not the amount of evidence that convinced people of the value of the gospel or the authenticity of Jesus as the long-awaited Messiah. Many who followed Jesus were very simple people. Some had very little education, while others were teachers and civic leaders.

Let's look at the experience of John the Baptist and some of Jesus' disciples so that we can see what evidence they found and the level of trust they placed in it. In fact, they were willing to die for their belief in Jesus. John the Baptist had very little "face time" with Jesus, yet he believed that He was the One who would take away the sin of the world.

We must ask ourselves, "How much more evidence do we need to see to be willing to risk all for the kingdom? Do we have enough evidence now or will it take more to keep us on the right side in the great battle of the spirits? Our faithfulness to our beliefs, if they are founded on a correct understanding of the Word of God, is a life or death matter. Our eternal life is literally hanging in the balance as we respond to the evidence that God gives us.

John the Baptist is one of the most remarkable characters in all the Bible. Think about how he related himself to the word of God in his day. He never went to any formal school. He was obviously not a graduate of a theological seminary. He had no grandiose pedigree. He was a simple country boy.

His father was a minister. A priest. A descendant of Aaron. We would never have heard of Zacharias if it were not for his son John. One afternoon while Zacharias was offering incense at the golden altar of the Temple, the angel Gabriel told him he was to have a son. Zacharias didn't believe it, and he was struck dumb. He remained speechless all the nine months that his wife was pregnant.

When his boy was born, the Scriptures record Zacharias's magnificent ode to the prophetic ministry of his son. A beautiful poem in which inspiration used his mind to describe the way his son would introduce the Messiah.

And for 30 years that boy grew up. Who knows where. We are simply told that it was the hill country of Judea. The hill country of Judea is no park in living green. It has no beautiful and bounteous trees. It is a desert. It had very few inhabitants. And in the solitude John grew to manhood. He was a contemplative boy. He had been told, of course, about the experience of his father when his birth was predicted. He knew about his father's punishment for unbelief. And he must have thought many times about the picture of his ministry that his father had given under inspiration. What he did during his growing-up years we are not told. But when he turned 30 years of age he came preaching.

The story begins in Matthew 3:1: "In those days John the Baptist came preaching in the wilderness of Judea, and saying," No sound of trumpets. No band. No impressive academic robes. No pastoral introduction or *vitae* calling attention to what he had accomplished. John came preaching, with a burning intensity in his soul. This is what we ought to contemplate. There were millions of men and women in Israel far better educated than John the Baptist. Many held down far more prestigious positions than his dad ever held or that he had ever held. What list of achievements did he have? What background did he have that they didn't have? But they didn't come preaching. They made no proclamation of a coming Messiah.

Six hundred years before, the prophet Isaiah had predicted a voice crying in the wilderness "prepare a way for the Lord. In the desert a highway for our God." John prepared the way for Jehovah—the Son of God, the Son of Man, Emmanuel, Jesus of Nazareth. Why didn't anyone else do it? Why didn't those with proper credentials do it? This is one of the great mysteries of life. And this same mystery is working today—as we shall see.

It has happened in every age. Every age! What fired John Wycliffe? From that tiny little village of Lutterworth—way off the tourist path—in the center of England. What fired him to gather about him young men who were later known as the Lollards? He sent them out preaching the ever-lasting gospel. What did it?

What about John Huss, the Goose of Constance, as he was called? What raised him up? What fired his heart?

What of Luther? His father was a miner. And as he said, "I was a poor monk going from door to door begging my food." What raised him up?

Why did the Spirit of God choose these persons? What did they have that the others didn't have? Not many wise are called. Not many powerful. Not many noble. But God hath chosen the poor of this world. Those rich in faith.

Those 30 years that John had lived in the wilderness he thought; he read; he prayed; he studied. And there converged in his consciousness—his mind—all the messages of Scripture that threw light on the face of the coming One. Though he had never seen Him, he came to know the Messiah. The time, the place, the family, the character, the mission, all had been predicted. We must ask, "Why didn't Annas see this? Why didn't Caiaphas discern it? Why didn't the learned Nicodemus know it?

Jesus asked the inquiring Nicodemus, "Art thou a teacher in Israel and don't know these things?" What happens in circumstances like this? This is the point that I want to make—the evidence of eternal truth is in the air. And whether we perceive it and breathe it depends more on us than it. It passes by the learned. It passes by those of position. It passes by the powerful. And lodges in the mind of an unknown—John the Baptizer!

And so he comes. Matthew tells us and Luke tells us precisely when he came. Let's look at this fascinating verse. Luke 3:1, 2:

[1] "Now in the fifteenth year of the reign of Tiberius Caesar,
[2] Pontius Pilate being governor of Judea,
[3] Herod being tetrarch of Galilee,
[4] his brother Philip tetrarch of Iturea and the region of Trachonitis,
[5] and Lysanias tetrarch of Abilene,
[6] while Annas and Caiaphas were high priests,
the word of God came to John the son of Zacharias in the wilderness."

Six points. Six significant points of evidence that to a lawyer, a scholar, or a Bible student are extremely significant. When you plot all of those time lines they converge precisely in only one year. Six clear points of evidence. So the coming of John the Baptist, six months before the coming of Christ, can be nailed down historically. These six points synchronize the Bible narrative. There is only one point in time. In the spring of A.D. 27 John began to preach. All of the prophecies focus on that precise moment. All heaven was looking down at that moment.

Isaiah had declared the mission of John the Baptist without naming him—he would come in the Spirit and power of Elijah. The Tishbite was another anonymous proclaimer of the truth. He suddenly came. You would be hard put to make a biography of Elijah before He appeared before Ahab. But God had prepared His man. Just as He prepared John 800 years later. And John came—fully convinced. In his mind all the evidence pointed irrefutably to the coming of the Messiah. And he came preaching. "The time is fulfilled. The kingdom of heaven is at hand. Repent! There cometh one after me, the latches of whose shoe I am not worthy to loose."

In another sermon he said, "There standeth among you one!" He knew. And again I must ask the question "Why didn't anyone else know?" What was there so special about him? And again the answer is simple: his personal relationship with God. His personal relationship with the Scriptures. People today talk about their relationship with Jesus. But how shallow it seems in comparison to these great men of the Bible. John's vertical connection gave him 20/20 vision in his horizontal view of life.

I hope you are seeing the overtones for all the revelation that has been given for us today. We, too, are living in a time when prophecies are focusing—converging. We, too, are looking for the coming of a Saviour. There are literally hundreds of pieces of evidence for this. Whether we read that evidence, whether we interpret it correctly, depends, too, more on us than the evidence. There are people who apparently see very little evidence that the coming of Christ is right at our door. Some even make fun of those of us who study the signs of the end as given in the Bible and seek to compare them with our day.

Our relationship with God is vital. John 7:17 reveals who will know and understand, "Whosoever willeth to do His will; he shall know the teaching." Willing to do His will. Willing to investigate the evidence. And because of his relationship to God, his relationship to the Scriptures, John could see the logic and the clarity of all the evidence he had at his fingertips. So when the time came, all the Spirit had to do was to nudge his mind. There in the wilderness of Judea, he began to proclaim. He came preaching and saying, "This is that which was spoken by the prophet Isaiah." He knew who he was. He knew where the biblical prophecies pointed. And nobody was going to shake his conviction.

They asked him, "Who are you? Are you one of the prophets? Are you Elijah? Are you the Messiah who is to come?" He had no doubt of his personal identity. "I am that voice that was to cry in the wilderness prepare a way for the Lord—in the desert a highway for my God. I am an announcer." And as he preached from day to day, he kept that focus. His total ministry was only about 6 months—and half that time he spent in Herod's dungeon before his execution. But his short ministry had the brilliance of a meteorite passing through a darkened sky. It was enough to call attention to the One who was coming.

In his short ministry John was joined by other sincere young men. And two disciples heard John speak, "Behold the Lamb of God" and followed the Lamb of God (John 1:37). And when Jesus saw them following Him He said to them, "What are you seeking?" And they said to Him, "Rabbi, where dwellest thou?" And He said, "Come and see." Where did He dwell? "Foxes have holes," He said later on, "the birds of the air have nests, but the Son of Man hath not where to lay His head." Where did He sleep? Perhaps under a bush? Where did He wash the next morning? Where He could find a stream. Sometimes people invited Him to their homes. We have come to understand that His favorite place was in Bethany at the home of Mary, Martha, and Lazarus. Sometimes they asked Him to a meal. And when the meal was over, He went out and found somewhere to sleep.

And when the two disciples of John saw where He abode, (verse 40) one of the two, Andrew, Simon Peter's brother, found his brother Simon and said to him, "We have found the Messiah." Found the Messiah? Sleeping under a hedge? Where did they get the evidence? The evidence was in the air. Whether we understand it or not depends more on us than on the evidence. And when Andrew found Peter, he brought him to Jesus. And Jesus said to Andrew's brother, "Thou art Simon, thou shalt be called Cephas." Which translated into Greek becomes petros, which is by interpretation a stone.

There was another young man. We are told in verse 43 that his name was Philip. And he went and found his friend, Nathaniel. And Philip proclaimed, "We have found Him of whom Moses and the prophets spake. Jesus of Nazareth, the son of Joseph." To which Nathaniel responded, "Can any good thing come out of Nazareth?" And Philip said, "Come and see." Come and see. And as he came, Jesus said to him, "Behold an Israelite indeed in whom is no guile." And Nathaniel said, "Whence knowest thou me?" Jesus answered and said, "Before Philip called thee when thou wast under the fig tree, I saw thee." Then He says (in verse 51), "Ye shall see the heavens opened and the angels of God ascending and descending upon the Son of Man." Nathaniel had been reading Genesis 28 about the ladder going up to heaven. When Jesus revealed to him that He was aware of what he was doing, the evidence came together within Nathaniel's mind. Jesus was that mystic ladder that connected earth to heaven. He was the Lord Jesus Himself. He is the way from here to there. At His command, the angels ascend and descend. Now suddenly in these few verses we see three disciples who were all absolutely convinced that they had found the Messiah.

And each with different little pieces of evidence. Much of which would be scientifically interpreted as subjective. What proof did they have? Let me pause a moment on that word "proof." There are very, very few things that we can prove. We don't function on proof. Day by day we function based on evidence. There are many things that you can't prove. I couldn't prove to you that my wife, Kathy, loves me. I could give you evidence a yard long. She has put up with me for 35 years. She must have some motivation. I couldn't tell you how many of my clothes she has washed. But I could get them done in a laundromat, and the laundromat doesn't love me. She can do the same thing, and it is evidence to me of love. It's purely subjective. No outside proof. You cannot prove love. You have evidences for an experience.

And in these relationships to the Messiah the evidence was much more experiential than it was coldly scientific. Let me tell you how that can work. You are reading the Bible. You may be John the Baptist. You may be Nathaniel sitting under a tree. You may be Bob or Sarah sitting in your study or in your living room, reading your Bible. And you are thinking thoughts. And when you are reading one passage, many other ideas from other passages you have read keep floating through your mind. And then suddenly there is a Spirit-indited synapse. Ideas that are separate suddenly come together. For example, you are reading the first few verses of Revelation 13 regarding the description of a beast with features of a lion, a bear, and a leopard, and you think, *I have seen this before. It sounds very much like Daniel 7.* And so two thoughts converge into one. The picture becomes clearer. And when this happens what has come together is much larger than the sum of the parts. You have a vision. You have a picture.

One Sabbath morning you listen to testimonies by others of how they are certain that God has been working with them. Then you remember the time when you were driving down the highway and you wanted to change lanes and you started to do so and something kept you from doing so and then you saw the car that was right there at your elbow—in your blind spot. You lifted up your heart to God and said, "God, thank You." Can you prove to anyone else that it was the Lord? No. You don't even mention it. But there within your soul something has happened. You asked God to bless you when you started out on that highway. You asked Him to protect you. And there in that split second something happened, and you know that God answered your prayers. The evidence is within you. The Spirit finds your reaction within your heart. And you say, "Thank You for the angel ministry."

The men we are discussing were willing to put themselves where the Spirit of God could use them. They knew that it was right. We have all heard children answer when asked why they did something, "Because." Did you ever say that? You can't argue with "Because." You ask John the Baptist, "Why do you believe this?" and he says, "Because. I have lots of reasons. Many things have happened."

You ask Philip, "You mean that you went to see where He spends the night and you then believe He is the Messiah? Why? How do you know He is the Messiah?" "Well, because. Something happened when I was there. I know. No one else could do that to me. Only the Messiah could do that. The way He did it. What happened came together in my mind and brought conviction."

I want to ask you just now, "Have you found the Messiah?" Jesus of Nazareth? Really found Him. Like John the Baptist are you ready to even have your head chopped off because of Him? Like Peter, are you ready to be crucified upside down because of Him? "We have found the Messiah," they said. "We have found Him of whom Moses and the prophets spoke." Have you found Him? Can you say of Him as Nathaniel said, "Rabbi, thou art the Son of God, thou art the king of Israel"? Why? Because within his mind, Genesis 28 and the ladder had now put on sandals and was walking in Palestine. "Thou art the Son of God, Thou art the king of Israel."

Have you found the Messiah? Many of us have encountered Him years ago. Now and as you read this book will you review the evidence that God has given to you? We must see Jesus more clearly, more precisely, in sharper focus than ever before. We must see Jesus come in the clouds of heaven with power and great glory. One day this same Jesus is coming again. And He has given us much evidence—that when taken together points clearly to our day! Have we found Him? Would we recognize Him? Are we searching for the evidence?

As you recall from your reading of Scripture, there were all kinds of false christs in the days of John the Baptist. Two years later Gamaliel made a list of all the false messiahs. Jesus said that in the last days many false christs would come to deceive if possible even the very elect. Have we found Him, the only true Christ? Do we have all the evidence that will fix in our mind a faith in Jesus that will never be shaken? If I am not willing to return to Him a tithe of my increase which is His, have I really found the Messiah? If I am willing to rob Him, would I die for Him? And so today, all the prophecies are converging. Six millennia of prophetic revelation are concentrating their light upon us.

Just now all the ages of prophecy look down on us. Their consummation is tomorrow—very soon. Jesus is coming. And if we don't find Messiah now we probably won't find Him then.

What is our relationship to the Scriptures? How much time do we spend in the carpenter shop or in the hill country of Judea? Or under a tree in the village? Or mending our nets by the seaside? Are we thinking about that prophetic word? How much time do we invest in allowing the Spirit to bring the cluster of memories back into our minds of what we have read that the evidences may be clear? So that when Jesus invites us here or there, or somewhere else, to come and see, we are ready to respond? Our conviction will be firm and resolute? The evidence is in the air. We can accept it or we can reject it. We can find the Messiah or we can turn our backs indifferently and go our way. Those are the only alternatives.

These stories are in the Bible for our benefit. We must realize that as we face the decisions of our lives in the end-time, God has given us plenty of evidence upon which to base our decisions. And those decisions will tell for life or death.

CHAPTER 12

Rome's Rebirth

Early one morning a number of years ago, when we were living in Jackson, Mississippi, I received a call from a nurse who was a member of our church. She was at work at the hospital and she explained that they needed a chaplain to minister to a grieving family.

Upon arriving at the hospital I learned that there had been a terrible traffic accident on Interstate 55 just north of town in the very early morning. A family of five had been returning home from a vacation on the Gulf Coast. Likely mom and dad were up front driving—trying to keep each other awake as they headed back home to school and work. The three children, two boys and a girl, were sleeping: one was probably in the second seat and the other two in the back part of the station wagon. Then something very unexpected happened. A man traveling south on the same interstate had stopped to rest or get gas, and when he entered the interstate again he mistakenly entered on the northbound side. I was not a party to the legal ramifications of this experience, but apparently he was confused by fatigue or alcohol and drove right past the "Wrong Way" signs on the northbound exit as he entered the freeway.

Just a few moments later the car driven by the family and the one with the lone driver met at interstate speeds in a head-on collision. Four people were killed instantly—the lone driver, and the husband and wife and one child in the other car. The two children who survived, a boy and the girl, were seriously injured and unconscious. Now they were just regaining consciousness, and the hospital staff called me to be the one to explain to them what had happened—that the accident had proved fatal to their mom, dad, and brother. It was an experience that I shall never forget. Four lives ended because one person had mistakenly gone the wrong way.

What could have been done to avoid the fatal crash? The most sensible thing, of course, would have been to stop and sleep when bedtime came. But suppose that you were in a position to warn one of the drivers what was likely to occur under the circumstances. What if you were traveling south on the same interstate at the same time of night and looked across the median and saw a car traveling the same direction as you? What if you had a CB radio and made a call, or flashed your lights, or sounded your horn, or done anything that might have alerted the other driver to the danger?

What do you think might have been the response from the other driver? Maybe he would have said, "What is that crazy guy doing on the other side of the road? He must be high on something." But then maybe he might have received your warning with understanding and said, "Oh, I am going the wrong way. I'm in the wrong lane. I must quickly change directions." Under these circumstances, would it be bigotry or an act of self-righteousness for someone to give a warning of danger ahead? Obviously not. But today, as predicted by Scripture, many of life's travelers are going in the wrong direction, with potentially eternal consequences, and society is plagued with such a penchant for "political correctness" and extreme tolerance that it is considered bigotry and self-righteousness to give a warning of the danger ahead!

But there is danger ahead—right ahead. The prophetic picture laid out in the Bible and reconfirmed to the end-time remnant church is finally coming into sharp focus. The end-time resurgence of the Roman Catholic Church* has, as we used to say, "shifted into high gear." Revelation 13 contains the prediction that even though that power would receive a deadly wound at the end of the Middle Ages, during the time of the end the deadly wound would be healed and all the world would wonder after it and the power behind it. We can say with all candor, "The perils of the last days are upon us, and in our work we are to warn the people of the danger they are in. Let not the solemn scenes which prophecy has revealed be left untouched. If our people were half awake, if they realized the nearness of the events portrayed in the Revelation, a reformation would be wrought in our churches, and many more would believe the message. We have no time to lose; God calls upon us to watch for souls as they that must give an account" (*Maranatha*, p. 140).

The New World Religion

This is not an easy chapter to write. But by the grace of God I will attempt to do so in the spirit of love and concern. As I have mentioned elsewhere in the book, we are living in an age of extreme tolerance. In fact, it could be a defining sin of our day. To take a stand for biblical, moral, or religious truth often causes one to be called prejudiced and bigoted. But we are all fellow travelers on our earthly and spiritual journey. I believe that we are duty bound before God to help our fellow travelers find the straight and narrow way that leads to life.

I want to share with you some very straightforward information. I will not be "beating around the bush," but rather it will be very pointed and direct. First, we will consider the prophetic picture given many years ago.

I am going to share with you some predictions from the book *The Great Controversy* regarding the world players at the end, and then we will examine how these words are being fulfilled today.

The Prophetic Warning

"As the time comes for it [the message of the third angel] to be given with greatest power [during the latter rain], the Lord will work through humble instruments, leading the minds of those who consecrate themselves to His service. The laborers will be qualified rather by the unction of His Spirit than by the training of literary institutions. Men of faith and prayer will be constrained to go forth with holy zeal, declaring the words which God gives them. The sins of Babylon will be laid open. The fearful results of enforcing the observances of the church by civil authority, the inroads of spiritualism, the stealthy but rapid progress of the papal power—all will be unmasked. By these solemn warnings the people will be stirred. Thousands upon thousands will listen who have never heard words like these. In amazement they hear the testimony that Babylon is the church, fallen because of her errors and sins, because of her rejection of the truth sent to her from heaven. As the people go to their former teachers with the eager inquiry, Are these things so? the ministers present fables, prophesy smooth things, to soothe their fears and quiet the awakened conscience. But since many refuse to be satisfied with the mere authority of men and demand a plain 'Thus saith the Lord,' the popular ministry, like the Pharisees of old, filled with anger as their authority is questioned, will denounce the message as of Satan and stir up the sin-loving multitudes to revile and persecute those who proclaim it" (*The Great Controversy*, p. 606).

This point can well be illustrated in the fact that politicians and others tried to paint George W. Bush as a bigoted, self-righteous, intolerant extremist when he visited Bob Jones University during the 2000 presidential primary. All this because the university has maintained a historic Protestant view of the Roman Catholic Church.

In a very well researched and written article titled *"Solely, Totally, and Only Rome,"* printed in the *Adventist Review,* December 23, 1999, author Clifford Goldstein concluded, "When we compromise on Rome (an entity that began through compromise) we become like what we have condemned. Thus, when we compromise on Rome, we condemn ourselves."

Forces that cannot be stopped are working to establish the Roman Catholic Church-State as the world's moral authority. The Papacy is working steadily to enter into agreements with countries and religions around the world to bring peace and brotherhood to the earth.

Many readers will appreciate a greater foundation in the prophetic picture. I recommend that you carefully read *The Great Controversy,* chapters 35-38. I will quote a few lines from chapter 35:

"Romanism is now regarded by Protestants with far greater favor than in former years. In those countries where Catholicism is not in the ascendancy, and the papists are taking a conciliatory course in order to gain influence, there is an increasing indifference concerning the doctrines that separate the reformed churches from the papal hierarchy; the opinion is gaining ground that, after all, we do not differ so widely upon vital points as has been supposed, and that a little concession on our part will bring us into a better understanding with Rome. The time was when Protestants placed a high value upon the liberty of conscience which had been so dearly purchased. They taught their children to abhor popery and held that to seek harmony with Rome would be disloyalty to God. But how widely different are the sentiments now expressed!

"The defenders of the papacy declare that the church has been maligned, and the Protestant world are inclined to accept the statement. Many urge that it is unjust to judge the church of today by the abominations and absurdities that marked her reign during the centuries of ignorance and darkness. They excuse her horrible cruelty as the result of the barbarism of the times and plead that the influence of modern civilization has changed her sentiments.

"Have these persons forgotten the claim of infallibility put forth for eight hundred years by this haughty power? . . .

"The papal church will never relinquish her claim to infallibility. All that she has done in her persecution of those who reject her dogmas she holds to be right; and would she not repeat the same acts, should the opportunity be presented? Let the restraints now imposed by secular governments be removed and Rome be reinstated in her former power, and there would speedily be a revival of her tyranny and persecution. . . .

"There are many who are disposed to attribute any fear of Roman Catholicism in the United States to bigotry or childishness. Such see nothing in the character and attitude of Romanism that is hostile to our free institutions, or find nothing portentous in its growth. . . .

"The pacific tone of Rome in the United States does not imply a change of heart. She is tolerant where she is helpless. Says Bishop O'Connor: 'Religious liberty is merely endured until the opposite can be carried into effect without peril to the Catholic world.'. . . The archbishop of St. Louis once said: 'Heresy and unbelief are crimes; and in Christian countries, as in Italy and Spain, for instance, where all the people are Catholics, and where the Catholic religion is an essential part of the law of the land, they are punished as other crimes.' . . .

"It is true that there are real Christians in the Roman Catholic communion. Thousands in that church are serving God according to the best light they have. . . . They have never seen the contrast between a living heart service and a round of mere forms and ceremonies. God looks with pitying tenderness upon these souls, educated as they are in a faith that is delusive and unsatisfying. He will cause rays of light to penetrate the dense darkness that surrounds them. He will reveal to them the truth as it is in Jesus, and many will yet take their position with His people.

"But Romanism as a system is no more in harmony with the gospel of Christ now than at any former period in her history. The Protestant churches are in great darkness, or they would discern the signs of the times. The Roman Church is far-reaching in her plans and modes of operation. She is employing every device to extend her influence and increase her power in preparation for a fierce and determined conflict to regain control of the world, to re-establish persecution, and to undo all that Protestantism has done. Catholicism is gaining ground upon every side. See the increasing number of her churches and chapels in Protestant countries. Look at the popularity of her colleges and seminaries in America, so widely patronized by Protestants. Look at the growth of ritualism in England and the frequent defections to the ranks of the Catholics. **These things should awaken the anxiety of all who prize the pure principles of the gospel.**

"Protestants have tampered with and patronized popery; they have made compromises and concessions which papists themselves are surprised to see and fail to understand. Men are closing their eyes to the real character of Romanism and the dangers to be apprehended from her supremacy. The people need to be aroused to resist the advances of this most dangerous foe to civil and religious liberty" (*ibid.*, pp. 563-566).

The news items that follow have been taken from the general public press and include several Catholic authors.

The book *Ecclesiastical Megalomania,* The Economic and Political Thought of the Roman Catholic Church (1999) was written by John W. Robbins, who holds his Ph.D in political philosophy from the Johns Hopkins University. I will quote a few excerpts to show that many Christians today are beginning to see the dangers and the evil practices of Rome. In his book Dr. Robbins refers to the Roman Catholic Church as "The Roman Church-State." The parenthesis following the selections are the page numbers in his book.

"The Roman Church-State is the oldest institution continually in existence, tracing its roots at least to the sixth century, and if one believes the Church's own claims, to the time of Christ himself. For much of that time, it has been the most powerful institution in Europe, and though its fortunes fell after the Reformation in the sixteenth century, it has made a remarkable resurgence in the past century." (9)

"Worldwide, of course, the Roman Church-State's roster of members ranks behind the entire populations of only two nations: China and India.

"In addition to being the world's oldest, largest, most powerful and most influential politico-ecclesiastical institution, the Roman Church-State may also be the world's wealthiest. . . . Only the assets of a handful of civil governments might surpass its massive wealth. It is difficult to ascertain the assets of the Roman Church-State; the organization does not report its holdings to anyone, including its members, and researchers who have endeavored to discover its riches have found no limits to them. . . . According to Canon Law, the control of all property of the Roman Church-State belongs to the pope, its supreme emperor. That property includes tens of thousands of buildings; millions of acres of land; tons of gold, silver, and precious stones; art collections; rare documents; and millions of shares in business corporations throughout the globe." (9, 10)

[Through the Reformation] "The Protestants of Europe were religiously, politically, economically, and psychologically liberated from a totalitarian Church-State that had browbeaten and beaten their fathers for generations." (17)

"And if there be any Roman Catholic readers who are inclined to favor freedom and free enterprise, may they understand that their church does not, and therefore they must choose to be either good Catholics or good Christians." (25)

"Roman Catholic economic thought, as developed by the popes in their encyclicals and by the Roman Church-State councils, has been a contributor to, if not the only source of, several forms of anti-capitalist political and economic organization during the long hegemony of the Roman Church-State. Among these forms are:

(1) feudalism and guild socialism in Europe during the Middle Ages;

(2) fascism in Italy, Spain, Portugal, Croatia, and Latin America in the twentieth century;

(3) Nazism in Germany in the twentieth century;

(4) liberation theology in Latin America and Africa in the twentieth century. (30)

"To understand how the economic thought of the Roman Church-State spawned these anti-capitalist systems, we begin with Thomas Aquinas' discussion of private property. . . . Private property, according to Thomas, is neither part of the natural law nor an absolute right, but an invention of human reason. It is a creation of and regulated by positive law. Rather than private property being part of the natural law, the possession of all things in common is the natural law." (30, 31)

Accordingly, "because the goods of some are due to others by the natural law, there is no sin if the poor take the goods of their neighbors." (32)

"These Thomistic notions—that private property is merely a construct of human reason and government, and that need gives title to the goods of others—are the reason the Roman Catholic bishops in Brazil in 1998 pronounced that looting is neither a sin nor a crime. The needs of the looters give the looters title to the goods they are taking. According to Roman Catholic doctrine, the looters are, by natural and divine law, the rightful owners of those goods." (35, 36)

"Much of the interference by federal, state, and local governments in the affairs of [U.S.] citizens, both Joe Klein [*Newsweek,* author, Feb. 19, 1996] and the papacy have told us, is due to Roman Catholic influence in American politics. Corrupt municipal political machines were constructed and operated by Roman Catholics, following the Church-State's support for a policy of effective interference: Tammany Hall, the Daley machine [in Chicago], the Curley machine, and so on. . . . Following Vatican directives, Roman Catholic politicians, legislators, and intellectuals brought us the Progressive movement, the labor union movement, the graduated income tax, the New Deal, and the growth of government in the United States." (47)

"Now it is this economic system of capitalism [the free enterprise system], . . . it is this biblical, moral, and productive system that the Roman Church-State views as one of her greatest enemies. The Roman Church-State rightly understands this system to be the economic counterpart of Protestantism, and it is determined to destroy both Protestantism and capitalism." (52)

"Leo XIII lamented the destruction of the medieval guild system, the guild socialism that had rendered the medieval economy virtually stagnant for a thousand years." (55)

"In the major documents that emerged from Vatican II, capitalism is condemned, but Communism is not even mentioned." (56)

"When the Roman Church-State sometimes may appear to defend private property, it is defending property only in the formal sense. Private property, which is not part of the natural law, is condemned on moral grounds, because of inequality. So while the Roman Church-State seems to defend private property at times, it uses the term in an equivocal manner." (59)

"Concern for human poverty is not the Vatican's primary motive. The Roman Church-State was in no position to ask any questions about economic development, for its own teachings and hegemony were the cause of economic stagnation, poverty, and suffering. Where those teachings have been abandoned and its hegemony cast off, economies developed rapidly, after more than a millennium of economic stagnation under its rule." (62)

"The Roman Catholic Middle Ages saw the development of almost no significant technical innovations." (75)

"In the United States, the influence of the Roman Catholic economic thought has resulted in the creation of a redistributive state, in which the government intervenes in the economy and society in order to protect the 'common good' and establish 'social justice.'. . . By the last third of the nineteenth century, the Roman Catholic Church had become the largest religious organization in the United States. By lending its moral authority to interventionist policies, the Roman Church-State played an indispensable role in the centralization, politicization, and socialization of American society and economy in the twentieth century." (81)

"In 1917, the Roman Church-State hierarchy in the United States formed the National Catholic War Council (later to be named the National Conference of Catholic Bishops). In 1919 its administrative committee issued a plan written by John Ryan, the *Bishops' Program of Social Reconstruction.* The plan advocated government unemployment, sickness, invalidity, and old age insurance; a federal child labor law; legal enforcement of labor's right to organize; public housing; graduated taxation on inheritance, incomes, and excess profits; regulation of public utility rates; worker participation in management, and so on. It is not surprising, then, that when Franklin Roosevelt was elected President in 1932, he invited Professor Ryan to join his administration." (84)

"What the papacy has realized is that by constantly enlarging the Rights of Man, to use the Vatican's own phrase, it can offer ever new moral arguments for enlarging the size, scope, and power of government." (86)

"The Roman Church-State has taken much of the credit for creating the entire field of labor law through the influence of *Rerum Novarum* [a papal encyclical]. In the United States, that law is a complex and unintelligible body of statutes, regulations, and decrees that few can understand, let alone obey." (87)

"As the number of Roman Catholic rights multiplies, the larger the government becomes, and the smaller the sphere of freedom shrinks. . . . Sometimes it takes the Roman Church-State years to get its policies enacted into law, but it usually succeeds." (89)

"The goal of the Roman Church-State is a completely regulated economy." (90)

"Incomplete collectivism, otherwise known as fascism, is the goal." (91)

"This reference to 'school choice' [in Article 797 of the Canon Law] means that the Roman Church-State favors voucher programs. Roman Catholic schools in the United States, from kindergarten to university, already receive hundreds of millions of dollars of tax subsidies, not through their tax exempt status, but through the provision of transportation, textbooks, teacher salaries, research grants, construction loans and grants, food, and so forth. Voucher programs, however, will permit Roman Catholic schools to receive hundreds of millions, perhaps billions, more tax dollars." (93)

"The Roman Church-State endorses the same fascist approach to health care. 'Our approach to health care is shaped by a simple but fundamental principle: "Every person has a right to adequate health care." ' " (94)

"There is nothing in the Scriptures that either expressly states or logically implies the primacy of the church of Rome or the office of pope in the Christian church. Far from being divinely instituted, the Roman Church-State is entirely a development of ambitious and sometimes unscrupulous men, their dupes, frauds, and forgeries." (116)

"Since the Roman Church-State is itself an authoritarian institution in which none of the rulers is elected by the people, in which power flows from the top down, and in which there is to be no disagreement with the leadership, it has shown an affinity for civil governments that reflect its own totalitarian and authoritarian structure, governments made in its own image." (162, 163)

"The fountainhead and stronghold of the Nazi movement in Germany was Bavaria in south Germany, Roman Catholic Germany, not Protestant North Germany. German Roman Catholics joined the Nazi party *en masse* and enthusiastically supported the Hitler regime. Over half of Hitler's troops were Roman Catholic." (163)

"On July 20, 1933, the Roman Church-State signed a treaty with Hitler guaranteeing the loyalty of German Roman Catholics to the Hitler regime." (165)

"Not only did the Roman Church-State support Hitler and Mussolini [both lifetime Catholics in good standing], it also created its own fascist state in Croatia." (169)

"A fascist named Ante Pavelic was installed as head of the Ustacha regime in Croatia in 1941. The Roman Church-State archbishop issued a Pastoral Letter ordering the Croatian clergy to support the new Ustacha government. During the years in which the Ustasha government existed, a Franciscan monk, Miroslav Filipovic, managed the Jasenovac concentration camp for two years, during which time he directed the extermination of not less than 100,000 victims, mostly Serbs who were members of the Orthodox Church." (170)

"Between 1941 and 1945, the Roman Church-State in Croatia murdered an estimated 700,000 Orthodox Serbs and 90,000 Jews and gypsies. The Vatican neither defrocked nor excommunicated anyone responsible for the holocaust. . . . We can only conclude that one of the most brutal and inhuman regimes of the twentieth century—not just the medieval millennium—is the Roman Church-State." (172, 173)

"What the Roman Church-State accomplished on a small scale during the Middle Ages is what it desires to achieve on a global scale in the coming millennium. If it fails to reach that goal within the next hundred years, it will not quit. It will continue to work relentlessly for world power, even if it should take another millennia or two." (187)

"The Roman Church-State is a hybrid—a monster of ecclesiastical and political power. Its political thought is totalitarian, and whenever it has had the opportunity to apply its principles, the result has been bloody repression. If during the last 30 years, it has softened its assertions of full, supreme, and irresponsible power, and has murdered fewer people than before, such changes in behavior are not due to a change in its ideas, but to a change in its circumstances." (195)

"The Roman Church-State in the twentieth century, however, is an institution recovering from a mortal wound. If and when it regains its full power and authority, it will impose a regime more sinister than any the planet has yet seen." (195)

"Until the Roman Church-State abandons the theology and philosophy that preclude it from repenting, until it repudiates the doctrines that have justified its use of force and violence, either directly or through proxies, and until it dismantles its entire apparatus of command, coercion, and control that has enabled it to inflict harm on its many victims, ecclesiastical apologies, or, more accurately, 'remembrances' are both duplicitous and disingenuous. . . . The Roman Church is morally required to seek forgiveness from its victims, but its victims are dead." (198)

The quotations above from a political scientist portray the Roman Catholic Church-State from a historical and political perspective and, interestingly, the descriptions are quite similar to those given in *The Great Controversy*.

Another insightful book is *Papal Sin, Structures of Deceit,* by Gary Wills (June 2000). Dr. Wills was raised Catholic and educated by Jesuits. A Pulitzer Prize-winning author, he received his Ph.D. in classics from Yale and is currently an adjunct professor of history at Northwestern University. Wills is one of the most respected historians in America today. In reviews printed by the New York *Times* and the Washington *Post* his book is described as "an extraordinary indictment of the Church."

Wills documents a history of the church that he calls "evasions, disingenuous explainings, outright denials, pieties, dodges, lapses and funk." He writes that the fundamental problem with the Papacy, despite the popularity of the current pope, is that "to keep evading the truth is a worse embarrassment [than all the crimes it has committed down through history], an insult to those who have been wronged and whose wrong will not be recognized."

Wills states, "Most people are familiar with Acton's famous axiom, 'Power tends to corrupt, and absolute power corrupts absolutely' (Acton 2.383). Fewer people remember that he was speaking of papal absolutism—more specifically, he was condemning a fellow historian's book on Renaissance popes for letting them literally get away with murder."

He gives the following illustration of the corruption that is overlooked in much that is called history today. "In the tenth century a dissolute teenager could be elected pope (John XII) because of his family connections and die a decade later in the bed of a married woman." He adds that even today there is a two-faced approach to the church. "There is, for instance, a kind of double consciousness in the church revealed by this fact: News reports about Catholicism seem to return again and again to matters like birth control, abortion, clerical celibacy, or whether women can be priests—yet in twenty years of regular attendance at Mass in one church, followed by twenty years in another, I have never heard a sermon that touched on any one of those things. What can that mean?" (p. 2).

Hitler's Pope

Another very recent book that is relevant to the current discussion is *Hitler's Pope—The Secret History of Pius XII,* by John Cornwell (1999). Cornwell is an award-winning journalist and senior research fellow at Cambridge University. He contributes regularly to the London's *Sunday Times* and to religious affairs publications around the world on the Vatican and other subjects. He is a practicing Roman Catholic and lives near Cambridge in England. When in the early 1990s the Roman Catholic Church announced plans to begin the "beatification" process that would eventually make Pope Pius XII [Eugenio Pacelli] a Catholic saint, there was a worldwide outcry. Many voices questioned whether a pope who stood silently by and watched the execution of millions of Jews could really be a saint. As a Catholic scholar, John Cornwell felt that he could lay the matter to rest by a proper study. "I was convinced," he said, "that if his full story were told, Pius XII's pontificate would be vindicated." His work began in earnest and he, as a Catholic scholar, on the side of his subject was given access to crucial material in the Vatican. As he neared the end of his research he stated, <u>"By the middle of 1997, nearing the end of my research, I found myself in a state I can only describe as moral shock. The</u>

material I had gathered, taking the more extensive view of Pacelli's life, amounted not to an exoneration but to a wider indictment. Spanning Pacelli's career from the beginning of the century, my research told the story of a bid for unprecedented papal power that by 1933 had drawn the Catholic Church into complicity with the darkest forces of the era" (p. viii).

A summary paragraph from the dustcover flap of *Hitler's Pope* states: "In the first decade of the twentieth century, Pacelli was a brilliant Vatican lawyer who helped shape a new ideology of unprecedented papal power. As papal nuncio in Munich and Berlin in the 1920s, he used cunning and moral blackmail to impose Rome's power on Germany. In 1933, he negotiated a treaty with Hitler, the Reich Concordat, which ensured that the Nazis would rise unopposed by the most powerful Catholic community in the world— sealing, by Hitler's own admission, the fate of the Jews in Europe. Until now, historians have focused on only one episode and one issue regarding Pius XII: his silence during the Holocaust. But John Cornwell documents how Pius's wartime reticence was consistent with a career dedicated to enhancing papal power and that he had a personal antipathy toward the Jews—for which Cornwell offers striking new evidence."

The New York *Times* book review of *Hitler's Pope* stated: "By combining the painstaking research of other scholars with his own new documentation . . . Cornwell makes a case in Hitler's pope that is very difficult to refute."

The Washington *Post* review stated: "The title tells the tale. And a chilling tale it is: Eugenio Pacelli, then the Vatican's all-powerful secretary of state, made it possible for Adolf Hitler to achieve total power in Germany and, as Pope Pius XII, went on to appease him, maintaining inexplicable public silence as the Nazis destroyed and massacred millions of European Jews before and during World War II. . . . The conclusions and revelations presented by John Cornwell in meticulously researched *Hitler's Pope* . . . leave no doubt that Eugenio Pacelli was the Fuhrer's best imaginable ally."

I mention these three current books to show the agreement of historians that even in the twentieth century the Papacy has used craft, deception, cunning, blackmail, and murder to advance its power and position in the world. It has not changed.

As a current follow-up to the Roman Catholic Church's involvement with the Nazis the *Christian Century,* October 11, 2000, reported: "Catholics to compensate for Nazi labor program. The Roman Catholic

Church in Germany has agreed to set up a $4.6 million fund to compensate for the church's use of Nazi-forced slave labor during World War II."

Other Church News

The Third Secret of Fatima as reported in "Inside the Vatican" June-July 2000:

On May 13, 1917, three Portuguese shepherd children who were watching sheep on a hillside west of the village of Fatima claimed to have seen "a most beautiful lady" who said she had come "from heaven."

In subsequent apparitions "Mary" told the children that two of them would die in childhood and come to be with her, and the surviving child would live to see the second coming of Christ. Francisco and Jacinta did die of illness in childhood, and the surviving child, Lucia, is now 93 years of age.

On May 13, 2000, Pope John Paul II beatified Francisco and Jacinta—starting them on the road to sainthood.

The pope, who has dedicated his pontificate to the sacred heart of Mary, claims that she saved his life when the Turk Ali Agca tried to kill him on May 13, 1981. He has visited the Fatima shrine many times and prays to Mary and offers incense to her on a regular basis. By these actions, this man, who wants to be the religious leader of the world, has demonstrated that he is, in fact, a spiritualist.

The Roman Catholic weekly, *Our Sunday Visitor,* printed an editorial titled *Mary Our Hope* on October 11, 1998. It was written by Msgr. Owen Campion, the associate publisher of the paper. He stated, "As defined infallibly by Pope Pius XII [Eugenio Pacelli, whom we have just discussed above] in 1950, the Assumption means that at the end of her earthly life, Mary was assumed into heaven, body and spirit, by God's power." [No biblical evidence has ever been given for this.] He went on to say, "Mary was also sinless, because she chose to be sinless. She was the first and most perfect of the disciples."

To graphically portray the Catholic Church's cultural base, the cover of the March 18, 2001, issue of *Our Sunday Visitor* headlined "Dream Team." Then are pictured five young people, three boys and two girls. They are facing a basketball goal with their backs toward the camera. They are wearing basketball jerseys with large numerals on them. Then above the numbers where the player's name is usually printed each player in the picture has a different word printed there. The players are named Saints,

Scripture, Sacrament, Mary, and Tradition. The subtitle says, "It takes a solid game plan to raise your kids in the Catholic faith in today's culture."

While We Were Sleeping

I want to use a biblical metaphor to introduce the remainder of the material in this chapter. It is taken from Matthew 25:5: "While the Bridegroom was delayed, they all slumbered and slept."

While we were slumbering:

The Vatican has been pursuing ecumenism on a broad front. On the following dates the Vatican began formal talks with various Christian bodies:

1965—Ecumenical Council of Churches

1966—Anglican Church

1967—World Methodist Council, World Lutheran Federation

1970—World Reformed Alliance

1977—Disciples of Christ and other evangelical churches

1980—Orthodox Church

1982—Pentecostal Movement

1984—World Baptist Alliance

And in 1986 a more far-reaching event took place. The Vatican summoned 130 leaders from 12 major world religions (including snake worshipers, animists, fire worshipers, spiritists, witch doctors, Buddhists, Muslims, Hindus, Christians, and Catholics) to meet at Assisi, Italy, to pray for peace.

On that occasion the pope allowed his friend, the Tibetan spiritual leader, the Dalai Lama, as part of their "unified worship" to replace the cross with a Buddhist god, *Bubo-tar,* at St. Peter's Church in Assisi. Several other such meetings of the same group have convened in the years since.

Our Sunday Visitor reported that on October 17, 2000, Queen Elizabeth of England, as head of the Anglican or Church of England, met with the pope in the Vatican and each pledged to continue their commitment to the cause of Christian unity. The pope said that "the sad years of division between Catholics and Anglicans and between the Vatican and the United Kingdom have ended, but the task of Christian unity is far from complete. There can be no turning back from the ecumenical goal we have set for ourselves in obedience to the Lord's command." The Queen said that she was pleased with "the important progress that has been made in overcoming historic differences between Anglicans and Roman Catholics.

I trust that we shall continue to advance along the path which leads to Christian unity" (*Our Sunday Visitor,* October 29, 2000).

Catholics, Lutherans End Doctrinal Dispute

So reported the Washington *Post* on November 1, 1999. The article was headed, **AUGSBURG, Germany, Oct. 31**—"Four hundred and eighty-two years ago today, the blunt-speaking monk Martin Luther nailed his legendary attack on Catholic Church practices to a church door in Germany, an act of conscience that triggered the Protestant Reformation, the wrenching division of Western Christianity, and more than a century of religious wars that killed hundreds of thousands.

"Today the heirs of that acrimony and fracture, the leaders of the modern Lutheran and Roman Catholic churches, signed a document that officially settles the central argument about the nature of faith that Luther provoked. The agreement declares, in effect, that it was all a misunderstanding.

" 'In the one Spirit we were all baptized into one body. Let us then pursue all that makes for peace and builds up our common life,' proclaimed Catholic Cardinal Edward Idris Cassidy, Pope John Paul II's emissary, as he signed the Augsburg accord on behalf of more than a billion Roman Catholics worldwide. All but 3 million of the world's 61.5 million Lutherans were represented by Bishop Christian Krause, president of the Lutheran World Federation, and by the Rev. Ishmael Noko, the federation's general secretary.

"The agreement is significant beyond the dispute over doctrine that it resolves. It has deep implications for future relations among Catholics and Protestants, said theologians and church leaders. Many said this accord gives added promise to the ideal their denominations champion—of full communion, or merger, between the churches."

With another insightful comment regarding the Reformation, Chuck Colson addressed the Bob Jones University flap during the 2000 election in a New York *Times* article dated March 2, 2000. He stated, "Since when do legislators issue official denunciations of anyone's theology? This goes to the very core of what the protections of the First Amendment are intended to prevent—federal action condemning particular churches or doctrines." Then he lets slip out why the Bob Jones matter is so pivotal. "In truth," he explains, "the gulf between Evangelicals and Roman Catholics, opened by the Reformation, is being bridged. . . .

Today we stand shoulder to shoulder as the most significant religious block in America."

Two months earlier, ZENIT news service reported on January 18, 2000, from Vatican City: "A decisive step was taken today on the road to Christian unity with the ecumenical rite of the opening of the fourth Jubilee Holy Door in Rome.

"The ceremony took place at the Basilica of St. Paul Outside the Walls, where, 40 years ago, John XXIII convoked Vatican Council II.

"Today, 22 leaders of other Christian churches, as well as the World Council of Churches, a community embracing 337 Christian denominations, accompanied John Paul II during the ceremony. All were united by their faith in Christ, the one Savior, and by one baptism.

"The drama of the event reached its height at the instant of the opening of the bronze Holy Door. As sunlight poured into the basilica, the people gathered inside could make out three figures in the doorway: the silhouettes of Pope John Paul II, Orthodox Metropolitan Athanasius of the Ecumenical Patriarchy of Constantinople, and George Carey, archbishop of Canterbury and president of the Anglican Communion. The faithful broke out into applause. Everyone seemed aware of the privileged moment they were experiencing on the road of ecumenical dialogue.

"All passed in turn through the Holy Door: representatives of the Catholic Church and of the Eastern Orthodox Churches, Anglicans, Lutherans, Methodists, Pentecostals all went up to the place of the Gospel. The procession symbolized the centuries-old road that Christians have followed in pursuit of unity.

"The pope said in his homily, 'We know we are brothers and that we are still divided, but we have directed ourselves with decisive conviction on the path that leads to full unity in the Body of Christ.' "

Ecumenical Bombshell

Not long after all of these ecumenical gestures the Catholic Church released a "bombshell" document titled *Dominus Iesus*, which claims that salvation is possible only in the Roman Catholic Church and that other "ecclesiastical communities" are no longer to be referred to as "Sister Churches." We are not sisters—Rome is the mother church, it stated. With the pope's approval and blessing, the document was released on August 6, 2000, by Joseph Cardinal Ratzinger, the "prefect" of the Office of the

Congregation for the Doctrine of the Faith, formerly known as the Office of the Inquisition.

Amazingly, the Protestant response has been more positive than negative. *Christianity Today,* October 23, 2000, stated in an editorial titled "Honest Ecumenism" that "the Vatican's recent statement on the nature of the Church is a step forward, not backward, for Christian unity."

In fact, Protestants continue to flock to Rome. *Religion Today,* March 30, 2001, reported in a feature story titled "Presbyterians Travel to the Vatican in Search of Unity With Roman Catholics" that "both sides pledge to disavow bitter historic denunciations. In a historic three-day meeting [that included a private audience with the pope], Presbyterian and Roman Catholic officials inched closer to more visible unity between their churches.

"The formal talks were sometimes simple and direct, sometimes as labyrinthine as the streets of this ancient city. At their conclusion, on March 22 [2001], the 15-member delegation from the Presbyterian Church (USA) and five staff members from the Vatican's Pontifical Council for Promoting Christian Unity issued a joint statement in which they pledged to continue working toward a theological agreement on three major issues:

- The doctrine of justification
- Mutual recognition of each other's baptisms
- A joint study of Reformation-era documents in which the churches condemned each other, culminating in a declaration 'that they no longer reflect the reality of our views of each other.'"

Vatican Diplomacy

The Roman Catholic leaders, in addition to welcoming a growing number of Protestant churches seeking unity with them, are also welcoming record numbers of diplomats from foreign countries. The Roman Catholic publication *Inside the Vatican* gave an interesting insight into the Vatican Diplomatic Corps on pages 53-55 of the October 1999 issue. According to the article, "two weeks after U.S. Secretary of State Madeleine Albright met in March [1999] with Pope John Paul II and Vatican diplomats, the U.S. announced that it was relaxing some of its restrictions on dealing with Cuba. The State Department specifically cited the influence of the pope's January visit to Cuba in making this policy change. This episode of Vatican diplomacy, with a high-profile result, is only one example of the increasingly diverse diplomatic dealings conducted by world powers with the Vatican. Most of the diplomacy operates without the media attention that [the] Cuba episode received, and is carried out by embassies and diplomats working quietly in Rome.

"Few would have guessed that the late 20th century would see a renaissance of embassies to the Vatican, those ambassadors accredited to what was once the papal court. Rather than fading away as a Renaissance anachronism, countries have been establishing embassies 'To the Holy See' in record numbers in the past decade. The 170 and counting countries now accredited include everyone from Cuba to the Russian Federation to Iran and Libya, with only China and Vietnam noticeably absent.

"A resident diplomatic corps accredited to the Holy See dates back to the 1400s, when the pope controlled central Italy. The loss of the Papal States in 1870 caused many countries to discontinue relations with the Holy See. The British parliament decided that, since the pope had become just another religious leader, there was no more reason to send an ambassador to him than for the King of Italy to send an envoy to the Archbishop of Canterbury.

"The situation changed in 1929 when the Holy See and Italy signed the Lateran Pact, which acknowledged the pope's authority as head of the 'Vatican City state.' The Pact also recognized the pope as a soverign head of state with all the appurtenances, including his own diplomatic corps.

"When the United States established full diplomatic relations [with the Holy See] in 1984 it joined 109 others." Since that time 61 more nations have entered into diplomatic relations with the Holy See!

The Pope Uses Young People

While we were slumbering: The July 3, 2000, editions of *Time* and *U.S. News* reported that Superstars, Britney Spears, and other rock stars including 'N Sync, Steven Tyler, and others, had just cut an album, a CD with an unlikely costar—John Paul II. They recorded a CD titled "World Voice 2000," reading prayers penned by the pope on peace, spirituality, and unity. If the CD is successful, the producer plans a Spanish version with Ricky Martin and Jennifer Lopez.

These rock stars are being used by the pope to build his image among young people, not to highlight the Christian virtues of the singers. Shortly after her work on the CD Britney Spears announced that she would appear nude in *Playboy* magazine.

The Holy See at the UN

While we were slumbering: According to *Inside the Vatican,* April 2000: "An unlikely coalition of Jews, evangelical Protestants, and Mormons joined with Catholics at the UN in March to defend the Holy See's UN Status which is under attack."

On July 12, news services all over the world reported that the U.S. House of Representatives, "by a vote of 416 to 1, overwhelmingly supported the presence of the 'Holy See' [the official designation for the Vatican] at the United Nations. The House also condemned the efforts of pro-abortion groups to remove the Roman Catholic Church from its Permanent Observer status there—a position it has held for 36 years."

House Majority Leader, Dick Armey (R-Texas), said in the Washington *Times* (7-12-00): "The Vatican is under attack by pro-abortion extremists, and Congress will not let that attack go unchallenged. . . . We will not tolerate the effort to silence the Vatican."

Rep. Christopher H. Smith (R-New Jersy) said, "If anything, the Holy See deserves a more prominent role at the United Nations."

U.S. House Gets a Catholic Chaplain

While we were slumbering:

Early in the year 2000, the U.S. House of Representatives needed a new chaplain. After a diligent search they selected a Protestant pastor who was appointed and notified of the decision. According to *Time,* March 6, 2000: "In November, House Speaker Dennis Hastert received a list of three finalists for the position of chaplain, winnowed from a group of some 50 candidates by a bipartisan committee. Hastert and majority leader Dick Armey outvoted minority leader Richard Gephardt to select the Rev. Charles Wright, a Presbyterian affiliated with the House's influential National Prayer Breakfast. In doing so they passed over the nominating committee's favorite, Father [Timothy] O'Brien, a Catholic priest."

Then the Catholic Church mounted a campaign, charging Hastert with bigotry and anti-Catholic bias. The Catholic weekly, *Our Sunday Visitor,* April 9, 2000, reported that "facing charges of bigotry, Republican leaders appoint a Catholic chaplain. The appointment [of Father Daniel Coughlin] came as Hastert's choice for the job, the Rev. Charles Wright, agreed to step aside and spare the House leaders further embarassment."

The bottom line: the Protestant pastor was asked to withdraw his name, and a Catholic priest, Father Daniel Coughlin, is now the new chaplain of the United States House of Representatives.

A Growing Presence in Society and Government

<u>While we were slumbering:</u> the power, presence, and influence of the Roman Catholic Church has been steadily growing in America. Much of what is happening in this arena happens in secret and is not open even to those of us who try to keep up with it. For example, the November 15, 1999, issue of *Our Sunday Visitor* revealed under the title "Jimmy Carter's Man in Rome" the following information: "Former U.S. President Jimmy Carter secretly corresponded with a newly elected Pope John Paul II on such global issues as arms control, Soviet policies, and Catholic missionaries in China, a former Carter aide said.

"The 'Vatican hotline,' as it was called inside the White House, was established soon after the pope's election in 1978 in the belief that the pontiff would be a major player on the world stage, said James Rentschler, a staffer on Carter's National Security Council.

"Writing in the *International Herald Tribune* (October 30 [1998]), Rentschler said he was the council's 'designated papist' after council chief Zbigniew Brzezinski convinced Carter to open up the secret channel of communication between the White House and the Vatican.

"'It was a link that Jimmy Carter and Pope John Paul II soon made operational with a personal correspondence of extraordinary breadth,' Rentschler said. Numbering about 40 still-classified letters, they covered a range of issues: human rights, famine relief, unrest behind the Iron Curtain, Cuban military activities in Africa, the Middle East peace process and terrorism, he said."

Through biological growth, immigration, and proselytizing the Catholic Church membership continues to grow in the United States. Though it is likely even higher today, the 1998 membership total for the Catholic Church in America was just over 62 million people. It is by far the single largest religious group; with Southern Baptists coming in a far distant second at 15 million members—barely one fourth the size of the Catholic Church. The Methodist Church is the third largest church in the U.S., with 8 million members. (See *Christianity Today,* May 22, 2000, p. 21.)

"Catholics Remain Largest Bloc in Congress," reported *Christianity Today* in its February 5, 2001, issue following the 2000 election. "Catholics continue to dominate numerically in the U.S. Congress, followed by

Baptists and Methodists, the latest tally by Americans for Religious Liberty shows. Of the 535 members of the 107th Congress, 150 are Roman Catholic, including 91 Democrats and 59 Republicans."

It should be common knowledge that three of the U.S. Supreme Court justices are Roman Catholic. Justices Scalia, Thomas, and Kennedy frequently vote together as a bloc and did so with Rehnquist and O'Conner in the Supreme Court decision to grant George W. Bush's request to halt hand recounts of ballots in Florida (see the Washington *Post,* December 10, 2000.) It should also be noted that Rehnquist and O'Conner have indicated that they will likely retire soon, leaving George W. Bush the duty of nominating their replacements. When this happens Bush may well appoint Catholic jurists to take their places, since he was told in effect by Congress "We will confirm John Ashcroft as Attorney General, but don't send us another conservative Protestant [Ashcroft is a Pentecostal] when you fill the Supreme Court positions."

Pope Awarded Congressional Gold Medal

Though very few Americans know of it, on May 24, 2000, Congressman Chris Smith introduced legislation supporting the awarding of the Congressional Gold Medal to Pope John Paul II. It was passed by the House, and the Senate followed suit in early July. President Bill Clinton signed the measure on July 27. The Catholic News Service reported on January 2, 2001, that "more than a dozen members of the U.S. Congress and the chaplain of the House of Representatives [the Catholic priest we have discussed above] will present Pope John Paul II with the Congressional Gold Medal Jan. 8 at the Vatican. The delegation will be led by Rep. Dennis Hastert, R. Ill., Speaker of the House, and by Sen. Sam D. Brownback, R-Kan., Senate sponsor of the bill. It will include Republicans and Democrats, according to the U.S. Embassy to the Holy See. Father Daniel P. Coughlin, the first Catholic-appointed House chaplain, was scheduled to join the delegation flying to Italy aboard a U.S. military aircraft."

The Associated Press carried the story on Tuesday, January 9, 2001: "Vatican City (AP)—Pope John Paul II was awarded the Congressional Gold Medal on Monday, joining a select list that also includes George Washington, Bob Hope, and Mother Teresa.

"U.S. House and Senate leaders presented the medal to the pontiff during a ceremony in the Apostolic Palace's fresco-covered 17th-century

Clementine Room. The legislation to award John Paul the medal hails the 80-year-old, Polish-born pope for using 'his moral authority to hasten the fall of godless totalitarian regimes.'

" 'May your influence be as strong in the 21st century as it was in the 20th century,' House Speaker Dennis Hastert said.

" 'Your strong words inspire 1 billion Catholics and impress people of various faiths throughout the world,' Hastert, R-Ill., told the pope after noting that 'of all the recognitions the Congress of the United States can bestow, the gold medal is considered the most distinguished.'

"It is the highest civilian honor Congress can award. The medal, heavy enough to make a palm sink when placed on an outstretched hand, has an image of the pope on one side and the symbolic bald eagle on the other.

"Sen. Sam Brownback, R-Kan., said John Paul's message of hope 'urgently needs to be heard.'

"John Paul told the politicians he was 'honored by the gracious gesture which brought you here. It is not for the successor of the apostle Peter to seek honors, but I gladly accept the Congressional Gold Medal as a recognition that in my ministry there has echoed a word that can touch every human heart. I accept this award as a sign that you, as legislators, recognize the importance of defending human dignity without compromise, so that your nation may not fail to live up to its high responsibilities in a world where human rights are so often disregarded.' "

O'Connor Honored by Civil Leaders

When Cardinal John O'Connor, the leader of the New York Archdiocese, died in early May at the age of 80, his influence in American politics was visible at his funeral. The Associated Press reported on May 9, 2000, that President Bill Clinton, and Senate rivals Hillary Rodham Clinton and Mayor Rudolph Giuliani were sitting on the front pews at St. Patrick's Cathedral. Besides the Clintons and Giuliani, other notables at the mass included Vice President Al Gore and his Republican rival for the presidency, Governor George W. Bush; Bush's father, former President George Bush; Governor George Pataki; Senators Daniel Patrick Moynahan and Charles Schumer.

It is interesting to observe the deference given to Roman Catholic leaders in America.

Catholic Spy Caught

The daily headlines the third week of February told of an FBI agent that had been arrested and accused of spying. The AP story on February 21, 2001, stated: "A veteran FBI agent was accused Tuesday of spying for Russia for more than 15 years, betraying three Russian undercover agents to Moscow and disclosing volumes of U.S. secrets in return for more than $1.4 million in cash and diamonds. The FBI director called the case 'the most traitorous actions imaginable.'

"Robert Philip Hanssen, 56, the father of six, was only the third FBI agent ever accused of espionage. President Bush called it 'a difficult day,' particularly for the law enforcement and intelligence communities.

"Hanssen, a 25-year FBI agent, was arrested Sunday night at a park in suburban Virginia after dropping a package of documents for his Russian contacts, authorities said. FBI agents confiscated $50,000 hidden for him at a nearby drop site."

This is very interesting information, but the most significant information for the purpose of mention in this chapter is not that Hanssen was a Roman Catholic. People of all faiths succumb to sin. The most interesting and significant factor is that he was a member of Opus Dei—a specialized Catholic group. The Washington *Times,* National Weekly Edition, February 26–March 4, 2001, reported the information this way: **"Hanssen belonged to a Catholic group that proselytized elites.** Robert P. Hanssen, the FBI special agent and suspected spy, was a member of an elite religious group that works to spread the Catholic faith by recruiting members active in the upper echelons of government and business.

" 'They are trying to get people in their vocation to change the world. They believe that if you convert the king, you convert the country,' says the Rev. Franklyn McAfee of the organization called Opus Dei. [Father McAfee is the pastor of St. Catherine of Siena Catholic Church in Great Falls, Va.—and Hanssen's pastor.]

"Opus Dei, with around 3,000 members in the United States and 84,000 worldwide, was called a 'floating diocese' or a 'personal prelate' that falls under the direct purview of the pope.

"Other high-profile figures who attend St. Catherine's traditional mass include Sen. Rick Santorum, Pennsylvania Republican, and Supreme Court Justice Antonin Scalia. FBI Director Louis J. Freeh also attends the church, Father McAfee said.

"Father McAfee said a good number of Opus Dei members in the area attend his church because it is more conservative and sticks closer to traditional Catholic teachings."

It is most interesting to note that there is a Catholic organization that specializes in influencing the world's civil leaders, and that many of them attend the same Catholic church in the Washington, D.C., area.

The Bush Catholic Connection

Florida Governor Jeb Bush was defeated in his 1994 bid to become governor by Lawton Chiles. "After the election, Bush's life seemed to hover on the edge of collapse. In interviews, he admitted he had neglected his family while running for office. During the campaign, Bush said, his marriage had begun to unravel. One of his children developed a drug problem. Bush publically pledged to become a better person. He stopped working on Sundays and began going to church regularly. . . . On Easter eve 1995, he converted to Catholicism" (*The Weekly Standard,* May 17, 1999). He won the 1998 governor's race and was therefore the governor of Florida during the infamous Florida election. During the campaign he spoke frequently to Hispanic groups in his flawless Spanish. Of course these groups had strong Catholic backgrounds.

When George W. Bush, who is a practicing Methodist, became president of the United States, one of his first programs was to introduce what has been called his "Faith-based Initiatives." Before announcing this program he summoned 40 prominent Catholic leaders to the White House and then announced the appointment of a Catholic, John DiIulio, as the director of the program.

CBS news reported on the 7:00 a.m. (EDT) national newscast of April 16, 2001 [Tax day], that President Bush was already planning his strategy for a second term in office. The reporter stated that Bush knew he would need the Catholic vote, so he was planning to court Roman Catholic leaders during his first term.

All politicians realize that courting the Catholic vote is essential to winning because there are efforts underway in the Catholic Church to vote together as a bloc in future elections. In the 2000 presidential election the Catholic vote was split almost evenly between Bush and Gore.

Former mayor of Boston and U.S. Ambassador to the Vatican, Raymond Flynn, has recently been appointed head of the Catholic Alliance. Originally started by the Christian Coalition in 1995, the Catholic Alliance is now a separate organization with all Catholic leadership. The headline of the full center spread of the May 23, 1999, issue of *Our Sunday Visitor* states: **"Can he get out the Catholic vote?**—Boldly going where others have gone and failed before him, former ambassador Raymond Flynn says he's ready to try to turn the nation's largest religious group into a formidable political bloc." The article stated that "Flynn, a Democrat, will be encouraging Catholics to vote for candidates of either party who espouse pro-life, pro-family positions and who are faithful to the social teachings of the Church."

Catholic Proselytization

Officially, the Catholic Church condemns efforts by others to prose-lytize among their members. In fact, the church has attempted to get Protestants to agree not to proselytize. However, in actual practice, as in the case of Opus Dei, the church encourages proselytization by its members in the Protestant community. Early in 2001 I received a fund-raising letter from the "Coming Home Network." (Apparently *Our Sunday Visitor* sells their mailing lists to other Catholic organizations.) The letter stated: "I want to introduce you to the *Coming Home Network.* We're a lay Catholic apostolate that has helped hundreds of Protestant ministers convert to the Catholic faith. And right now, we're helping 200 more. However, a severe financial crisis threatens all our work unless emer-gency help arrives soon. Please read this important letter and consider helping us help more Protestant clergy convert to the Catholic faith."

Perhaps the most well-known Protestant convert to the Roman Catholic Church is "Father" Richard John Neuhaus. A Lutheran minister for 19 years before converting to Catholicism, he is now a major leader in the ecumenical movement and was the co-author with Chuck Colson in the *Evangelicals and Catholics Together* document of several years ago.

While we were slumbering: (*Our Sunday Visitor,* February 14, 1999)

In the last week of January 1999 Pope John Paul II visited the United States. He was greeted and welcomed at the St. Louis, Missouri, airport by President Clinton, who was under the heavy cloud of the Monica Lewinsky affair. A nonrelated, yet very significant event occurred on that visit.

Following a personal appeal by the pope, Missouri Governor Mel Carnahan, who was killed in a tragic plane crash while campaigning for the U.S. Senate, announced that he would not execute a convicted triple murderer.

The governor said, "In reaching this decision, I took into account the extraordinary circumstances of the pope's request and the historical signif-icance of the papal visit to St. Louis and the State of Missouri."

The governor, a Baptist, told the New York *Times:* "The pope asked me to show mercy. I'll have to say that I was moved by his concern for the prisoner. I continue to support capital punishment, but after careful consideration of his direct and personal appeal and because of a deep and abiding respect for the pontiff and all he represents, I decided last night to grant his request."

The convicted murderer, Darrell Mease, killed a man, his wife, and their handicapped teenage grandson in cold blood—intentional first-degree murder. He will now spend the rest of his life in jail.

The significance of this event is that the pope, who could hardly be against capital punishment—representing as he does an organization which throughout history has murdered literally millions—has come to the U.S. and pressured a sovereign state to violate its justice system.

And finally, while we were slumbering another prophetically significant event was unfolding. You are no doubt well aware that President Bill Clinton had been desperately seeking to bring peace to the troubled Middle East before he left the office of president. Observers say that he wanted something more than the Monica Lewinsky story and his subsequent impeachment as his legacy. At Camp David and other meetings around the world, the parties had been able to settle almost everything. There was just one major sticking point—the fate of Jerusalem.

Those of you who keep up with the news and world events know that the Vatican was contacted in person by U.S. Secretary of State, Madeleine Albright, who asked the pope and the Vatican to assist with the Jerusalem issue.

The Vatican responded with a plan to unify Jerusalem as a world religious and peace center under its leadership. It was also proposed that the civil leadership of the city be provided by the United Nations. These proposals were not implemented.

There is much more—but the constrains of time and space won't allow us to continue. We could talk about the role of the Catholic Church at the Great Millennial meeting of the United Nations, where the heads of state of 150 countries met together in New York. We could discuss the scandal of AIDS in the Priesthood, and much more. But what we have shared is easily enough to show that the prophetic understanding we have been given in the Bible and the Spirit of Prophecy is indeed correct and being confirmed each passing day. The battle of the spirits, the great controversy, is down to the critical stage. We must plan to stand firm, with our armor on, and be with Jesus on the winning side. It is time for us to give the message of Revelation 18. The call is to come out of Babylon. This call will lighten the entire world. It is God's last warning!

---

* The information contained in this chapter does not come from a personal bias. It is an update on a long-standing Protestant understanding—namely that the Roman Catholic Church/State system is the antichrist power that has been specifically identified in the Bible books of Daniel and the Revelation. If you desire a biblical foundation and a deeper understanding of this topic, I would refer you to the six-chapter appendix in my book *Sunday's Coming.* For many readers this will not be a new idea, and I must assume that before reading this chapter you have looked at the prophetic picture and reviewed the evidence for yourself.

CHAPTER 13

End Times in Focus

S igns of the end abound in the natural world. Many thousands of people have died in large earthquakes in India, El Salvador, and elsewhere around the globe. There are an increasing number of cyclones, tornadoes, and floods. For those who study these natural disasters the report is clear—the events are larger, more frequent, and more intensive that ever before. In fact, these "signs" are so common now that some consider them a normal part of life and fail to see any eschatological significance in them. But we have been clearly told that these events are signs of the end. "The coming of the Lord is nearer than when we first believed. The great controversy is nearing its end. Every report of calamity by sea or land is a testimony to the fact that the end of all things is at hand. Wars and rumors of wars declare it. Is there a Christian whose pulse does not beat with quickened action as he anticipates the great events opening before us?

"The Lord is coming. We hear the footsteps of an approaching God, as He comes to punish the world for its iniquity. We are to prepare the way for Him by acting our part in getting a people ready for that great day. . . . We are to give the message with as much more earnestness as the coming of the Lord is nearer. The message for this time is positive, simple, and of the deepest importance. We must act like men and women who believe it. Waiting, watching, working, praying, warning the world—this is our work.

"All heaven is astir, engaged in preparing for the day of God's vengeance, the day of Zion's deliverance. The time of tarrying is almost ended [written in 1913]. The pilgrims and strangers who have so long been seeking a better country are almost home. I feel as if I must cry aloud, Homeward bound! Rapidly we are nearing the time when Christ will come to gather His redeemed to Himself" (*Evangelism,* p. 219).

Even if man can explain the natural disasters as a part of El Niño, global warming, or some other "natural" phenomenon, that does not keep them from being genuine signs of the end. "The time is at hand when there will be sorrow in the world that no human balm can heal. The Spirit of God is being withdrawn. Disasters by sea and by land follow one another in quick succession. How frequently we hear of earthquakes and tornadoes, of destruction by fire and flood, with great loss of life and property! Apparently these calamities are capricious outbreaks of disorganized, unregulated forces of nature, wholly beyond the control of man; but in them all, God's purpose may be read. They are among the agencies by which He seeks to arouse men and women to a sense of their danger" (*Prophets and Kings,* p. 277).

Travel Disasters

Before the two great world wars of the last century, Ellen White wrote: "Thousands of ships will be hurled into the depths of the sea. Navies will go down, and human lives will be sacrificed by the millions." This was obviously fulfilled in the great wars. Nothing like this had ever happened before. But then she went on to describe a time just before the close of probation when there would be unexpected disasters in the civilian world. "Confusion, collision, and death without a moment's warning will occur on the great lines of travel. The end is near, probation is closing. Oh, let us seek God while He may be found, call upon Him while He is near!" (*Last Day Events,* p. 24).

The pride of the Russian submarine fleet, the *Kursk,* lies at the bottom of the Barents Sea under 350 feet of dark, cold water. On August 12, 2000, at around 11:30 local time two powerful explosions were picked up from the area of the *Kursk.* The 505-foot Oscar II-class submarine immediately sank to the bottom, taking 118 men to their death. A note found on one of the first four bodies retrieved said that at least 23 of the 118 crewmen survived the initial blast and retreated to the stern for safety. There they also perished as the lights dimmed and went out, the oxygen supply ran out, and water seeped into the compartment.

On September 27, 2000, the Greek passenger ferry *Express Samina* struck a patch of rocks in the Agean Sea and sank. Two American women, too excited to go below, had stayed on deck to watch the sunset. "Then, out of the darkness, rocks appeared," they said. The boat struck the rocks at 18 knots—near full speed. The lights went out, and the *Express Samina* began listing. Then confused passengers poured out onto the deck. The American women wondered if this was the end. It was for more than 75 of the passengers. It was later determined that at the time of the accident the captain was taking a nap; the officer in charge was off the bridge flirting with a passenger, and the other officers were watching a soccer game in the main lounge.

On July 25, 2000, an Air France supersonic Concorde took off from the Charles De Gaulle Airport near Paris and a few minutes later crashed into a hotel in the nearby town of Gonesse. Of the Concorde's 100 passengers, 97 were German tourists on the first leg of a luxury Caribbean cruise holiday. All 100 passengers died, along with the nine crew members and four people on the ground.

On October 31, 1999, Egypt Air Flight 990, a Cairo-bound Boeing 767, plunged 33,000 feet without warning into the sea a half hour after leaving Kennedy International Airport in New York. All 217 people on board were killed. Investigators later concluded that one of the flight officers, who was left alone briefly in the cockpit, may have deliberately sent the big plane into a nosedive and disabled the plane's recovery system.

And there are many more tragic headlines: "Alaska Airplane Spun Before Crash"; "Kenya Airways Jet Crashes Into Sea"; "143 Dead in Gulf Airplane Crash"; "Singapore Air Defends Storm Takeoff." The point is that the predictions are being fulfilled!

There Shall Be Plagues

Most people have no idea about the desperate situation of those with HIV-AIDS. The February 12, 2001, issue of *Time* dedicated the cover and an extensive feature story to AIDS. The article begins: **"Imagine your life this way**. You get up in the morning and breakfast with your three kids. One is already doomed to die in infancy. Your husband works 200 miles away, comes home twice a year and sleeps around in between. You risk your life in every act of sexual intercourse. You go to work past a house where a teenager lives alone tending young siblings without any source of income. At another house, the wife was branded a whore when she asked her husband to use a condom, beaten silly and thrown into the streets. Over there lies a man desperately sick without access to a doctor or clinic or medicine or food or blankets or even a kind word. At work you eat with colleagues, and every third one is already fatally ill. You whisper about a friend who admitted she had the plague and whose neighbors stoned her to death. Your leisure is occupied by the funerals you attend every Saturday. You go to bed fearing adults your age will not live into their 40s. You and your neighbors and your political and popular leaders act as if nothing is happening."

Of the 36 million adults and children in the world living with HIV-AIDS in 2000, more than 70 percent (25 million plus) were in sub-Saharan Africa. And some 3.8 million Africans were newly infected last year. A total of 17 million Africans have died since the AIDS epidemic began in the late 1970s, more than 3.7 million of them children. An additional 12 million children have been orphaned by AIDS. An estimated 8.8 percent of adults in Africa are infected with HIV-AIDS, and on average one adult in five living in the seven southernmost countries in Africa is living with HIV. Every continent on earth is now infected with HIV-AIDS, with the greatest concentration of victims in Africa and South/Southeast Asia. And the experts say that AIDS has only begun to take its deadly toll.

According to an April 17, 2001, news report doctors in Papua New Guinea have estimated that the country risks losing about 20 percent of its population to AIDS in the next nine years—a million people.

World magazine, October 21, 2000, reported that "since the virus was first identified, America's cities have acted as its primary incubators. In the mid-1980s the disease struck like an urban cobra, killing first in San Francisco, Miami, and New York—all homosexual meccas. Then it slithered out across the rest of the country, cutting an epic trail of death. As of 1999, AIDS has killed 430,411 people in the United States—nearly as many as live in the entire state of Wyoming. The cities still are hotbeds: Last year, 10 cities (New York, Los Angeles, San Francisco, Miami, Washington, D.C., Chicago, Houston, Philadelphia, Newark, and Atlanta) accounted for nearly half of cumulative reported AIDS cases." And the most sobering news is that "the promise of anti-AIDS drugs is yielding to the harsh reality that reckless behavior is driving up the rate of new HIV infections."

AIDS in the Priesthood

In late January 2000, the Kansas City *Star* newspaper printed a series of articles on AIDS in the Priesthood. "The *Star* began researching AIDS more than four years ago. In the last 18 months, the newspaper examined scores of death certificates and church documents and interviewed hundreds of priests, church officials and AIDS experts worldwide. The newspaper also visited a sex education school for priests in Maryland and an

AIDS hospice in Florida. Last fall, the newspaper conducted a random nationwide survey of 3,000 priests to learn their views on AIDS in the priesthood and how the Catholic Church has dealt with the issue."

Then in an article by Judy L. Thomas, the *Star* reported on January 29, 2000, that "hundreds of Roman Catholic priests across the United States have died of AIDS-related illnesses, and hundreds more are living with HIV, the virus that causes the disease.

"The actual number of AIDS deaths is difficult to determine [because it is kept secret by the priest or hidden by church leaders]. But it appears priests are dying of AIDS at a rate at least four times that of the general U.S. population, according to estimates from medical experts and priests, and an analysis of health statistics by the Kansas City *Star*.

"In Missouri and Kansas alone, at least 16 priests and two religious-order brothers have died of AIDS since early 1987.

"The deaths are of such concern to the church that most dioceses and religious orders now require applicants for the priesthood to take an HIV-antibody test before their ordination.

"For the nation's 60 million Catholics, served by 46,000 priests, the AIDS issue goes straight to the heart of church doctrine—a doctrine that teaches compassion and forgiveness but also considers homosexual relations a sin and opposes the modern practice of 'safe sex.' "

The Thomas article in the *Star* went on to report: "Another researcher who has extensively studied the issue of AIDS within the church is the Rev. Thomas Crangle, a Franciscan priest in the Capuchin order in Passaic, N.J. In 1990, Crangle conducted a mail survey of hundreds of priests selected at random.

"Crangle said that of the 500 surveys he sent, 398 were returned. About 45 percent of those responding volunteered that they were gay, and 92—nearly one fourth—said they had AIDS. 'I was surprised,' Crangle said. 'I felt there was a problem, but I didn't think it was of that magnitude.' "

The *Star* research report continued: "Exactly how many priests have died of AIDS or are infected with HIV is unknown, in part because many suffer in solitude. When priests do tell their superiors, the cases generally are handled quietly, either at the priests' request or because church officials are reluctant to discuss them.

"In 1995, Bishop Emerson J. Moore left the Archdiocese of New York and went to Minnesota, where he died in a hospice of an AIDS-related illness. His death certificate attributed his death to 'unknown natural causes' and listed his occupation as 'laborer' in the manufacturing industry. After a Minnesota AIDS activist filed a complaint, officials changed the cause of death to 'HIV-related illness.' The occupation, however, has not been corrected."

The immorality and deception continue.

Without Natural Affection

On August 4, 1999, the New Jersey Supreme Court ruled that the Boy Scouts of America is a "Public Accommodation" and must admit homosexuals as adult Scout leaders. In a unanimous (7-0) decision the court ruled that James Dale, a homosexual activist, must be readmitted as a Scout leader under the state's law against discrimination. This decision was later reversed by the U.S. Supreme Court, but it points out the feeling of many in society today.

The California legislature has enacted three measures that focus on civil rights "protections" for homosexuals. The legislation, which Governor Gray Davis signed on October 4, 1999, grants spousal benefits to same-sex couples, fines businesses and property owners who consider sexual orientation in hiring or housing, and authorizes the public education system to foster better understanding of homosexuals. (See *Christianity Today*, November 15, 1999.)

The March 20, 2000, edition of *Newsweek* devoted the cover and a major section in the magazine to a special report titled "Gay Today: How the Battle for Acceptance Has Moved to Schools, Churches, Marriage and the Workplace." The point of the article is that homosexuality and homosexual behavior are here to stay and are being accepted by all except those who are narrow and bigoted.

Fading Leader Accountability

There is much that could be said here, but I will let a Washington *Times* commentary summarize the current situation in America. "Hot on the heels of revelations that he fathered a love child with his mistress, the Reverend Jesse Jackson has tumbled further from the moral high ground. Mr. Jackson has added former Democratic congressman Mel Reynolds to the Rainbow/PUSH Coalitions' payroll. Reynolds was among the 176 criminals excused in President Clinton's last-minute forgiveness spree. Reynolds received a commutation of his six-and-a-half-year federal sentence for 15 convictions of wire fraud, bank fraud, and lies to the Federal

Election Commission. He is more notorious, however, for currently serving five years for sleeping with an underage campaign volunteer.

"This [the Reynolds saga] is a first in American politics. An ex-congressman who had sex with a subordinate won clemency from a president who had sex with a subordinate, then was hired by a clergyman who had sex with a subordinate."

And very few seem to care that the moral fabric of our country is being ripped apart.

Wizard Kids

Many people see nothing wrong with the Pokemon and Harry Potter materials and associated secular phenomena. However, those who have taken a closer look at the materials recognize that they are a not so subtle introduction to wizardry and the occult. Pokemon made the *Time* cover on November 22, 1999, with this subtitle: "For many kids it is now an addiction: cards, video games, toys, a new movie." It is all about pocket monsters! "Since last fall, Pokemon has become a $1 billion business for Nintendo of America, thanks to a full-fledged product line and an army of 100 U.S. licensees."

The Pokemon card game is made and distributed by Wizards of the Coast, the same company that made the best-selling, heavily occult-laced trading card game "Magic: The Gathering." Wizards of the Coast also owns TSR, the producers of all the Dungeons & Dragons materials. This material, as you may recall, was a favorite of the two young men who perpetrated the Columbine massacre. It should be obvious to all that the producers of this material have only one goal in mind—to make lots of money by addicting children to their products. And of course the effects on the children speak for themselves.

Forbes magazine, in its March 19, 2001, issue listed J. K. Rowling, the creator of the Harry Potter wizardry books for kids, as one of the "Celebrity 100," who is now worth $36 million. *Forbes* reported that "the latest installment of her Harry Potter series sold a magical 5.1 million copies in two days."

Adults are not left out of the world of the occult in the popular media. Clairvoyant John Edward's nightly séance is the top-rated show on the Sci Fi network. Under the bold title "Talking With the Dead," *Time,* March 5, 2001, reported that "none today is better known or more listened to than John Edward, a fast-talking, former ballroom-dancing instructor who is cleaning up on his proclaimed ability 'to connect with the energies of people who have crossed over.' Died, that is.

"Indeed, his nightly *Crossing Over with John Edward* is the highest rated show on the Sci-Fi network and is about to go into syndication. He has made appearances on *Larry King Live, Dateline,* an HBO special, *Entertainment Tonight* and other TV shows. Between his fees for individual appointments, tickets for his seminars and stage appearances, and sales of his books, audiotapes and videotapes, Edward seems to be one of the few growth industries in an otherwise lackluster economy."

Another *Time* issue (November 6, 2000) noted that Barbara Walters would air on *20/20* an interview with Barbra Streisand in which Streisand recalls visiting a Long Island, NY, psychic to contact her late father.

Are These Things "Signs"?

The Acts of the Apostles is directly on point in addressing the spirit of our age: "There are in the world today many who close their eyes to the evidences that Christ has given to warn men of His coming. They seek to quiet all apprehension, while at the same time the signs of the end are rapidly fulfilling, and the world is hastening to the time when the Son of man shall be revealed in the clouds of heaven. Paul teaches that it is sinful to be indifferent to the signs which are to precede the second coming of Christ. Those guilty of this neglect he calls children of the night and of darkness. He encourages the vigilant and watchful with these words: 'But ye, brethren, are not in darkness, that that day should overtake you as a thief. Ye are all the children of light, and the children of the day: we are not of the night, nor of darkness. Therefore let us not sleep, as do others; but let us watch and be sober' " (p. 260).

Mad Cow Disease

Some time ago on a business flight I had a conversation with a dentist. I learned that he was going to attend a convention and take some courses for his continuing education. He learned that I was going to speak at a camp meeting. When our meal was served I received my "special meal"—vegetarian. My seatmate asked why I had ordered or preferred vegetarian. I told him there were two reasons. One was for health reasons and that while studying for a Master of Public Health degree I had become more knowledgeable about nutrition and wanted to avoid the possibility of getting mad cow disease. We both laughed, because on the cover of all the national news magazines that week was the story of the mad cow disease outbreak in Great Britain. He then stated, "That makes sense, but I thought you said there were two reasons." Then I told him about my interest in prophecy and the second coming of Christ. I concluded by saying, "I am planning to go to heaven soon, and the best I can tell they are all vegetarians up there. So I am training my taste buds to enjoy the food of heaven." He said, "That makes sense, too."

We have been given adequate warning that animal products would someday be so diseased that we should learn to prepare vegetarian dishes to take the place of meat. Frankly, since I have been a vegetarian all my life, I have learned to enjoy that regimen. And I feel that I have enjoyed better overall health as a result. With the serious problems with meat today I am very thankful I have followed the counsel.

Read just a few of the hundreds of statements on this topic while keeping in mind the situation of the livestock industry today.

"Flesh was never the best food; but its use is now doubly objectionable, since disease in animals is so rapidly increasing. Those who use flesh foods little know what they are eating. Often if they could see the animals when living and know the quality of the meat they eat, they would turn from it with loathing. People are continually eating flesh that is filled with tuberculous and cancerous germs. Tuberculosis, cancer, and other fatal diseases are thus communicated" (*Child Guidance,* p. 382). One would think that with all our scientific advances we could protect animals from disease. We could, of course, but then we would have to stop feeding them their own manure and the byproducts of other animals. In other words, it would cost us something.

"Animals are becoming more and more diseased, and it will not be long until animal food will be discarded by many besides Seventh-day Adventists. Foods that are healthful and life sustaining are to be prepared, so that men and women will not need to eat meat" (*Counsels on Diet and Foods,* p. 267). Many besides Seventh-day Adventists are now vegetarians. In fact millions—a relatively high percentage of the U.S. population—are vegetarian. Most restaurants today offer vegetarian selections.

"Those who subsist largely upon flesh cannot avoid eating the meat of animals which are to a greater or less degree diseased. The process of fitting the animals for market produces in them disease" (*Healthful Living,* p. 103). How did Ellen White know this? Today many poultry growers keep the lights on 24 hours a day in the chicken houses and gorge the birds for the last few days before they are slaughtered. I dare say that if you visited a chicken operation the day before the trucks come to pick them up and observed their condition and behavior you would never eat another bite of chicken. It is widely reported that many farmers fatten their cattle on chicken manure to save money.

"I am instructed to say that if meat eating ever were safe, it is not safe now. Diseased animals are taken to the large cities and to the villages, and sold for food. Many of these poor creatures would have died of disease in a very short time if they had not been slaughtered; yet the carcasses of these diseased animals are prepared for the market, and people eat freely of this poisonous food" (*Medical Ministry,* p. 280).

"Educate yourself to discard all flesh meat. Soon butter will never be recommended, and after a time milk will be entirely discarded, for disease in animals is increasing in proportion to the increase of wickedness among men. The time will come when there will be no safety in using eggs, milk, cream, or butter" (*Manuscript Releases,* vol. 21, p. 286).

There have been many major outbreaks of disease that have made the news in recent years. In 1997 it was noted then that food-borne illness sickens up to 80 million Americans each year and that the most common causes were from meat eating. The September 1, 1997, issue of *U.S. News & World Report* carried a major story of the bad beef scandal. One paragraph stated: "The contents of animal feed are attracting more attention as a result of the outbreak of so-called mad cow disease in Great Britain and concern that similar problems could occur here. More than a dozen Britons died after eating beef from cattle infected with bovine spongiform encephalopathy (BSE). The cattle are thought to have contracted the disease by eating rendered brains and spinal cords of sheep infected with a condition called scrapie. While scrapie is far less common in the United States, on August 4 [1997] the FDA ordered a halt to feeding all slaughterhouse wastes to U.S. cattle and sheep as a BSE safety precaution. Seventy-five percent of the nation's 90 million cattle had been eating feed containing slaughterhouse byproducts, so the ban raises the possibility that more farmers and feed manufacturers will turn to cheap additives like manure and other questionable waste products."

In early 2001 most of the countries of Western Europe were stricken with mad cow disease—BSE-infected cattle. Now the countries of the Middle East and North Africa are also at high risk because they have imported meat and bonemeal from Europe.

The human version of mad cow disease, called new variant Creutzfeldt-Jakob disease (vCJD), was first diagnosed in a British teenager in 1995. Since then, 92 persons—almost all younger than 55— have died of or been diagnosed with vCJD. Eighty-eight were in Britain, three in France, and one in Ireland.

The Washington *Times,* National Weekly Edition, February 12-18, 2001, gave a two-full-page report of the mad cow epidemic. Their article began: "U.S. health officials are clamping down as 'mad cow disease'— and the fear of it—spreads throughout the world.

"Scientists say the chances of the brain-destroying illness appearing in the United States are slim. But several incidents here in the past two weeks have made calls for stricter regulation grow louder.

"The Food and Drug Administration confirmed that 1,222 head of cattle in Texas were mistakenly fed cattle remains, a practice banned in the United States since 1997 because scientists think it could help spread the disease."

Newsweek, March 12, 2001, bannered on the cover "The Slow Deadly Spread of Mad Cow Disease. How It Could Become an Epidemic." The nine-page article on mad cow disease contained the following explanatory paragraph: "Mad cow is the creepiest in a family of disorders that can make Ebola look like chickenpox. Scientists are only beginning to understand these afflictions. Known as transmissible spongiform encephalopathies, or TSEs, they arise spontaneously in species as varied as sheep, cattle, mink, deer and people. And once they take hold they can spread. Some TSEs stick to a single species, while others ignore such boundaries. But each of them is fatal and untreatable, and they all ravage the brain—usually after long latency periods—causing symptoms that can range from dementia to psychosis and paralysis. If the prevailing theory is right, they're caused not by germs but by "prions"—normal protein molecules that become infectious when folded into abnormal shapes. Prions are invisible to the immune system, yet tough enough to survive harsh solvents and extreme temperatures. You can freeze them, boil them, soak them in formaldehyde or carbolic acid or chloroform, and most will emerge no less deadly than they were."

Now the counsel I listed above seems quite appropriate, doesn't it? But wait. There is more. If the mad-cow problem weren't enough, now foot-and-mouth disease has returned with a vengeance. Already, thousands of animals have been slaughtered in Europe in an effort to stop the spread of the disease.

The Cell From Hell

Toxic algae that thrive on pollutants are killing fish, making people sick, and spreading nationwide. A report in *U.S. News & World Report* in the July 28, 1997, issue related this story: "Retired North Carolina fisherman David Jones struggles with symptoms similar to those of several chronic afflictions: the mental confusion of Alzheimer's, the physical crippling of multiple sclerosis, the wasting of AIDS. But Jones has none of these. Doctors say all the evidence points to a neurological assault by algae.

"Jones is one of about 100 North Carolina victims—fishermen, commercial divers, marine construction workers—who appear to have been poisoned by *pfiesteria,* a toxic alga found in the state's eastern rivers and estuaries. [It was noted later in the article that these rivers have been polluted by the runoff of fecal material from commercial chicken and hog operations.] The victims' symptoms can include open sores, nausea, memory loss, fatigue, disorientation, and the near-total incapacitation suffered by Jones.

"*Pfiesteria* was first discovered in 1991 and has since killed hundreds of millions of fish in North Carolina. State workers have used bulldozers to clear piles of dead menhaden from the beaches. A 1995 outbreak wiped out 14 million fish, temporarily closed parts of the Neuse River, and put 364,000 acres of shellfish beds off limits. Since then, the problem has been spreading to other parts of the country."

There is much more in the current literature regarding the concerns of health authorities regarding serious illnesses that result from contact with or eating flesh food.

Without Self-control—Brutal

In 2 Timothy 3:1-5 Paul gives a list of characteristics that would be evident in the lives of people in the last days. In verse three he says men will be "without self-control and brutal." In a similar description of the last days, Ellen White wrote: "Men possessed of demons are taking the lives of men, women, and little children. Men have become infatuated with vice, and every species of evil prevails" (*Testimonies for the Church,* vol. 9, p. 11).

The shocking details of the fulfillment of the end-time signs are so sickening that I will mention only the locations for some of the examples:

- The Oklahoma City bombing.
- Four women killed by one man in Yosemite National Park.

- Children shot and injured in a Jewish day-care center by a man on a hate-inspired killing spree.
- Students killing other students in elementary schools.
- Youth killing other youth and teachers in high schools.
- Employees killing fellow workers in Georgia, Hawaii, Washington, and Massachusetts.
- Seven people killed by one man at the Wedgewood Baptist Church in Ft. Worth, Texas.
- More than 2,000 children under the age of four are killed by their parents and guardians every year in the United States.
- Internationally, there have been terrible atrocities in Sudan, Kosovo, Chechnyah, Russia, and East Timor. In the West African country of Sierra Leone rebel soldiers have practiced an ugly ritual of amputating the arms of thousands of innocent men, women, and children.

The Dark Side of the Internet

The Internet, the much touted World Wide Web that is now available to schools, libraries, homes, and businesses around the world, has become so corrupt that even the most ardent techies admit that much of its current content is either worthless, degrading, or worse. The Internet has been responsible for I.D. theft, child pornography, securities swindles, stalking, false advertising, credit fraud, adoption scams, and much more. In many homes and other locations this material is available to children as well as adults.

Signs in the Religious World

In July 2000, Mexico elected a new president. The Washington *Post* carried a front-page story on August 6, 2000, with the headline "Church Reemerges in Mexico as First Openly Catholic Leader Fox Opens Door for Stronger Role." A very lengthy article followed. I will share just a couple short notes: "Shortly after winning the Mexican presidency last month, Vicente Fox returned to his ranch in hilly central Mexico, and together with family, bodyguards and reporters, attended Sunday Mass at a local church.

"With news cameras flashing, Fox stepped forward and accepted Holy Communion from a Roman Catholic priest. The effect was stunning. The next morning, photos of a president-elect publicly receiving the sacrament under headlines such as 'Broken Tradition' were splashed in newspapers across the country.

"Like so much here in this season of political revolution in Mexico, the role of the Catholic Church is fundamentally changing with the election of the country's most openly religious president in nearly a century.

"Although 90 percent of Mexicans consider themselves Catholic, the church was officially invisible for most of the 20th century. Relegated to the sidelines of political discourse by some of the world's toughest laws separating church and state, the church is now poised to take a more prominent role in public life and have an impact on policy."

Apparently the Catholics had already been "feeling their oats." The August 7, 2000, issue of *Christianity Today* reported that "in March about 70 Protestant families were expelled from the Mexican village of Plan de Ayala, in Chiapas state, by the town's Roman Catholic majority. 'Fourteen homes were demolished by the mob as the Protestants fled to the hills for refuge,' reports Seventh-day Adventist pastor Isaias Espinosa.

"The ethnic and political conflicts have fanned the flames of religious tensions between Roman Catholic (80 percent of the population) and the fast-growing Protestants, who have surged at three times the rate of population growth during the 1980s.

"The pope has aggravated the situation by expressing alarm about the growth of Latin American evangelicalism. During his 1999 visit to Mexico, Pope John Paul II urged Catholics to vigorously defend their faith against Protestant sects that have made inroads in Latin America. On previous visits to the region, the pontiff said that evangelicals are spreading 'like an oil stain' in the region and 'threaten to pull down the structures of faith in numerous countries.'"

Protestant Mergers

In an effort to maintain viability many mainline Protestant denominations are merging. "A sudden burst of ecumenical activity last week prompted some religious leaders to suggest—cautiously—that the new century would bring a resurgence in religious tolerance and tranquility. 'There is a kind of energy,' said the Rev. John Buchanan, editor of the ecumenical journal *The Christian Century,* 'a "moving of the Spirit" that the apostle Paul promised would bring all things together.'

"After decades of dialogue, prayer, and politicking, the 5.2 million-member Evangelical Lutheran Church in America and the 2.5 million-member Episcopal Church last week celebrated the launch of a 'full communion' agreement that will enable the two denominations to share clergy and pool other resources at a time of declining membership for both. More like a marriage than a merger, the arrangement calls for mutual recognition of each other's clergy, members, and sacraments while allowing both to retain their own creeds and structures.

"On the eve of a joint service at the Washington National Cathedral in Washington, D.C., celebrating the alliance, leaders of the two churches said the venture would enable Lutherans and Episcopalians to 'speak with one voice' and share opportunities for ministry. The agreement, said the Episcopal Church's presiding bishop, Frank T. Griswold, 'is a sign to a divided world' that the two churches 'have made common cause together and are entering full communion full of hope.' Other ecumenically minded churches, added the ELCA's presiding bishop, H. George Anderson, should take heart at the agreement, which took more than 30 years to negotiate. 'We're here today saying it can be done,' Anderson said" (*U.S. News & World Report,* January 15, 2001).

This ecumenical agreement becomes even more significant knowing that this same Lutheran group which is a party to the merger above had already entered into "full communion" in 1997 with the Presbyterian Church (USA), the United Church of Christ, and the Reformed Church in America.

Left Behind

So much has already been said about the phenomenal "success" of the *Left Behind* book series by Tim LaHay and Jerry Jenkins that it need not take up much space here. However, it should be noted that this series of <u>novels</u> has sold over 12 million copies to "Christians" who are being led astray by the secret rapture falsehood, the seven years of tribulation idea, and most deceptively, the notion that at the time of the rapture the wicked will have a second chance to be saved. The Bible simply does not teach a second chance at the Second Coming. Mankind is having his second chance right now! This error-filled series could well be part of the great false revival.

Strange Bedfellows

Much of what I know about Focus on the Family is very positive. Dr. James Dobson has had a significant impact on holding up the value of the traditional family unit. Though I don't know him personally, I have received some of his material in the mail and have heard his program on the radio. That is why what I am about to share with you now seems so out of character with him. Dave Hunt, author of *Global Peace and the Rise of the*

AntiChrist and *A Woman Rides the Beast,* among other books, also has a free newsletter that I have been receiving for several years. In the February 2001 issue of "The Berean Call," the following story was reported in the News Alert section as a quote from Religion News Service (12/00): "It was a striking image to one observer: evangelical Protestant powerhouses James Dobson and Chuck Colson visiting the headquarters of the Catholic Church, the very institution Protestants rebelled against centuries ago.

"Dobson and Colson joined a global cast of business executives and Catholic politicians, lawyers and scholars last month for a three-day conference at the Vatican on the world economy's impact on families. They also met briefly with the pope.

"For centuries, Catholics and Protestants have clashed over the role and infallibility of the pope, among other issues. That makes the brief meeting among Pope John Paul II; Dobson, president of Colorado Springs-based Focus on the Family; and prison ministry leader Colson a special moment.

"The significance was not lost on Colson who, according to one conference participant, noted that there would have been a time when he would not have been invited and he would not have come.

"Though Catholics and Protestants disagree frequently on theological matters, dialogue between the faith groups has been going on for years. On several social issues such as opposition to abortion and homosexuality, many Evangelicals and Catholics find common ground.

"Conference participant Rev. Robert Sirico, a Catholic priest and president of the Acton Institute, said <u>Vatican officials told him they could not recall a similar meeting involving such high-level evangelical Protestants taking place at the Vatican.</u>"

I wanted to check out this story and make sure that it had been reported correctly. I called Focus on the Family and asked if they could determine whether or not Dr. Dobson had attended the meeting in the Vatican. They confirmed that indeed he had attended and faxed me a press release of the event.

Apparently, what Dr. Dobson wasn't aware of is that when you "go to see the pope" or attend meetings that he calls, you are in fact responding to one who claims to occupy a place above yours. For example, in the many times the pope has visited the United States, he has never visited the president at the White House. Most recent U.S. presidents have gone to see him, but he doesn't come to see them. They even "come to see him" when he comes to the U.S. Presidents have gone to New York, Miami, St. Louis, Denver, and other places to see the pope, but he has never come to see them.

Faith-based Initiatives

Barely 10 days in office President Bush announced plans to create a "faith-based initiative" to enlist churches and other charitable organizations to deliver billions of dollars' worth of aid to the needy in America. The Catholic weekly, *Our Sunday Visitor,* reported in its February 18, 2001, issue the following headline: "Bush Sees New Era for Church-State Cooperation—Consulting With Catholic Leaders, Bush Pushes His Agenda for Government-backed, Faith-based Social Programs." The accompanying article noted: "President George W. Bush, who stunned some politicos last year when he said that Jesus Christ was his favorite philosopher, has placed an unprecedented emphasis on religion during his early days in office.

"Bush, a Methodist, told 4,000 attendees at the National Prayer Breakfast Feb. 1 that his faith has 'sustained me in moments of success and in moments of disappointment. Without it, I'd be a different person, and without it, I doubt I'd be here today.'

"The previous day, he met with more than 40 Catholic leaders, including Cardinal-designate Edward M. Egan of New York and Archbishop Charles J. Chaput of Denver. He also met with Cardinal Bernard F. Law of Boston the following week.

"Bush was rallying support for his proposal to enlist faith-based organizations as allies in delivering certain social services. 'Government,' he said, 'cannot be replaced by charities, but it can welcome them as partners instead of representing them as rivals.'"

To accomplish this goal, Bush signed executive orders creating a White House Office of Faith-based and Community Initiatives and Centers for Faith-based and Community Initiatives in five cabinet departments.

"The White House office is headed by Dr. John J. DiIulio, Jr., of the University of Pennsylvania, an expert in the field and a Catholic.

"DeIulio's office will encourage faith-based and secular groups to deal with such community problems as homelessness, drug addiction, crime and family dysfunction. It will attempt to remove legal barriers by promoting new legislation and regulations."

Then the article pointed out that "the administration has stressed that there would be no proselytizing and that participants would be served without regard to their religious affiliation. <u>Existing **models** include Catholic Relief Services overseas and Catholic Charities USA at home. About 62 percent of Catholic Charities' money [already] comes from government.</u>"

Many churches and organizations are very eager to get money from the government; others are cautious. It may sound good on the surface, but the devil, as always, may be in the details. The United States has become a great country by keeping a separation between church and state. The Founding Fathers were well aware of the serious problems that arise when the church seeks the support of the state or vice versa. In this case, will the church end up running the government, or will the government end up running the church?

Dr. Derek H. Davis, director of the J. M. Dawson Institute of Church-State Studies at Baylor University, made some very insightful observations in a press release February 1, 2001. The following are typical: "Government funding of religion is a wolf in sheep's clothing." Charitable Choice is an example of "right motive, wrong method." "The policy of funding churches and other communities of faith will have some positive impact in the short term, but it will do much damage in the long term. People are forgetting about the government regulation that must accompany government funding and they do not think about the climate of government dependency that will result."

Davis continued, "This initiative could result in religion eventually just being thought of by the American people as another government program. As government takes over more and more responsibility for tending to those in need, people in the pews will be much less inclined to fill the offering plates. Religion in America is dynamic because the people know that they must support their religious institutions because the government does not do it for them."

Davis concluded, "America has thrived in large part because of its deep religious commitments. If these commitments decline, and I believe they will under these initiatives, then America will suffer and lose part of the secret to its success. Once lost, it will be very hard to recapture."

It Gets Even More Complicated

Now the Bush administration is exploring a proposal to channel all U.S. foreign aid though faith-based organizations. Senator Jesse Helms

(R-N.C.), chairman of the senate Foreign Relations Committee, says he wants all U.S. foreign aid channeled through private charities and religious groups. Helms stated, "The time has come to reject what President Bush correctly labels the 'failed compassion of towering, distant bureaucracies' and, instead, 'empower private and faith-based groups who care most about these issues'" (*Christian Century,* January 31, 2001).

An Image to the Beast

I was shocked when I first heard about what is now being revealed about what is happening in the background of American politics. In a direct parallel fulfillment of the traditional Adventist interpretation of Revelation 13, the president of the United States has began the journey down the road to cooperation with the Church of Rome. The Washington *Post* printed a full article on this topic on April 16, 2001. The headline read, **"Bush Aims to Strengthen Catholic Base."** The article that followed stated in part: "Since taking over the White House, President Bush and top advisers have been assiduously cultivating Catholic voters in an attempt to realign a once-Democratic constituency in much the same way that the Republican Party in the 1970s and 1980s won over Southern evangelical Protestants.

"A number of Republican operatives view the Catholic vote as the linchpin of a larger Republican strategy to gain solid majorities among all White religious voters—critical to Bush's reelection prospects.

"'Religiously active voters have been gradually migrating to the Republican Party, leaving the Democrats as the party of the religiously indifferent as well as the politically liberal,' pollster Steve Wagner, who is a member of the informal Catholic advisory group to the White House, recently wrote the conservative Catholic magazine *Crisis.*

"Bush, seeking to capitalize on those trends, has met privately with at least three high Catholic Church officials and has adopted Catholic themes in speeches; his staff has instituted a weekly conference call with an informal group of Catholic advisers; and the Republican National Committee is setting up a Catholic Task Force.

"Wagner's findings are supported by broader trends. The more religious a voter is—based on church attendance—the more likely the voter is to be a Republican. At the two extremes, voters who attend services more than once a week voted for Bush by 63 percent to 36 percent, said VNS, while those who never attend services voted for Gore, 61 percent to 32 percent.

"Bush, bidding to improve on those margins in 2004, has met with Archbishop Justin Rigali of St. Louis, Bishop Donald Wuerl of Pittsburgh, and Washington's Cardinal Theodore McCarrick. His staff has created an informal advisory group that includes *Crisis* publisher Deal Hudson and Princeton University political scientist Robert George.

"Perhaps most important, Bush has incorporated language familiar to Catholics—what strategists call Catholic 'buzzwords'—into speeches. In a March 22 address for a new Catholic University center honoring Pope John Paul II, Bush told a gathering that included Detroit Archbishop Adam Cardinal Maida and McCarrick:

> "'The culture of life is a welcoming culture, never excluding, never dividing, never despairing, and always affirming the goodness of life in all its seasons. In the culture of life we must make room for the stranger. We must comfort the sick. We must care for the aged. We must welcome the immigrant. We must teach our children to be gentle with one another. We must defend in love the innocent child waiting to be born.'"

The pope could have written the above quote. It sounds, intentionally, just like his speeches. The article continues with two amazing and revealing statements:

"The effort to recruit Catholic voters has led to a striking change in the political climate in Washington. George noted in an interview last week that 'in 1960, John Kennedy went from Washington down to Texas to assure Protestant preachers that he would not obey the pope. In 2001, George Bush came from Texas up to Washington to assure a group of Catholic bishops that he would.'

"'It's almost too good to be true, how much they have come to understand what appeals to religiously active Catholics,' Hudson said. 'We have a leader who is not afraid of sharing his vision of a country that welcomes life, protects it by law, but does it in a way that is not moralistic or self-righteous.'"

Welcome to the time of the end! What an awesome time to be alive. How should we then live? Our salvation is so clearly nearer than when we first believed.

CHAPTER 14

My Spirit Will Not
Always Strive With Man

Before God destroyed the ancient world with a flood, He told Noah, "My Spirit shall not strive with man forever" (Genesis 6:3). In other words, God has set a boundary on evil and our involvement in it. In the New Testament, after Peter talks about God's longsuffering nature, he adds, "But the day of the Lord will come as a thief in the night, in which the heavens will pass away with a great noise, and the elements will melt with fervent heat; both the earth and the works that are in it will be burned up" (2 Peter 3:10).

Apparently, just before the end, the Spirit of God, and consequently an understanding of His Word, will be slowly withdrawn from the earth. "Behold the days are coming," says the Lord, "that I will send a famine on the land, not a famine of bread, nor a thirst for water, but of hearing the words of the Lord. They shall wander from sea to sea, and from north to east; they shall run to and fro, seeking the word of the Lord, but shall not find it" (Amos 8:11, 12). These verses are likely speaking of the time right after the close of probation, but "the restraining Spirit of God is even now being withdrawn from the world. Hurricanes, storms, tempests, fire and flood, disasters by sea and land, follow each other in quick succession. Science seeks to explain all these. The signs thickening around us, telling of the near approach of the Son of God, are attributed to any other than the true cause. Men cannot discern the sentinel angels restraining the four winds that they shall not blow until the servants of God are sealed; but when God shall bid His angels loose the winds, there will be such a scene of strife as no pen can picture" (*Testimonies for the Church,* vol. 6, p. 408).

In order to put our time to best use, we should "dwell on present truth, on Christ's second coming. The Lord is coming very soon. We have only a little while in which to present the truth for this time—the truth that is to convert souls. This truth is to be presented in the utmost simplicity, even as Christ presented it, so that the people can understand what is truth. Truth will dispel the clouds of error" (*Evangelism,* p. 624).

Since I have written about God's great prophetic time line in my other books, I will not repeat that evidence here. We are indeed living in the time of the end, and time is running out. Those who lived in the days of Christ's first coming could and should have known when He was coming. So we today can and should know when it is time for the Second Coming. Both comings are based on Bible prophecies.

God's purposes, of course, know no haste and no delay. Like the stars in their appointed courses His plans move steadily, unshakably to their consummation. In the fullness of time, Paul tells us, God sent forth His Son. He waited. Many things converged to that point of waiting. There are parallels to the second coming of Christ. Many things converge to our time also. Heavenly plans, Satanic plans, earthly plans all move, and in the divine providence our heavenly Father is aware of those movements. And in the fullness of time Jesus came. And in the same manner, "in the fullness of time," He will come the second time.

There are hundreds of predictions in the Old Testament concerning the first coming of Christ. Some scholars have said that the first coming of Christ is the best attested fact in history. Prophetic details are precise in their implications. They were all fulfilled! Jesus was born of the virgin Mary in the little town of Bethlehem, as prophesied. His parents' home was in Nazareth in Galilee, but the emperor, Augustus, needing more revenue, required a registration, a head tax. And so every family in the Roman Empire had to go to the town of its birth. Prophecy was being fulfilled as Joseph and Mary, who was great with child, came out of the hills of Nazareth, across the hogsback that goes up the center of Judea past Jerusalem, four miles to the little town of Bethlehem.

Many observed the events that were taking place. In the gospel story these individuals are brought to our attention one by one through various circumstances. The Pharisees, the rabbis, and the scribes are mentioned. They were the learned or educated men of Judea. They were well aware of the prophets of the Old Testament. When Herod inquired of them where He should be born they said in Bethlehem. They turned to the prophet Micah immediately. They could pinpoint the time He was to be born. So when Herod made his decree to massacre the babies he knew the year, so he went plus or minus one each side—2 years and younger—and he would get Him either way.

Prophecies almost 3,000 years old that inform us of the place, the time, the tribe—He must be of the tribe of Judah. The census was being taken. The tribesmen of Judea were being identified. The Messiah would come from the tribe of Judah. He was to come as a descendant of Abraham and David. The genealogies recorded in the Gospel of Matthew give these facts precisely and accurately. There could be no question, they knew. It was the right time, the right line, the right tribe, and the right city.

And then God piled evidence upon evidence. When Joseph and Mary came to Bethlehem there was no room for them in the local motel. But they were able to find a stable close by, and there it was that Mary gave birth to Jesus. All heaven rejoiced. From the celestial heights a select band of angels was dispatched to serenade the newborn king. Their choir robes were glorious light—not unlike the robes originally given to Adam and Eve. No one had ever heard singing like the song of the angels. But the only people who listened were shepherds. Wouldn't it have been great if someone had made a tape recording of it? Wouldn't you like to hear the angels sing? One day soon it will be our privilege to hear similar angelic praise at the celebration of the redeemed.

Who heard them then? They were singing just outside of Bethlehem. There is no notice made in the records of the Jewish chroniclers of a band of glorious angels singing on the hillside: singing to the new king and proclaiming peace and goodwill among men. No one recorded it in Palestine. But somewhere, a long way from Palestine in the East, some men saw that star of shining angels. Maybe it was east to Iraq, India, or Iran. They saw the star hundreds of miles away. But the people in Palestine weren't even looking. Maybe they were stuck to their TV's and couldn't see outside. The glory faded near Bethlehem, but it was marked by the men of the East and they were able to follow it by traveling at night. Arriving in Palestine, they announced, "We have seen His star." Whose star? They said, "His star." A man from the East, named Balaam, had made a prediction 1,400 years earlier. He had been bribed by the king of Moab to curse Israel. And he had gone. But he promised, wisely, "I will say only what God's Spirit tells me to say." And under inspiration he predicted that the star of Judah would arise to mark the birthday of the king (Numbers 24:17). And in his homeland that prediction of the star was remembered.

The Wise Men were apparently interested in astronomy, the movement of heavenly bodies. Then one evening they saw in the West a new heavenly body. They were curious. And their curiosity gave way to deep interest. They did some research. And the prediction in the writings of the East that had been lying there dormant for 1,400 years spoke to their hearts. Now that is incredible to me. They read in what was even at that time an ancient scroll in a distant land, a word that had been spoken by a renegade prophet 14 centuries before. A word that had been given by the Holy Spirit was suddenly made luminous and powerful in their minds.

As these Wise Men pondered the star and its prediction they said to themselves, "Let's go see it." It was shining in the West and was obviously a long way from home. They decided to investigate. Can you imagine what their friends said? And so they began the journey. It is likely that the trip took several months. Finally in Bethlehem they found a young child. When the shepherds came, the babe was wrapped in swaddling clothes and lying in a manger. But according to the Bible, when the Wise Men found Him, they found a young child. He was no longer a baby; He was a young child. Months had passed in the long trek of those Wise Men. It would have been very difficult to take a newborn on a trip to Egypt. And so in the providence of God this baby became a young child. Jesus was maybe a full year of age. But He was a young child, and these Wise Men came and found Him. He had absolutely nothing to distinguish Him. His parents were poor. They weren't in some fancy suite. They were among the homeless! Staying in a cattle shed. And as those Wise Men looked at Him they believed. It is an incredible story.

Where was the evidence? That is what we must think about in our day. Where is the evidence? It is not found in great propositional statements nailed down in bold type. It was a glimmer of a star that they had seen in the West. And the Wise Men saw, and followed, and believed, and accepted. And so they found confirmation of their quest as they looked into the eyes of a young child. Just 4 or 5 miles away in Jerusalem the Jewish scholars had all the ancient scrolls and all the evidence in front of them. They could have listed dozens of items of evidence. They had evidence enough, but they didn't believe. The glory of the angels shone in the nearby fields around Bethlehem and the southern part of Jerusalem with the glory of heaven. Yes four or five shepherds believed, but the rest of them didn't. Where was the innkeeper at that time? Do you think the shepherds kept their mouths shut? Not likely! But why didn't the others believe? Didn't they see the sign? What made some people believe and some people not believe?

When Jesus was 40 days old Joseph and Mary took Him up to the

Temple to be registered as their firstborn, according to God's law. And as Leviticus 12 mandates, an offering had to be offered. They could offer a bull, or a ram, or a lamb. And if one didn't have the money for one of these, one could capture two turtledoves and bring them instead. Joseph brought the two turtledoves. He didn't have any money to buy anything else. The Wise Men hadn't yet arrived with their gifts. And so they took their two turtledoves and the 40-day-old baby and went up to Jerusalem and the Temple.

The priest who was on duty at the Temple welcomed them. That was his job. He accepted the offerings, and offered them. Then he took the baby in his arms and offered Him to Jehovah. And then he invoked the blessings of God and handed the baby back to His parents. He had done his job. He accepted the registration fee, wrote His name in the register, and the job was done. He didn't even recognize that he had just held the Messiah. The shepherds who looked into the eyes of the baby believed. Wise Men looked into the face of the young child and believed. The priest held Him in his arms and was unmoved.

As the parents were leaving the Temple they met an old man— Simeon. We don't know much about him. He was just there. He loved the Temple. He loved the Scriptures. He loved the Lord. He apparently spent a lot of time in the Temple. He studied and understood the Scriptures. And most of all, he longed for the Lord to fulfill His promise. And now he saw this baby of a poor couple, and the scriptural evidence clicked in his mind. The time was right. The tribe was right. Everything was right. And within his heart the Spirit awakened a response. This was He. He walked right up to them, took the baby, and glorified God. "Now, Lord, let me go to sleep. My eyes have seen the fulfillment of Thy promise." Hardly had he finished speaking and returned the babe to His mother than an old woman who lived near the Temple—Anna—saw Him. She recognized Him. Accepted Him. Committed her life to Him. I wonder what the priest thought as he watched these two. They were old and a bit slow, with failing memory. Perhaps a little bit weepy in their old age. *Humor them—but I have other things to do.*

And Jesus of Nazareth moved out of their lives. Evidence? Enough for some. Not enough for others. The Holy Spirit gave the evidence, and awakened in the mind the response to the evidence. One of the purposes of the Spirit is to convince (John 16:9, 10). He comes into the heart. And the mind responds, *This is it. This is the truth. This is right.* But what we do after that conviction is up to us. And the wonderful part about this is that God knows all our lives. He chooses the opportune moment to focus the evidence and bring the witness. To some of us He comes when we are children. While for others it's as young people or young adults. To some He waits for a long time.

A number of years ago, while working with evangelist Dale Brusett in a meeting in Jacksonville, Florida, I visited a 75-year-old man who had been coming to the meetings. He told me that he had attended a similar meeting in New York City when he was a young man. He remembered that the meetings had been conducted by a man named Everson. He said, "I enjoyed the meetings, but didn't make a decision to join the church then. But now it is all coming together. I want to be baptized." Some respond when they are young, and some when they are older. Of course we don't know if other opportunities will come to us, so that's why the Bible says, "Today, while you hear His voice. . . . Today."

Now is the day of salvation. When we become aware of it. When it suddenly dawns in our minds, *This is the program. This is the Saviour that I must follow. This is the way of life that I must internalize. And allow the Spirit of God to replicate in me as I look to Jesus.* It's the time when that awareness comes to us. That is the fullness of time. That is the best time. He may come again. But every time you delay it gets harder to respond. When you talk to people who have delayed—people who have played with the Spirit of God, and brushed aside His urgings—you sense how difficult it is to respond later on. It becomes increasingly difficult to get your thinking straight, to get your life organized the right way.

Look to those people whose lives touched the life of Jesus—imagine them in your mind. Think of them as faces looking at a crib lined with straw on which a babe is lying. Herod is there, at once fearful and yet cruel, arrogant, murderous. He sees a baby that must be killed—who is a threat to him. He is not some terrorist with an automatic rifle in His hand, but just a baby. Conviction is stabbing at his heart. Perhaps this is a real king.

We can imagine the high priests looking on, too. A curl in their lips, cynicism in their eyes. They had built up their own pictures of what Messiah was to be. Their wishful thinking of the design they had for their own lives made the Messiah in their own image. His coming to Bethlehem, in a stable, was enough to crowd out all the evidence that they had uncovered in two dozen prophetic writers. Yes, they met Christ several times thereafter: when He was 12 years old, and then in a series of encounters from when He reappeared at 30 years of age until they silenced Him a little over three years later. By then they had steeled their minds, and the evidence passed them without a thought. They would destroy Him with it.

We see the nameless shepherds and the nameless Wise Men. There was the nameless innkeeper. The elderly Simeon and Anna. And there was the trusting Joseph, and submissive Mary. They are all there around that crib in ancient Bethlehem, and above them is the star. And the divine narrative is complete. There was no one else. In all the world—no one else. There was no one to chronicle that birth. No one to record the birth of that boy in illuminated sheets. No fanfare to announce His arrival. And when the angel choir returned to their heavenly business it was silent again in the fields of Bethlehem. But the evidence was there, all right. The evidence was powerful enough to change some lives. And the same evidence awakened resentment, hatred, and indifference in others.

Matthew 2:12 says of these Wise Men that "they departed to their own country another way." No one encounters Jesus and departs on the same path he was traveling when he came to Christ. There is always another way. There are other thoughts. There are other philosophies. There are other priorities. They saw the young child, and they worshiped and went back to their country another way.

It might be appropriate to look at the evidence that the Lord has given you. Every one of us is different. Every one of those faces looking over the crib was different. They came from different backgrounds. They had different outlooks on life. God didn't serenade the Wise Men with an angel choir as He did the shepherds. God didn't give Joseph and Mary a large number of scrolls containing the prophetic writings on them as He did to the people in Jerusalem.

God gives evidence adequate to our needs and backgrounds. We each stand in our places today totally different from each other. And the Holy Spirit comes into our minds with different evidences. We need to see Jesus. The self-emptying, wise Creator God. In a manger, He was giving Himself and everything He had. And when He comes into your life you dare not ignore the evidence for change. From now on you are going home to the Father's house another way.

The Wise Men returned to their country, and we look for a country. We look for a city—a home, whose builder and maker is God. It may cost us to go another way—changing directions in our lives. We have to decide as the

Spirit works on our mind. Which road have you come? What evidence have you accepted? What impact of the Spirit in your life have you failed to respond to? When the Spirit comes with a small, quiet voice saying *This is what you ought to do,* how have you responded, in your own heart, in your devotional life, in your own family, in your relationship to your spouse, or your parents, or your children?

You have now seen Jesus. Your journey needs to be carefully structured to put your feet just where He would have you. Through the Spirit Jesus has been manifest to us. What are we going to do about that? In the quietness of this moment you should decide. I can't tell you what to do. I can only alert you to the evidence and the ministry of the Spirit of God. You must do the deciding. You must decide what you are going to do with all the evidences of God's guidance in your life. Are you ready to take those steps—wherever He leads?

Are you ready to go to the new country that He has prepared for you? To go His way? Another way from yours? To walking in His footsteps? To be led by His Spirit?

"There are in the world today many who close their eyes to the evidences that Christ has given to warn men of His coming. They seek to quiet all apprehension, while at the same time the signs of the end are rapidly fulfilling, and the world is hastening to the time when the Son of man shall be revealed in the clouds of heaven. <u>Paul teaches that it is sinful to be indifferent to the signs which are to precede the second coming of Christ.</u> Those guilty of this neglect he calls children of the night and of darkness. He encourages the vigilant and watchful with these words: 'But ye, brethren, are not in darkness, that that day should overtake you as a thief. Ye are all the children of light, and the children of the day: we are not of the night, nor of darkness. Therefore let us not sleep, as do others; but let us watch and be sober'" (*The Acts of the Apostles,* p. 260). (See 1 Thessalonians 5:1-6.)

After Jesus died, the presence of God was withdrawn from the Temple and the Jewish people were no longer considered God's chosen people, but they didn't realize it. "When God's presence was finally withdrawn from the Jewish nation, priests and people knew it not. Though under the control of Satan, and swayed by the most horrible and malignant passions, they still regarded themselves as the chosen of God. The ministration in the temple continued; sacrifices were offered upon its polluted altars, and daily the divine blessing was invoked upon a people guilty of the blood of God's dear Son and seeking to slay His ministers and apostles. So when the irrevocable decision of the sanctuary has been pronounced and the destiny of the world has been forever fixed, the inhabitants of the earth will know it not. The forms of religion will be continued by a people from whom the Spirit of God has been finally withdrawn; and the satanic zeal with which the prince of evil will inspire them for the accomplishment of his malignant designs, will bear the semblance of zeal for God" (*The Great Controversy,* p. 615).

God through the prophet appeals to us, "Seek the Lord while He may be found, call upon Him while He is near. Let the wicked forsake his way, and the unrighteous man his thoughts; let him return to the Lord, and He will have mercy on him; and to our God, for He will abundantly pardon" (Isaiah 55:6, 7).

We are way down the stream of probationary time. Most of the major signs have taken place. "The exact day and hour of Christ's coming have not been revealed. The Saviour told his disciples that he himself could not make known the hour of his second appearing. But he mentioned certain events by which they might know when his coming was near. 'There shall be signs,' he said, 'in the sun, and in the moon, and in the stars.' 'The sun shall be darkened, and the moon shall not give her light, and the stars of heaven shall fall.' Upon the earth, he said, there shall be 'distress of nations, with perplexity; the sea and the waves roaring; men's hearts failing them for fear, and for looking after those things which are coming on the earth.

" 'And they shall see the Son of man coming in the clouds of heaven with power and great glory. And he shall send his angels with a great sound of a trumpet, and they shall gather together his elect from the four winds, from one end of heaven to the other.'

"The signs in the sun, moon, and stars have been fulfilled. Since that time earthquakes, tempests, tidal waves, pestilence, and famine have multiplied. The most awful destructions, by fire and flood, are following one another in quick succession. The terrible disasters that are taking place from week to week speak to us in earnest tones of warning, declaring that the end is near, that something great and decisive will soon of necessity take place.

"Probationary time will not continue much longer. Now God is withdrawing his restraining hand from the earth. Long has he been speaking to men and women through the agency of his Holy Spirit; but they have not heeded the call. Now he is speaking to his people, and to the world, by his judgments. The time of these judgments is a time of mercy for those who have not yet had opportunity to learn what is truth. Tenderly will the Lord look upon them. His heart of mercy is touched; his hand is still stretched out to save. Large numbers will be admitted to the fold of safety who in these last days will hear the truth for the first time.

"The Lord calls upon those who believe in him to be workers together with him. While life shall last, they are not to feel that their work is done. Shall we allow the signs of the end to be fulfilled without telling people of what is coming upon the earth? Shall we allow them to go down in darkness without having urged upon them the need of a preparation to meet their Lord? Unless we ourselves do our duty to those around us, the day of God will come upon us as a thief. Confusion fills the world, and a great terror is soon to come upon human beings. The end is very near. We who know the truth should be preparing for what is soon to break upon the world as an overwhelming surprise.

"As a people, we must prepare the way of the Lord, under the over-ruling guidance of the Holy Spirit. The gospel is to be proclaimed in its purity. The stream of living water is to deepen and widen in its course. In fields nigh and afar off, men will be called from the plow, and from the more common commercial business vocations, and will be educated in connection with men of experience. As they learn to labor effectively, they will proclaim the truth with power. Through most wonderful work-ings of divine providence, mountains of difficulty will be removed. The message that means so much to the dwellers upon earth will be heard and understood. Men will know what is truth. Onward, and still onward, the work will advance, until the whole earth shall have been warned. And then shall the end come" (*Review and Herald,* November 22, 1906).

CHAPTER 15

It's Time for the Latter Rain

What is the latter rain? Is it necessary for every Christian to experience it? When does it occur in the life of the Christian and the history of the church? The term "latter rain" has little significance for those not acquainted with biblical terminology. But to those who recognize its significance the term brings a feeling of anticipation and joy. When this topic is studied in depth its tremendous implications are readily apparent.

Much of the Bible, especially the prophetic portions, is written from the perspective of one living in the land of Israel. Therefore, to fully understand a topic such as this, we need to try to look through the eyes of the prophets themselves and investigate the culture of their time.

Many of the stories and illustrations of the Bible and particularly those of Jesus Himself are taken from nature. They in turn have applications to the spiritual life of the individual and the church. By and large, the people of Israel were farmers, and theirs was an agrarian lifestyle. Even today many parts of the world have very predicable weather patterns, with dry seasons and rainy seasons. So it was for the land of Israel in biblical times. In the lands of the East the former, or early, rain fell at the time of sowing. Farmers depended on it to germinate the seed. The latter rain fell near the close of the growing season, and farmers depended upon it to ripen the grain in preparation for the harvest. "The Lord employs these operations of nature to represent the work of the Holy Spirit" (*Last Day Events,* p. 183).

The latter rain was absolutely imperative for a successful harvest, and the people looked forward to it with great anticipation. God had promised, "Then I will give you rain in its season, the land shall yield its produce, and the trees of the field shall yield their fruit" (Leviticus 26:4). "I will give you the rain for your land in its season, the early rain and the latter rain, that you may gather your grain, your new wine, and your oil" (Deuteronomy 11:14). The people asked for and waited for the latter rain. "Ask the Lord for rain in the time of the latter rain," they were instructed. "The Lord will make flashing clouds; He will give them showers of rain, grass in the field for everyone" (Zechariah 10:1). One very interesting text is reminiscent of baby birds in a nest waiting eagerly for food from their parents. "They waited for me as for the rain, and they opened their mouth wide for the latter rain" (Job 29:23, KJV).

The Bible makes an awesome transition from the natural rain to the spiritual rain. "Let us know, let us pursue the knowledge of the Lord. His going forth is established as the morning; He will come to us like the rain, like the latter and former rain to the earth" (Hosea 6:3). "He shall come down like rain upon the mown grass: like showers that water the earth" (Psalm 72:6).

There is a timeliness to the latter rain, both in its natural and symbolic applications. "Sow for yourselves righteousness; reap in mercy; break up your fallow ground, for it is time to seek the Lord, till He comes and rains righteousness upon you" (Hosea 10:12). And in the context of the Second Coming we are encouraged to "therefore be patient, brethren, until the coming of the Lord. See how the farmer waits for the precious fruit of the earth, waiting patiently for it until it receives the early and latter rain. You also be patient. Establish your hearts, for the coming of the Lord is at hand" (James 5:7, 8). Twice here patience is encouraged. Just so there are many references to patience and the blessings of God in the Spirit of Prophecy: "The rain is not seen until it begins to fall, and it often comes wholly unexpectedly. So the Lord's precious gift of grace is often nearer than we think. If we will only have faith, and wait patiently for a little while, His help will come, and will surprise us as He surprised the woman of Samaria. He shall come down like showers upon the fruitful earth" (*Signs of the Times,* April 22, 1897).

Christians longing for the return of Christ in glory have long discussed and prayed for the latter rain. We are told what preparation is necessary to receive the latter rain. We are also given the time parameters within which the latter rain will come in its fullness. We are given the purpose of the latter rain, and can conclude that among those living on the earth at the second coming of Christ only those who receive the latter rain will be translated to heaven. This is quite a sobering thought, and reason enough to study more deeply into the topic. In addition we are told the results of the latter rain coming in its abundance—like waters covering the entire earth.

How to Prepare

When the rich young man came to Jesus he asked, "What shall I do to inherit eternal life?" When Jesus told him what to do "he went away sorrowful, for he had great possessions" (Matthew 19:16-22). The young man knew what it would take, but he was not willing to meet the conditions. In the same manner, God has outlined through the prophetic gift to us what is necessary to receive the latter rain. The question then becomes, "Are we willing to meet the conditions?" The conditions are not very complex, but they do require a commitment on our part.

Some points we can understand by simple logic. For example, if the early rain in the biblical illustration is to germinate the seed, and the latter rain is to bring the grain to maturity and harvest stage, then if the seed is not germinated no amount of rain at harvesttime will bring it to maturity. The natural analogy is that if we have not been converted by the early rain, then the latter rain will be of no benefit to us.

"Many have in a great measure failed to receive the former rain. They have not obtained all the benefits that God has thus provided for them. They expect that the lack will be supplied by the latter rain. When the richest abundance of grace shall be bestowed, they intend to open their hearts to receive it. They are making a terrible mistake. The work that God has begun in the human heart in giving His light and knowledge must be continually going forward. Every individual must realize his own necessity. The heart must be emptied of every defilement and cleansed for the indwelling of the Spirit. **It was by the confession and forsaking of sin, by earnest prayer and consecration of themselves to God, that the early disciples prepared for the outpouring of the Holy Spirit on the Day of Pentecost. The same work, only in greater degree, must be done now.** Then the human agent had only to ask for the blessing, and wait for the Lord to perfect the work concerning him. It is God who began the work, and He will finish His work, making man complete in Jesus Christ. But there must be no neglect of the grace represented by the former rain. Only those who are living up to the light they have will receive greater light. Unless we are daily advancing in the exemplification of the active Christian virtues, we shall not recognize the manifestations of the

Holy Spirit in the latter rain. It may be falling on hearts all around us, but we shall not discern or receive it" (*Testimonies to Ministers,* p. 507).

Here and in many other places we are told to pray earnestly for the latter rain. "We may have had a measure of the Spirit of God, but by prayer and faith we are continually to seek more of the Spirit. It will never do to cease our efforts. If we do not progress, if we do not place ourselves in an attitude to receive both the former and the latter rain, we shall lose our souls, and the responsibility will lie at our own door" *(ibid.).*

Most of us are very familiar with the biblical counsel "And let us consider one another in order to stir up love and good works, not forsaking the assembling of ourselves together, as is the manner of some, but exhorting one another, and so much the more as you see the Day approaching" (Hebrews 10:24, 25). There are likely many good reasons why we should get together as church members near the end, but one of the most important should surely be to pray for the early and latter rains. "We should improve every opportunity of placing ourselves in the channel of blessing. Christ has said, 'Where two or three are gathered together in My name, there am I in the midst.' The convocations of the church, as in camp meetings, the assemblies of the home church, and all occasions where there is personal labor for souls, are God's appointed opportunities for giving the early and the latter rain.

"But let none think that in attending these gatherings, their duty is done. A mere attendance upon all the meetings that are held will not in itself bring a blessing to the soul. It is not an immutable law that all who attend general gatherings or local meetings shall receive large supplies from heaven. The circumstances may seem to be favorable for a rich outpouring of the showers of grace. But God Himself must command the rain to fall. Therefore we should not be remiss in supplication. We are not to trust to the ordinary working of providence. We must pray that God will unseal the fountain of the water of life. And we must ourselves receive of the living water. Let us, with contrite hearts, pray most earnestly that now, in the time of the latter rain, the showers of grace may fall upon us. At every meeting we attend our prayers should ascend, that at this very time God will impart warmth and moisture to our souls. As we seek God for the Holy Spirit, it will work in us meekness, humbleness of mind, a conscious dependence upon God for the perfecting latter rain. If we pray for the blessing in faith, we shall receive it as God has promised" (*Testimonies to Ministers,* pp. 508, 509).

Several factors are involved in preparing for the latter rain. The first is to receive the early rain. Then we should assemble with believers as often as we can to pray for God's Spirit, and, of course, this special latter rain blessing. Then we are to preach God's Word, work for the lost, and put away dissensions. "Instead of man's speculations, let the word of God be preached. Let Christians put away their dissensions, and give themselves to God for the saving of the lost. Let them in faith ask for the blessing, and it will come. The outpouring of the Spirit in apostolic days was the 'former rain,' and glorious was the result. But the 'latter rain' will be more abundant. Joel 2:23" (*The Desire of Ages,* p. 827).

And we must add character development—the battle with self. We must understand that this is accomplished only by the indwelling Christ through His Holy Spirit. "I saw that none could share the 'refreshing' [the latter rain] unless they obtain the victory over every besetment, over pride, selfishness, love of the world, and over every wrong word and action. We should, therefore, be drawing nearer and nearer to the Lord and be earnestly seeking that preparation necessary to enable us to stand in the battle in the day of the Lord. Let all remember that God is holy and that none but holy beings can ever dwell in His presence" (*Early Writings,* p. 71).

This character preparation also becomes a prerequisite for the seal of God. "Not one of us will ever receive the seal of God while our characters have one spot or stain upon them. It is left with us to remedy the defects on our characters, to cleanse the soul temple of every defilement. Then the latter rain will fall upon us as the early rain fell upon the disciples on the Day of Pentecost" (*Testimonies for the Church,* vol. 5, p. 214).

It is the work of God's Spirit all along the way that germinates our spiritual interest and helps to bring our experience to maturity. That maturing includes victory over our besetting sins. And now is the time to make the necessary preparation. "I saw that many were neglecting the preparation so needful and were looking to the time of "refreshing" and the "latter rain" to fit them to stand in the day of the Lord and to live in His sight. Oh, how many I saw in the time of trouble without a shelter! They had neglected the needful preparation; therefore they could not receive the refreshing that all must have to fit them to live in the sight of a holy God. Those who refuse to be hewed by the prophets and fail to purify their souls in obeying the whole truth, and who are willing to believe that their condition is far better than it really is, will come up to the time of the falling of the plagues, and then see that they needed to be hewed and squared for the building. But there will be no time then to do it and no Mediator to plead their cause before the Father. Before this time the awfully solemn declaration has gone forth, 'He that is unjust, let him be unjust still: and he which is filthy, let him be filthy still: and he that is righteous, let him be righteous still: and he that is holy, let him be holy still' " (*Early Writings,* p. 71).

Since probation's days and hours are fast running out, we must get serious about getting ready. "The third angel's message is swelling into a loud cry, and you must not feel at liberty to neglect the present duty, and still entertain the idea that at some future time you will be the recipients of great blessing, when without any effort on your part a wonderful revival will take place. Today you are to give yourselves to God, that he may make of you vessels unto honor, and meet for his service. Today you are to give yourself to God, that you may be emptied of self, emptied of envy, jealousy, evil-surmising, strife, everything that shall be dishonoring to God. Today you are to have your vessel purified that it may be ready for the heavenly dew, ready for the showers of the latter rain; for the latter rain will come, and the blessing of God will fill every soul that is purified from every defilement. **It is our work today to yield our souls to Christ, that we may be fitted for the time of refreshing from the presence of the Lord—fitted for the baptism of the Holy Spirit**" (*Review and Herald,* March 22, 1892).

We know that in the grand scheme of things—from the prophetic/historical perspective—we are living at the time of the Laodicean or lukewarm church. Jesus says of that church, "You say, 'I am rich, have become wealthy, and have need of nothing'—and do not know that you are wretched, miserable, poor, blind, and naked" (Revelation 3:17). Wonderfully in the power of revival this church eventually becomes the church militant and the church triumphant. But we are warned, "Ministers and people are unprepared for the time in which they live, and nearly all who profess to believe present truth are unprepared to understand the work of preparation for this time. In their present state of worldly ambition, with their lack of consecration to God, their devotion to self, they are wholly unfitted to receive the latter rain and, having done all, to stand against the wrath of Satan, who by his inventions would cause them to make shipwreck of faith, fastening upon them some pleasing self-deception. They think they are all right when they are all wrong" (*Testimonies for the Church,* vol. 1, p. 466).

Two Latter Rains?

Reading through all the biblical references to the latter rain, as well as those in the Spirit of Prophecy, one sees a picture emerging of two latter rains. One is for us as individuals: all this will become more clear as we study the purpose for the latter rain. The other is the general latter rain upon God's remnant church. Individually it comes when we are sealed and prepared to give the loud cry. And there will also be a great outpouring of the Spirit upon the church. But "the great outpouring of the Spirit of God, which lightens the whole earth with His glory, will not come until we have an enlightened people, that know by experience what it means to be laborers together with God. When we have entire, wholehearted consecration to the service of Christ, God will recognize the fact by an outpouring of His Spirit without measure; but this will not be while the largest portion of the church are not laborers together with God" (*Counsels on Stewardship,* p. 52). Another reference that indicates that there will be a time when the church as a whole will receive the latter rain states: "When the latter rain is poured out, the church will be clothed with power for its work; but the church as a whole will never receive this until its members shall put away from among them, envy, evil-surmisings, and evil-speaking" (*Review and Herald,* October 6, 1896).

We are also told that "when the churches become living, working churches, the Holy Spirit will be given in answer to their sincere request. . . . Then the windows of heaven will be open for the showers of the latter rain" (*Last Day Events,* p. 193). The Spirit is given to empower those who are involved in ministry! And countless thousands will be!

But beware! If you are seeking fellowship with Christ and a place in His kingdom—this ensures that Satan and His evil angels will work to discourage and sidetrack you from the necessary preparation. We need to be aware of this and realize that much of what we encounter in the world today, though it may seem quite harmless to some, is being used by Satan to take our time away from developing a genuine relationship with Jesus. Think of the time many spend in front of the television: it can be measured in many hours per week! We could add time spent on the Internet, etc. The point is that this all takes time away from spiritual nurture and even diminishes interest in it. Satan knows that God is eagerly waiting to transform our characters by the power of His Spirit. He fears that we will determine to take the time to do it.

"There is nothing that Satan fears so much as that the people of God shall clear the way by removing every hindrance, so that the Lord can pour out His Spirit upon a languishing church and an impenitent congregation. If Satan had his way, there would never be another awakening, great or small, to the end of time. But we are not ignorant of his devices. It is possible to resist his power. When the way is prepared for the Spirit of God, the blessing will come. Satan can no more hinder a shower of blessing from descending upon God's people than he can close the windows of heaven that rain cannot come upon the earth. Wicked men and devils cannot hinder the work of God, or shut out His presence from the assemblies of His people, if they will, with subdued, contrite hearts, confess and put away their sins, and in faith claim His promises. Every temptation, every opposing influence, whether open or secret, may be successfully resisted, 'not by might, nor by power, but by my spirit, saith the Lord of hosts' (Zech. 4:6)" (*Selected Messages,* vol. 1, p. 124).

When Will the Spirit Fall?

In the biblical illustration, the latter rain fell just before the harvest. It was depended on to ripen the grain in preparation for the harvest. According to Jesus the harvest is the end of the world (see Matthew 13:39). There are two closely related purposes for the latter rain. It is both to prepare the grain (the people) for the end of the world *and* to empower them to take the gospel to all the world—which will be a sign of the end or harvest. So by definition the latter rain will fall just before the end of time.

The latter rain will actually fall just before the seven last plagues begin, at the beginning of the time of trouble, and in connection with the Sunday law agitation. At that point the end is very near. The gospel must go to all of the world in the power that lightens the entire world. The Bible gives this a clear focus: "After these things I saw another angel coming down from heaven, having great authority, and the earth was illuminated with his glory. And he cried mightily with a loud voice, saying, 'Babylon the great is fallen, is fallen. . . . Come out of her, my people, lest you share in her sins, and lest you receive of her plagues" (Revelation 18:1, 2, 4). Babylon's final fall, the enforcement of Sunday worship through the power of the state, is proclaimed with a loud voice. The power of the latter rain, given just before the plagues are poured out, enables the proclamation of this message.

Ellen White gives a detailed and explicit picture of this time: "At the commencement of the time of trouble, we were filled with the Holy Ghost as we went forth and proclaimed the Sabbath more fully.

" 'The commencement of that time of trouble,' here mentioned, does not refer to the time when the plagues shall begin to be poured out, but to a short period just before they are poured out, while Christ is in the sanctuary. At that time, while the work of salvation is closing, trouble will be coming on the earth, and the nations will be angry, yet held in check so as not to prevent the work of the third angel. At that time the 'latter rain,' or refreshing from the presence of the Lord, will come, to give power to the loud voice of the third angel, and prepare the saints to stand in the period when the seven last plagues shall be poured out" (*Maranatha*, p. 170).

We know from the parable of the sower in Matthew 13 that there are tares in the church. They are called by many names in the Bible. The fact is that during times of peace such people make a profession of godliness, while denying its life-changing power. But when hard times come— Sunday law agitation and the stressful situations that bring it on—the "bad guys" will quickly leave the church (see Matthew 13:20, 21). This faithful group left in the church (the wheat) is then joined by honest people from all sectors of society and the world. This new group—the remnant, if you please—will then commit all their resources to "finishing the work." It is this group that receives the latter rain.

Apparently there are those, even among the ministry, who are not sanctified and will leave the church when the Sunday laws are enforced. "The great issue so near at hand [enforcement of Sunday laws] will weed out those whom God has not appointed and He will have a pure, true, sanctified ministry prepared for the latter rain" (*Last Day Events*, p. 179).

God waits until the threat of persecution purges the church of the unconverted before He pours out the latter rain on the corporate church. Then while probation lingers the last message of mercy is given to a dying world. It is commonly understood that human probation ends when the seven last plagues begin. This is the pouring out of God's wrath unmixed with mercy.

Purpose of the Latter Rain

Character development and personal fortitude are gifts inherent in the latter rain. God prepares His church to live with Him and to finish the work in the world. Both of these tasks are impossible without His power. "Near the close of earth's harvest, a special bestowal of spiritual grace is promised to prepare the church for the coming of the Son of man. This outpouring of the Spirit is likened to the falling of the latter rain; and it is for this added power that Christians are to send their petitions to the Lord of the harvest 'in the time of the latter rain.' In response, 'the Lord shall make bright clouds, and give them showers of rain.' 'He will cause to come down . . . the rain, the former rain, and the latter rain.' Zechariah 10:1; Joel 2:23" (*The Acts of the Apostles,* p. 55).

The descriptions of conditions in the world near the Second Coming are quite frightful to many people. In fact the Bible says the situation was so disturbing that "men's hearts fail them for fear" (Luke 21:26). But God's people have His gift of power and assurance that allows them to sanely pass through this time. "It is the latter rain which revives and strengthens them to pass through the time of trouble" (*Last Day Events,* p. 201).

In the great battle of the spirits all will ultimately align themselves with one side or the other. But it will take an intentional choice to join God's side. Because the devil is now the prince of this world, all defaults or neutral choices go to his side. But God has promised that those who choose to follow Him will be transformed or regenerated by the Holy Spirit. "As the dew and the rain are given first to cause the seed to germinate, and then to ripen the harvest, so the Holy Spirit is given to carry forward, from one stage to another, the process of spiritual growth. The ripening of the grain represents the completion of the work of God's grace in the soul. By the power of the Holy Spirit the moral image of God is to be perfected in the character. We are to be wholly transformed into the likeness of Christ" (*ibid.,* p. 183). The awesome part of this transformation is that it fits us for translation. "Those who come up to every point, and stand every test, and overcome, be the price what it may, have heeded the counsel of the True Witness, and they will receive the latter rain, and thus be fitted for translation" (*Maranatha,* p. 43).

Results of the Latter Rain

We have already noted the results of the latter rain in those who receive it. They are brought to spiritual maturity. They are fitted to live with holy beings in heaven. They are given power for their witnessing. They are ready to go to work in sharing with others when the power comes. They don't just observe, they are active participants in taking the gospel to the entire world. It will be obvious to others that the power of God is at work.

Some time ago during the Friday evening meeting of camp meeting I felt that the Spirit of God was present and that the material I was presenting was apparently meeting the needs of those who had come. And yes, a speaker can tell if the audience is receptive and responsive. At the close of the meeting I gave an invitation for a recommitment and dedication. Many responded to the appeal as God moved their hearts. After the meeting closed a number of people spoke to me of their appreciation for the meeting.

Then one dear lady approached me and said, "You said 'I' two different times when you should have said 'me.'" Apparently I had used the subjective form of the pronoun instead of the correct objective form. I felt sorry that I had made that error, but I felt even worse about the fact that the dear lady missed the primary focus of the message. Evidently, under the great moving of the Spirit at the end no one will notice this type of blunder. "Under the showers of the latter rain the inventions of man, the human machinery, will at times be swept away, the boundary of man's authority will be as broken reeds, and the Holy Spirit will speak through the living, human agent, with convincing power. No one then will watch to see if the sentences are well rounded off, if the grammar is faultless. The living water will flow in God's own channels" (*Selected Messages,* vol. 2, p. 58).

The Power of the Final Warning

We know that at the end the message doesn't change. It is the same three angels' messages that we have always given, but now it is given with "ten times the power" (*Spaulding and Magan Collection,* p. 4). "As the message of the third angel swells to a loud cry, great power and glory will attend the closing work. It is the latter rain" (*Signs of the Times,* November 27, 1879). "Thousands of voices will be imbued with the power to speak forth the wonderful truths of God's Word. The stammering tongue will be loosed, and the timid will be made strong to bear courageous testimony to the truth" (*Early Writings,* p. 383). And there won't be just a hot spot for the gospel presentation here and there. The whole earth will be lightened with the glory of God!

Not only will the timid speak boldly but those who have held back about accepting and practicing the truth of God's Word will now take their stand with the people of God. "I heard those clothed with the armor speak forth the truth in great power. It had effect. I saw those who had been bound; some wives had been bound by their husbands, and some children had been bound by their parents. The honest who had been held or prevented from hearing the truth, now eagerly laid hold of it. All fear of their relatives was gone. The truth alone was exalted to them. It was dearer and more precious than life. They had been hungering and thirsting for truth. I asked what had made this great change. An angel answered: 'It is the latter rain, the refreshing from the presence of the Lord, the loud cry of the third angel'" (*Testimonies for the Church,* vol. 1, p. 182).

Yes, those who had held back on making a decision earlier, through fear of relatives and other factors, now respond. Also responding to the loud cry message under the latter rain will be civil leaders—those who are lawmakers. Many of these leaders join the faithful. We know that once the Sunday agitation begins, and it is likely to begin during a crisis, there will be no stopping it. But we speak out against it anyway in order that those who are honest in heart and have reasonable minds will understand the true will of God about the day of worship. They will then have the opportunity to make an informed response. "Thus the work will go on until the third message has done its work, and at the loud cry of the third angel, these agents [some of earth's civil lawmakers] will have an opportunity to receive the truth, and some of them will be converted, and endure with the saints through the time of trouble" (*Testimonies for the Church,* vol. 1, p. 203).

At the time of the early rain at Pentecost, God's people were given the gift of languages in order to able to clearly communicate with those who had assembled at Jerusalem from around the world to celebrate the feast. This experience will be repeated in connection with the latter rain. Writing about a special prayer meeting she experienced with the church members in Switzerland, Ellen White wrote, "It is with an earnest longing that I look forward to the time when the events of the day of Pentecost shall be repeated with even greater power than on that occasion. John says, 'I saw another angel come down from heaven, having great power; and the earth was lightened with his glory.' Then, as at the Pentecostal season, the people will hear the truth spoken to them, every man in his own tongue. God can breathe new life into every soul that sincerely desires to serve Him, and can touch the lips with a live coal from off the altar, and cause them to become eloquent with His praise" (*Review and Herald,* July 20, 1886).

Sabbath Significance

The keeping of the commandments is a hallmark of God's remnant church. The Sabbath is a particularly significant point. "I saw that the holy Sabbath is, and will be, the separating wall between the true Israel of God and unbelievers; and that the Sabbath is the great question to unite the hearts of God's dear, waiting saints. I saw that God had children who do not see and keep the Sabbath. They have not rejected the light upon it. And at the commencement of the time of trouble, we were filled with the Holy Ghost as we went forth and proclaimed the Sabbath more fully" (*Early Writings,* p. 85). In another statement this thought is amplified: "I saw that we sensed and realized but little of the importance of the Sabbath, to what we yet should realize and know of its importance and glory. I saw we knew not what it was yet to ride upon the high places of the earth and to be fed with the heritage of Jacob. But when the refreshing and latter rain shall come from the presence of the Lord and the glory of His power we shall know what it is to be fed with the heritage of Jacob and ride upon the high places of the earth. Then shall we see the Sabbath more in its importance and glory. But we shall not see it in all its glory and importance until the covenant of peace is made with us at the voice of God, and the pearly gates of the New Jerusalem are thrown open and swing back on their glittering hinges and the glad and joyful voice of the lovely Jesus is heard richer than any music that ever fell on mortal ear bidding us enter" (*Maranatha,* p. 245).

Heaven, too, will take on a new significance at this time. As conditions on the earth continue to deteriorate, the things of earth will grow strangely dim and Jesus and heaven will be seen as the treasure hid in a field; the pearl of great price that is worth more than anything of earthly value.

Opposition to the Latter Rain

It would seem that the latter rain, with its awesome power, would be welcomed by those inside and outside the church. It has such a positive effect on those who give the message and there is a response from those who are seeking truth. However, some church members of long standing will resist and criticize the manifestation of the latter rain. "There is to be in the churches a wonderful manifestation of the power of God, but it will not move upon those who have not humbled themselves before the Lord, and opened the door of their heart by confession and repentance. In the manifestation of that power which lightens the earth with the glory of God, they will see only something which in their blindness they think dangerous, something which will arouse their fears, and they will brace themselves to resist it. Because the Lord does not work according to their expectations and ideal, they will oppose the work. 'Why,' they say, 'should we not know the Spirit of God, when we have been in the work so many years?' Because they did not respond to the warnings, the entreaties, of the messages of God, but persistently said, 'I am rich, and in-creased with goods, and have need of nothing'" (*ibid.,* p. 219).

When the last message of warning is made powerful by the latter rain, the wicked raise up in opposition to it. "The last great warning had sounded everywhere, and it had stirred up and enraged the inhabitants of the earth who would not receive the message" (*Early Writings,* p. 279). This powerful end-time message will polarize those living on the earth. What the wicked cannot defend with the Bible they will seek to do with force. It is this physical resistance to truth in the context of the troubles on the earth that will finally bring about the death decree and the intervention of Christ at the Second Coming.

We must, therefore, pray for the latter rain to perfect our characters, empower us to take the gospel to the entire earth, and to prepare us to stand firm during the time of trouble. "Therefore be patient, brethren, until the coming of the Lord. See how the farmer waits for the precious fruit of the earth, waiting patiently for it until it receives the early and latter rain. You also be patient. Establish your hearts, for the coming of the Lord is at hand" (James 5:7, 8).

CHAPTER 16

Putting On the Armor of God

The battle of the spirits intensifies as we approach the end of time. There are casualties all around us. The devil is using all of his cunning and craftiness—his meanness and hatred. He hurls his weapons at those who would follow Jesus. He intends to intimidate them. He would cause them to turn away from Jesus to avoid the problems Satan himself brings. But we must always remember that God has given us awesome promises of protection and encouragement.

Knowing that we will face very trying times near the end Paul outlined a God-inspired plan of protection: "Finally, my brethren, be strong in the Lord and in the power of His might. Put on the whole armor of God, that you may be able to stand against the wiles [schemings] of the devil. For we do not wrestle against flesh and blood, but against principalities, against powers, against the rulers of the darkness of this age, against spiritual hosts of wickedness in the heavenly places. Therefore take up the whole armor of God, that you may be able to withstand in the evil day, and having done all, to stand. Stand therefore,

[1] having girded your waist with truth,

[2] having put on the breastplate of righteousness,

[3] and having shod your feet with the preparation of the gospel of peace;

[4] above all, taking the shield of faith with which you will be able to quench all the fiery darts of the wicked one.

[5] And take the helmet of salvation,

[6] and the sword of the Spirit, which is the word of God;

[7] praying always with all prayer and supplication in the Spirit,

[8] being watchful to this end with all perseverance and supplication for all the saints" (Ephesians 6:10-18).

Twice in this passage we are counseled to take up not just the armor of God but the *whole* armor of God. We must take advantage of every provision that God has made for our protection, so that we will not have any vulnerable spots or areas. Our defense is no stronger than our weakest point. The whole armor is all eight recommended items. The armor is said to be "the armor of God," because He is the one who provides it for us. And He asks us to put it on and fight the good fight of faith. God guarantees the effectiveness of His armor. It is the only armor that enables us to stand against the devil. So the entire armor is necessary.

The primary purpose of armor is, of course, protection. But soldiers don't put on their armor and then just stand there in the battle letting the enemy take shots at them. The Christian soldier is to be on the offensive. The armor simply provides protection while we are fighting.

This passage is one of many in the Bible to use the warfare/soldier motif. We gain additional insights into the many army parallels from this statement: "The church of Christ may be fitly compared to an army. The life of every soldier is one of toil, hardship, and danger. On every hand are vigilant foes, led on by the prince of the powers of darkness, who never slumbers and never deserts his post. Whenever a Christian is off his guard, this powerful adversary makes a sudden and violent attack. Unless the members of the church are active and vigilant, they will be overcome by his devices" (*Testimonies for the Church,* vol. 5, p. 394).

We Are in the Army Now

Historically, wars have been fought mostly by young men, with older, wiser, and more experienced officers. In some modern armies women are also actively involved in many roles. But everyone who is a Christian is in God's army and must be fitted with His armor. There is a place for men, women, and young people! "The fallen world is the battlefield for the greatest conflict the heavenly universe and earthly powers have ever witnessed. It was appointed as a theater on which would be fought out the grand struggle between good and evil, between heaven and hell. Every human being acts a part in this conflict. No one can stand on neutral ground. Men must either accept or reject the world's Redeemer. All are witnesses, either for or against Christ. Christ calls upon those who stand under His banner to engage in the conflict with Him as faithful soldiers, that they may inherit the crown of life" (*God's Amazing Grace,* p. 36).

As Christians we are all in God's army, and we all have a position to fill on this earth just as surely as there is a place for us in heaven. (See *Christ's Object Lessons*, p. 327.) We are not all officers, but the role of every soldier is vital to success. "All who enter the army are not to be generals, captains, sergeants, or even corporals. All have not the care and responsibility of leaders. There is hard work of other kinds to be done. Some must dig trenches and build fortifications; some are to stand as sentinels, some to carry messages. While there are but few officers, it requires many soldiers to form the rank and file of the army; yet its success depends upon the fidelity of every soldier. One man's cowardice or treachery may bring disaster upon the entire army" (*Testimonies for the Church*, vol. 5, p. 394).

In this age of specialists in medicine, law, teaching, information technology, and most other areas of work, we sometimes feel that the work of God is largely placed on the trained professional pastors. But *all* of us, pastors and laymen, are to be involved. "It is a fatal mistake to suppose that the work of soul-saving depends alone upon the ministry. The humble, consecrated believer upon whom the Master of the vineyard places a burden for souls is to be given encouragement by the men upon whom the Lord has laid larger responsibilities. Those who stand as leaders in the church of God are to realize that the Saviour's commission is given to all who believe in His name. God will send forth into His vineyard many who have not been dedicated to the ministry by the laying on of hands.

"Hundreds, yea, thousands, who have heard the message of salvation are still idlers in the market place, when they might be engaged in some line of active service. To these Christ is saying, 'Why stand ye here all the day idle?' and He adds, 'Go ye also into the vineyard.' Matthew 20:6, 7. Why is it that many more do not respond to the call? Is it because they think themselves excused in that they do not stand in the pulpit? Let them understand that there is a large work to be done outside the pulpit by thousands of consecrated lay members" (*The Acts of the Apostles*, p. 110).

This great battle over the souls of men is deadly serious, and will eventually determine the eternal consequences of every life. But the good news is that when it is all over there will never again be sin, heartache, pain, or death. As Christian soldiers, it is comforting to realize and visualize that we are not just marching—we are marching to Zion! And Jesus has already been over the ground we are traveling. He knows the power of temptation. He has promised to guide us through the danger spots. "They [God's followers] are to contend with supernatural forces, but they are assured of supernatural help. All the intelligences of heaven are in this army. And more than angels are in the ranks. The Holy Spirit, the repre-sentative of the Captain of the Lord's host, comes down to direct the bat-tle. Our infirmities may be many, our sins and mistakes grievous; but the grace of God is for all who seek it with contrition. The power of Omnipotence is enlisted in behalf of those who trust in God" (*The Desire of Ages,* p. 352).

Girded With Truth

The fabric of our society has changed radically in our own lifetimes. The inroads of pluralism and relativism have left many with no moral compass. The words "Does it work?" have replaced "Is it right?" Extreme tolerance of evil has become politically correct. Truth hardly even enters into the picture. The concepts of "If it works for you, it's OK with me" and "Your way is no better than my way" have permeated society. Men no longer seem to care if another is going the wrong direction on the path of life. In fact, many consider it bigotry to question the beliefs of others or to encourage a change in their life direction. Proselytizing—evange-lism among those already professing Christianity—is strongly criticized by many, since "we are all on our way to heaven and my way is as good as yours." For many there is no such thing as absolute truth, anyway.

New Age mysticism, astrology, science fiction, Eastern religions, ma-terialism, Communism, and other voices call to people today. But God has given ample evidence to the reasonable man that His Word is true and can be trusted as the standard for faith and practice. He desires that we worship Him in spirit and in truth. Truth is the first item listed in the armor of God (Ephesians 6:14). Jesus told us that His Word is truth. Accordingly, the Bible and the Bible only must be our standard for all doctrine and the basis for all reforms. We cannot look to the opinions of wise and educated men, the deductions of science, the creeds or decisions of ecclesiastical coun-cils—no matter what church they represent, or the voice of the majority. None of these should be regarded as evidence for or against any point of religious faith. Before we accept any doctrine or teaching we should de-mand a plain explanation from the Bible for its support!

Those who plan to be on the winning side in the battle of the spirits must stand on the foundation of truth—"Thy Word is truth." It is not big-otry or self-righteousness to share with others what one believes to be the truth. In fact, it is quite selfish not to share with others. As a matter of fact, if a person doesn't believe that his church tradition is teaching the truth, then he should prayerfully search for one that does. We are encouraged to "speak the truth in love" (Ephesians 4:15), but it must be spoken. Paul asks, "Have I therefore become your enemy because I tell you the truth" (Galatians 4:16)?

Our daily prayer should be that of King David, "Teach me Your way, O Lord; I will walk in Your truth; unite my heart to fear Your name" (Psalm 86:11).

We can recognize the significance of life's journey and where we are in the stream of time only as we seriously consider the Word of God, which He says is truth (John 17:17). Some in their haste to bring about worldwide Christian unity belittle others who are reluctant to drop their long-held beliefs. Of course, it is not possible for anyone to say that they know the "truth," the complete facts, about anything. But when it comes to spiritual things and the way to our eternal destiny, God has given us directions in His Word and through His life, both of which He says are truth. In spiritual things, then, by the grace of God, we can know what is truth. Truth is what God says it is. We have His word on that.

Jesus promised that when He returned to heaven He would send the Spirit and His general and special gifts. Ephesians 4 tells us that the gifts were to bring about unity of faith and solidify doctrinal understanding, so that believers might not be tossed on the waves of uncertainty.

Unity does not come naturally to the unconverted heart. It takes the indwelling of God's Spirit to bring this about.

And truth is basic to real unity. In Jesus' "unity" prayer in John 17, He prayed, "Sanctify them by Your truth. Your word is truth" (John 17:17). This most touching and wonderful prayer reaches down the ages, even to our day. It's for us. "I do not pray for these alone, but also for those who will believe in Me through their word" (John 17:20).

We are all as different as snowflakes. We have different backgrounds, different personality types, different ways of looking at things, yet, in Christ, we can be one in purpose. We can love one another. The disciples were a very diverse group, yet in Christ and by His Spirit they formed a team that changed the world. It is important to note that not until they submitted to the infilling of the Spirit of Christ did they become effective in their witnessing.

Church members today are of many different temperaments and dispositions. We have come together from different denominations and religious backgrounds. God's great cleaver of truth has cut us out of the world and placed us together in His church. It is by His power we learn to work together and become one in faith, doctrine, and spirit.

Apparently, one of the reasons why there are different spiritual gifts and different personality types in the church is that there are different minds to be reached in the great harvest field. Some will reject the message when it is presented by one worker, only to open their hearts to the same message when presented in a different manner by another worker. Our different talents should all be under the control of the same Spirit. The world will then know that we are Christ's disciples. We can all be kind, courteous, and tenderhearted in God's power. We must all pray earnestly that all our inherited and cultivated prejudices will be taken away, so that the world will recognize our love for one another and give God the glory.

We know that there is a great work before us. As Jesus told the repentant Peter, when we are converted we will strengthen the brethren. With God's promised blessing, mighty things will happen. The closer we come to Christ as individuals, the closer we will come to each other, and the more focused will be our ministry. The secret of true unity in the church and in the family is not diplomacy, not management, not a superhuman effort to overcome difficulties—though there will be much of this to do—but union with Christ.

As the end-time battle intensifies, our friends in the church should be the closest people to us on the earth. The bond between Christians is to be cemented by the Spirit of God. Some have left, or been abandoned by, family members as a result of their Christian commitment. As Jesus said, they become our brothers and sisters. Such people will love to gather together for Christian fellowship and, in fact, are encouraged to do so. "Not forsaking the assembling of ourselves together, as is the manner of some, but exhorting one another, and so much the more as you see the Day approaching" (Hebrews 10:25).

Each of us should show our interest in the prosperity of the church by identifying ourselves with it and working with our fellow believers for the completion of the Great Commission. Precisely because unity is such a positive blessing to the church and a witness to the world, Satan works to bring about division.

Unity is very important. But the unity that Christ spoke of was unity of faith and doctrine based on the platform of truth. True unity can never be at the expense of truth. Truth is more important than unity. It is the work of God's Spirit to bring unity, and to guide us into all truth. Accordingly, we can't have Spirit-inspired unity apart from truth.

There are many calls today for Christians to join some great ecumenical church or to drop "denominational barriers" and become one happy Christian family. On the surface this sounds great, but let us remember that God has called the last-day church to uphold unity on the platform of truth. The last message to the world and to those in apostate religions is to "come out of her, My people" (Revelation 18:4). Jesus prayed that His followers might be one; but we are not to sacrifice truth in order to secure this union, for we are to be sanctified through the truth.

Truth or Tradition

There are good traditions and there are bad traditions; just as there are good and bad habits. The standard of Bible truth outlines which teachings are right and which are in error. Both Old and New Testaments tell us this. "To the law and to the testimony! If they do not speak according to this word, it is because there is no light in them" (Isaiah 8:20). "All Scripture is given by inspiration of God, and is profitable for doctrine, for reproof, for correction, for instruction in righteousness" (2 Timothy 3:16).

All true Christians are eager to be guided by God's Spirit. But since there are also evil spirits, we are counseled, "Do not believe every spirit, but test the spirits, whether they are of God; because many false prophets have gone out into the world" (1 John 4:1). We should test teachings and spirits by God's Word. Yes, Scripture pulls rank on everything! That is always our standard of last resort. Jesus called those who put tradition above Scripture hypocrites! "Well did Isaiah prophesy of you hypocrites, as it is written: 'This people honors Me with their lips, but their heart is far from Me. And in vain do they worship Me, teaching as doctrines the commandments of men.' For laying aside the commandment of God, you hold the tradition of men" (Mark 7:6-8). As we prepare to meet our Saviour, live our lives, and share with others, we must be certain that our religious experience has no traditions that are contrary to Scripture.

Many years ago someone with much experience shared with me his observation that all individuals become involved with a particular church for one of three reasons. And over the years I have noted the truth of his observation. Here are the reasons:

1. Most people are members of a particular church because

they were raised in that church. Their family has been members for years. They were born in that church. They were dedicated or baptized in that church. Perhaps they were married in that church. Almost all of their close friends are in that church.

2. The second, and quite common, reason is that people are members of a particular church out of convenience. For example, let's say a Baptist and a Methodist get married. They are not going to be members of both churches or alternate between them on Sundays. Most of the time one will join the other's church out of convenience, and that is the end of the story. Another example of this convenience idea might be if a person who is a member of a Congregational church in New England moves to Alabama. He can't find a Congregational church near his home, so he joins a nearby Presbyterian church.

3. The third, and last, reason for church membership is quite different from the first two. It involves personal belief. A person decides to study the Bible in an effort to determine what it says and means. This may be a private, personal study, with a group, or in a seminar or evangelistic meeting. Discovering a basic knowledge of God and His will, the person then seeks fellowship with those who are following what he believes the Scriptures teach. This reason for church membership involves theology—what a person understands about God and His will. In my personal judgment this is the only justifiable reason for being a church member. Membership that is based on an understanding of truth, rather than heritage or convenience, is the only biblical reason.

Truth Matters

Between the laws of men and the law of God will come the last great conflict of the controversy between truth and error. We are now entering onto this battlefield. This battle is not between rival churches contending for the supremacy, but between the religion of the Bible and the religion of fable and tradition. The agencies which have united against truth are now actively at work. God's Holy Word, which has been handed down to us at so great a cost of suffering and bloodshed, is little valued by most. There are very few who really accept it as the rule of life. Infidelity prevails to an alarming extent, not just in the world, but in the church as well. Many who call themselves Christians have come to deny doctrines that are the very pillars of the Christian faith. The great facts of Creation as presented by the inspired writers, the fall of man, the atonement, the perpetuity of God's law—these are practically rejected by many who are professedly Christian.

But thank God millions of men, women, and young people today are sincerely asking, "What is truth?" And to them Jesus says, "I am the way, the truth, and the life: no one comes to the Father, except through Me" (John 14:6). And again in His prayer to His Father, Jesus said, "And this is eternal life, that they may know You, the only true God, and Jesus Christ whom You have sent" (John 17:3).

In his first Epistle, John used very pointed language to emphasize the value of truth. "He who says, 'I know Him,' and does not keep His commandments, is a liar, and the truth is not in him" (1 John 2:4). In the mind of God, obedience to the commandments and the way of truth are one and the same. It should be for us as well.

The Breastplate of Righteousness

Many commentators suggest that the breastplate of righteousness is equivalent to the robe of righteousness, spoken of so frequently in the Bible. One verse makes a direct comparison: "He put on righteousness as a breastplate" (Isaiah 59:17). Just as the part of a soldier's armor, the breastplate covers the heart, so righteousness preserves the life of the believer, and protects the "vital organs" of our spiritual life.

When you see a man dressed in tough pants, leather boots, leather gloves, and a hard hat, you would likely think him a construction worker. If you see a person dressed with a helmet, shoulder pads, a jersey with numbers, tight pants with a stripe down the side, and spiked shoes, you are probably looking at a football player. If you see a family leaving their home on Sabbath morning all dressed up, with shoes shined and Bibles under their arms, you could well be seeing Seventh-day Adventists going to church. It is quite appropriate to dress for the occasion. In addition, our dress and mannerisms tell a story about who we are and where we are going.

What would you expect to see a person wearing on their way to heaven to live with Jesus and the angels? Would any of the outfits I have described above be appropriate? If really serious about going to live with Jesus, they will be wearing the robe of Christ's righteousness—the wedding garment. Though you might not to be able to see the actual weave of the white robe, you could tell it was being worn. By their mannerisms—you could tell.

The Robe of Righteousness

There are numerous references in the Bible to the robe that must be worn by those who are saved and taken to the eternal kingdom. This robe of righteousness is the same as the wedding garment in the New Testament. One quickly sees that the clothing we have devised is not what God had in mind. Adam and Eve tried to form garments of fig leaves to take the place of the covering of light God had given at Creation. But God has something much better in mind. It is an expensive, spotless robe, woven in the loom of heaven. It is provided to the repenting, believing sinner as a vital part of his armor.

Isaiah described his delight in having received such a garment. "I will greatly rejoice in the Lord. My soul shall be joyful in my God. For He has clothed me with the garments of salvation, He has covered me with the robe of righteousness, as a bridegroom decks himself with ornaments, and as a bride adorns herself with her jewels" (Isaiah 61:10). When the lost (prodigal) son came to himself and returned home, his father said to his servants, "Bring out the best robe and put it on him" (Luke 15:22).

Ellen White makes the application this way: "He [Jesus] bids you exchange your poverty for the riches of His grace. We are not worthy of God's love, but Christ, our surety, is worthy, and is abundantly able to save all who shall come unto Him. Whatever may have been your past experience, however discouraging your present circumstances, if you will come to Jesus just as you are, weak, helpless, and despairing, our compassionate Saviour will meet you a great way off, and will throw about you His arms of love and His robe of righteousness. He presents us to the Father clothed in the white raiment of His own character" (*Thoughts From the Mount of Blessing,* pp. 8, 9). As a financial counselor and teacher I find this a very intriguing statement. Christ is my "surety." He "co-signs" for me. I counsel folks never to do this for anyone else, because so often the cosigner ends up paying the debt. And Christ does so in this case as well! I am not credit worthy. But He becomes my surety. I am worthy of death for my sins. He died for me! He has already paid my debt!

Paul described conditions in the last days exactly as we see them now.

Think about the current state of society when you read his words. "But know this, that in the last days perilous times will come: for men will be lovers of themselves, lovers of money, boasters, proud, blasphemers, disobedient to parents, unthankful, unholy, unloving, unforgiving, slanderers, without self-control, brutal, despisers of good, traitors, headstrong, haughty, lovers of pleasure rather than lovers of God, <u>having a form of godliness, but denying its power.</u> And from such people turn away" (2 Timothy 3:1-5)!

A form of godliness with no power. Another name for it would be nominal Christianity. Profession without practice. But what is the power that is lacking? Is this description given because the volume is too low on the music? Hardly. The power is the grace of God that provides not only pardon, but transformation. It is the miracle-working power of God. It is also a power for witnessing that will eventually lighten the whole earth. The powerless Christians Paul identifies are those who have not really experienced conversion. They don't enjoy Bible study, are not in love with their Saviour, and they have not accepted heaven as their real home.

Only the Creator can accomplish the creative work of transforming our lives. He is willing and able to do this. "Now may the God of peace Himself sanctify you completely; and may your whole spirit, soul, and body be preserved blameless at the coming of our Lord Jesus Christ. <u>He who calls you is faithful, **who also will do it**</u>" (1 Thessalonians 5:23, 24). Our sanctification is the work of God. However, He does not sanctify us without our participation. We must place ourselves in the channel of the Spirit's working, which we can do by beholding Christ. As we meditate on Christ's life, study His Word, and share what God has done for us with others, the Holy Spirit restores the physical, mental, and spiritual faculties. "According to His mercy He saved us, through the washing of regeneration and renewing of the Holy Spirit" (Titus 3:5).

In the first chapter of his second letter, Peter explains how we can partake of the divine nature. "Grace and peace be multiplied to you in the knowledge of God and of Jesus our Lord, <u>as His divine power has given to us all things that pertain to life and godliness, through the knowledge of Him who called us by glory and virtue,</u> by which have been given to us **exceedingly great and precious promises,** <u>that through these **you may be partakers of the divine nature,**</u> having escaped the corruption that is in the world through lust" (2 Peter 2:2-4).

Then after giving God the credit for "all things that pertain to life and godliness," Peter outlines the part that man is to play in the sanctification process. "Giving all diligence, add to your faith virtue, to virtue knowledge, to knowledge self-control, to self-control perseverance, to perseverance godliness, to godliness brotherly kindness, and to brotherly kindness love." Peter starts his ladder to sanctification by saying, "Giving all diligence." Then he goes on to say, "Therefore brethren, be even more diligent to make your calling and election sure, for if you do these things you will never stumble; for so an entrance will be supplied to you abundantly into the everlasting kingdom of our Lord and Saviour Jesus Christ" (2 Peter 1:5-11).

There is no point in being "born again" if we are just going to go on living as we did before we accepted Christ. In the true new-birth process, brought about by the Holy Spirit, a real transformation takes place. If we cooperate with Him, God will change our fallen natures into His image by transforming our wills, minds, desires, and characters.

"We must comply with the terms of salvation, or we are lost. At the hour when we leave the service of Satan for the service of Christ, when true conversion takes place, and by faith we turn from transgression to obedience, the severest of the heart struggles take place. But many accept the theory of truth, and compromise with the world, the flesh, and the devil. The soul that has truly experienced the transforming grace of Christ has chosen Christ for its portion; it yields to the gracious influence of His Holy Spirit, and thus the character is formed according to the divine pattern. We are to feel, to act, as one with Christ" (*Review and Herald,* January 31, 1893).

The Holy Spirit brings a decided change to believers. Instead of the "works of the flesh"—things such as adultery, hatred, contentions, temper tantrums, selfishness, and intemperance (see Galatians 5:19-21)—the fruit of the Spirit starts to grow in the life of the believer. The fruit is manifested in its various forms: love, joy, peace, longsuffering, kindness, goodness, faithfulness, gentleness, and self-control (Galatians 5:22, 23).

As we contemplate the soon return of Christ, we might ask the same rhetorical question as Jesus did: "Will He find faith on the earth?" (Luke 18:8). Many "have nominally accepted the truth, but they do not practice it" (*Testimonies for the Church,* vol. 6, p. 296). How can we really feel that we are ready to meet our Saviour when half of us don't even bother to attend church and an even larger number rob Him with impunity by withholding tithes and offerings? We are a privileged generation. We stand on the shoulders of the apostles, the Reformers, our pioneers, Ellen White, and see much more than they saw. We not only have all the light that God gave them; we have also the ability to see the amazing fulfillment of world conditions that tell us the end is near.

Nature provides a good illustration of man's part in salvation through the biblical imagery of the early and latter rains in bringing crops to harvest. "God has given man land to be cultivated. But in order that the harvest may be reaped, there must be harmonious action between divine and human agencies. The plow and other implements of labor must be used at the right time. The seed must be sown in its season. Man is not to fail of doing his part. If he is careless and negligent, his unfaithfulness testifies against him. The harvest is proportionate to the energy he has expended.

"So it is in spiritual things. We are to be laborers together with God. Man is to work out his own salvation with fear and trembling, for it is God that worketh in him, both to will and to do of his good pleasure. There is to be co-partnership, a divine relation, between the Son of God and the repentant sinner. We are made sons and daughters of God. 'As many as received him, to them gave he power to become the sons of God.' Christ provides the mercy and grace so abundantly given to all who believe in Him. He fulfills the terms upon which salvation rests. But we must act our part by accepting the blessing in faith. God works and man works. **Resistance of temptation must come from man, who must draw his power from God.** Thus he becomes a co-partner with Christ" (*Review and Herald,* May 28, 1908).

When one has come to Christ he no longer tries to "just get by." He actually enjoys being obedient! "I delight to do Your will, O my God, and Your law is within my heart" (Psalm 40:8). No more does he question, "What is wrong with this or that?" Or rationalize "Just a little won't hurt, will it? God is love; He is not picky." "When, as erring, sinful beings, we come to Christ and become partakers of His pardoning grace, love springs up in the heart. Every burden is light, for the yoke that Christ imposes is easy. Duty becomes a delight, and sacrifice a pleasure. The path that before seemed shrouded in darkness, becomes bright with beams from the Sun of Righteousness" (*Steps to Christ,* p. 59).

Can I know that I have passed from death to life? The answer is "Yes." I can tell *if* my life has been changed. "There is no evidence of genuine repentance unless it works reformation. If he restore the pledge, give again that he had robbed, confess his sins, and love God and his fellow men, the sinner **may be sure** that he has passed from death unto life" *(ibid.).*

We can be ready! Jesus provides both the terms of salvation and the power to meet them. Note this next tremendous promise—every sentence is power-packed: "All who have put on the robe of Christ's righteousness will stand before Him as chosen and faithful and true. Satan has no power to pluck them out of the hand of the Saviour. Not one soul who in penitence and faith has claimed His protection will Christ permit to pass under the enemy's power. His word is pledged: "Let him take hold of my strength, that he may make peace with me; and he shall make peace with me" (Isa. 27:5). The promise given to Joshua is given to all: "If thou wilt keep my charge, . . . I will give thee places to walk among these that stand by" (Zech. 3:7). Angels of God will walk on either side of them, even in this world, and they will stand at last among the angels that surround the throne of God" (*God's Amazing Grace,* p. 316).

The Preparation of the Gospel of Peace

When our feet are shod with the preparation of the gospel of peace we can stand firm in the midst of the battle. The stresses of this life, even when we are not in the heat of the battle, can be almost overbearing. In fact, without the wonderful promises of God's Word, men's hearts fail them for fear. But we have the promise, "You will keep him in perfect peace, whose mind is stayed on You, because he trusts in You" (Isaiah 26:3).

This piece of armor gives us good footing spiritually because we have confidence and assurance in what God has done for us and what He has provided for us. Instead of worrying about the necessities of life we heed the counsel of Jesus to "seek first the kingdom of God and His righteousness, and all these things shall be added to you" (Matthew 6:33).

There is nothing quite like doubt to bring on discouragement. On the other hand, the assurance that God offers brings the peace that passes understanding. We can know of the provisions made by our Commander in Chief and be sure that we are on the winning side and that we will be victorious in the end.

Taking the Shield of Faith

To those living in Bible times the shield was the primary defensive piece of armor. In the Christian warfare it is called the shield of faith. "This is the victory that overcometh the world, even our faith" (1 John 5:4, KJV).

Our faith is active, like the shield that is raised to catch the fiery darts; it is also passive in that it trusts in God for deliverance. When temptations come, it is faith that trusts in the power of God for victory and enables a person to carry on the battle. This piece of armor is so important that the Bible says, "But without faith it is impossible to please Him, for he who comes to God must believe that He is, and that He is a rewarder of those who diligently seek Him" (Hebrews 11:6).

The shield of faith stops the arrows of temptation before they reach the vulnerable parts of the spiritual body. It was faith that enabled the heroes of God to excel for Him (Hebrews 11). "We are altogether too faithless, and too narrow in our views. Gideon's army prevailed, not because of their numbers, but because in living faith they followed the special directions of God" (*Gospel Workers* (1892), p. 297). And so, we too, can join the list of God's faithful. "Putting our trust in God, we are to move steadily forward, doing His work with unselfishness, in humble dependence upon Him, committing to His providence ourselves and all that concerns our present and future, holding the beginning of our confidence firm unto the end, remembering that we receive the blessings of heaven, not because of our worthiness, but because of Christ's worthiness and our acceptance, through faith in Him, of God's abounding grace" (*God's Amazing Grace,* p. 38).

The Helmet of Salvation

The head needs special protection during warfare because from it emanates the will and the intelligence. The helmet is designed to protect the head so that the body can function properly. It was because the giant Goliath did not have his helmet in its proper place that David was able to kill him. He was able to kill him with a single stone to the forehead.

Paul suggests in 1 Thessalonians 5:8 that the helmet is "the hope of salvation." Hope is a primary motivator of mankind. In some cases it may be the only thing that keeps individuals from total despair. And it is hope that helps to motivate us to faithfulness as we wait for the Second Coming. "For the grace of God that brings salvation has appeared to all men, teaching us that, denying ungodliness and worldly lusts, we should live soberly, righteously, and godly in the present age, looking for the blessed hope and glorious appearing of our great God and Savior Jesus Christ" (Titus 2:11-13).

The Sword of the Spirit

The sword is used both defensively and offensively. In the Ephesian passage, the sword is defined as the Word of God. The Bible becomes our offensive weapon in the battle with Satan and his evil spirits. It is our offensive weapon as we take the gospel to every person on earth. And it becomes our defensive weapon to protect us against the attacks of Satan. Since all eight of the pieces of armor are essential, we are encouraged to "put on the whole armor" of God. But so much counsel is given regarding this element of our armor that it almost seems the most important. For example, we are warned: "The people of God are directed to the Scriptures as their safeguard against the influence of false teachers and the delusive power of spirits of darkness. Satan employs every possible device to prevent men from obtaining a knowledge of the Bible; for its plain utterances reveal his deceptions. At every revival of God's work the prince of evil is aroused to more intense activity; he is now putting forth his utmost efforts for a final struggle against Christ and His followers. The last great delusion is soon to open before us. Antichrist is to perform his marvelous works in our sight. So closely will the counterfeit resemble the true that it will be impossible to distinguish between them except by the Holy Scriptures. By their testimony every statement and every miracle must be tested.

"Those who endeavor to obey all the commandments of God will be opposed and derided. They can stand only in God. In order to endure the trial before them, they must understand the will of God as revealed in His word; they can honor Him only as they have a right conception of His character, government, and purposes, and act in accordance with them. None but those who have fortified the mind with the truths of the Bible will stand through the last great conflict. To every soul will come the searching test: Shall I obey God rather than men? The decisive hour is even now at hand. Are our feet planted on the rock of God's immutable word? Are we prepared to stand firm in defense of the commandments of God and the faith of Jesus?" (*The Great Controversy*, p. 593).

A major purpose of the Bible is to aid our spiritual growth. Just spending time in the Bible allows our mind to grasp spiritual themes and to view the examples of the men and women of faith. "The creative energy that called the worlds into existence is in the word of God. This word imparts power; it begets life. Every command is a promise; accepted by the will, received into the soul, it brings with it the life of the Infinite One. It transforms the nature and recreates the soul in the image of God.

"The life thus imparted is in like manner sustained. "By every word that proceedeth out of the mouth of God" (Matthew 4:4) shall man live.

"The mind, the soul, is built up by that upon which it feeds; and it rests with us to determine upon what it shall be fed. It is within the power of everyone to choose the topics that shall occupy the thoughts and shape the character. Of every human being privileged with access to the Scriptures, God says, "I have written to him the great things of My law." "Call unto Me, and I will answer thee, and show thee great and mighty things, which thou knowest not." Hosea 8:12; Jeremiah 33:3.

"With the word of God in his hands, every human being, wherever his lot in life may be cast, may have such companionship as he shall choose. In its pages he may hold converse with the noblest and best of the human race, and may listen to the voice of the Eternal as He speaks with men. As he studies and meditates upon the themes into which "the angels desire to look" (1 Peter 1:12), he may have their companionship. He may follow the steps of the heavenly Teacher, and listen to His words as when He taught on mountain and plain and sea. He may dwell in this world in the atmosphere of heaven, imparting to earth's sorrowing and tempted ones thoughts of hope and longings for holiness; himself coming closer and still closer into fellowship with the Unseen; like him of old who walked with God, drawing nearer and nearer the threshold of the eternal world, until the portals shall open, and he shall enter there. He will find himself no stranger. The voices that will greet him are the voices of the holy ones, who, unseen, were on earth his companions—voices that here he learned to distinguish and to love. He who through the word of God has lived in fellowship with heaven, will find himself at home in heaven's companionship" (*Education,* pp. 126, 127).

Those who spend time in the Word of God will recognize the voice of God. They will become acquainted with those heroes of faith from the past who will be their companions in heaven! If we really want to know what truth is as we investigate God's Word, we must read with our minds open and receptive. "Our salvation depends on a knowledge of the truth contained in the Scriptures. It is God's will that we should possess this. Search, O search the precious Bible with hungry hearts. Explore God's word as the miner explores the earth to find veins of gold. Never give up the search until you have ascertained your relation to God and His will in regard to you. . . . You must lay your preconceived opinions, your hereditary and cultivated ideas, at the door of investigation. If you search the Scriptures to vindicate your own opinions, you will never reach the truth. Search in order to learn what the Lord says. If conviction comes as you search, if you see that your cherished opinions are not in harmony with the truth, do not misinterpret the truth in order to suit your own belief, but accept the light given. <u>Open mind and heart that you may behold wondrous things out of God's word"</u> (*Christ's Object Lessons,* pp. 111, 112).

Praying Always in the Spirit

Prayer is the seventh item in the armor of God. It is indispensable; as are the other items. As you read the great stories of the Bible, it is clear that those who prevailed in the battle with Satan were all men and women of prayer. Abraham, Isaac, Jacob, Daniel, Moses, Joshua, Gideon, Jesus, Peter, Paul, and a host of others were all people of prayer. God encourages us to pray—to call upon Him. All of the great revivals mentioned in the Bible and recorded in the history of the Christian church have been accompanied by much prayer.

We are told that the angels are mystified that we pray so little. "What can the angels of heaven think of poor helpless human beings, who are subject to temptation, when God's heart of infinite love yearns toward them, ready to give them more than they can ask or think, and yet they pray so little and have so little faith? The angels love to bow before God; they love to be near Him. <u>They regard communion with God as their highest joy; and yet the children of earth, who need so much the help that God only can give, seem satisfied to walk without the light of His Spirit, the companionship of His presence"</u> (*Steps to Christ,* p. 94).

An attitude of prayer maintains our connection with the Omnipotent One. Likely this is the reason that Paul counseled us to "pray without ceasing" (1 Thessalonians 5:17). Our contact with God through prayer is the vital relationship that gives us power over Satan's constant temptations. <u>"The darkness of the evil one encloses those who neglect to pray. The whispered temptations of the enemy entice them to sin; and it is all because they do not make use of the privileges that God has given them in the divine appointment of prayer.</u> Why should the sons and daughters of God be reluctant to pray, when prayer is the key in the hand of faith to unlock heaven's storehouse, where are treasured the boundless resources of Omnipotence?" *(ibid.).*

There are certain conditions upon which we may expect that God will hear and answer our prayers. They are:

1. We must feel our need of help from God.
2. We must put away sin from our lives.

3. We must have faith that God can do what He says He can do.

4. We must have a spirit of love and forgiveness in our own hearts.

5. We must be persevering in our petitions.

6. We must have distinct views of Jesus and eternal realities.

7. We must pray in the name of Jesus.

8. We must come in an attitude of praise and gratitude.

(See *Steps to Christ,* pp. 95-104.)

Being Watchful . . . With All Perseverance

Being watchful connotes being awake and observant. In the Gospels Jesus encourages His followers to watch for two primary reasons. Watch, He says, so that you will be ready for the Second Coming; and watch, lest you enter into temptation. "But take heed to yourselves, lest your hearts be weighed down with carousing, drunkenness, and cares of this life, and that Day come on you unexpectedly. For it will come as a snare on all those who dwell on the face of the whole earth. Watch therefore, and pray always that you may be counted worthy to escape all these things that will come to pass, and to stand before the Son of Man" (Luke 21:34-36).

We are told that we should watch for "signs" of the Second Coming, so that we will know when it is near. In the Bible "signs" and "wonders" are frequently linked as supernatural events that indicate that God is at work.

We have been given a word picture of the final battle. "In vision I saw two armies in terrible conflict. One army was led by banners bearing the world's insignia; the other was led by the bloodstained banner of Prince Immanuel. Standard after standard was left to trail in the dust as company after company from the Lord's army joined the foe and tribe after tribe from the ranks of the enemy united with the commandment-keeping people of God. An angel flying in the midst of heaven put the standard of Immanuel into many hands, while a mighty general cried out with a loud voice: 'Come into line. Let those who are loyal to the commandments of God and the testimony of Christ now take their position. Come out from among them, and be ye separate, and touch not the unclean, and I will receive you, and will be a Father unto you, and ye shall be My sons and daughters. Let all who will come up to the help of the Lord, to the help of the Lord against the mighty.'

"The battle raged. Victory alternated from side to side. Now the soldiers of the cross gave way, 'as when a standardbearer fainteth.' Isaiah 10:18. But their apparent retreat was but to gain a more advantageous position. Shouts of joy were heard. A song of praise to God went up, and angel voices united in the song, as Christ's soldiers planted His banner on the walls of fortresses till then held by the enemy. The Captain of our salvation was ordering the battle and sending support to His soldiers. His power was mightily displayed, encouraging them to press the battle to the gates. He taught them terrible things in righteousness as He led them on step by step, conquering and to conquer.

"At last the victory was gained. The army following the banner with the inscription, 'The commandments of God, and the faith of Jesus,' was gloriously triumphant. The soldiers of Christ were close beside the gates of the city, and with joy the city received her King. The kingdom of peace and joy and everlasting righteousness was established" (*Testimonies for the Church,* vol. 8, p. 41).

The armor of God is available to each of us. We can be successful in the struggles and battles of life only if we use the armor. May God help us to awaken to the seriousness of this important offer.

CHAPTER 17

Laodicean, Militant, and Victorious

T he church of God has at least three distinct phases in the final stage of earth's history. The church of our day is described in the book of Revelation as Laodicean—lukewarm (see Revelation 3:14-22). Jesus even describes the people in the church as being asleep—not aware of the impending crisis (Matthew 25:5). But then something happens. There is a great change—a metamorphosis, if you like. This same end-time church becomes awake, alert, and a virtual fighting machine. It becomes the church militant—a working church (see Revelation 14:6-12; 18:1-4). And, thank God, the final phase is the church victorious (see Revelation 19:6-8; 21:1-4). These three phases are real and observable—and the transformation is as real as a caterpillar becoming a butterfly.

The Laodicean Phase

Of course not every member of God's church during this phase is lukewarm, asleep, and indifferent. Many have opened their heart's door in answer to the knock of Jesus. They have welcomed Him into their hearts to accomplish His awesome work of transformation. In anything but a mixed metaphor they are being "refined in the fire," have "covered themselves with the robe of Christ's righteousness," and had their "eyes opened by the anointing of eye salve." Praise God for their willing response. Of course God is pleased with such a preparation.

But when we look at the church in general, if we are honest with ourselves, we can see that God's description of Laodicean is quite accurate. We see lukewarmness, sleepiness, misused wealth, spiritual blindness, and "nakedness." Moses, in his last sermon to Israel, encouraged God's people to faithfulness and obedience, and then listed the many blessings that would follow faithfulness. He also listed the curses that would come as a result of their disobedience. He began by saying, "Now it shall come to pass, if you <u>diligently obey</u> the voice of the Lord your God, to <u>observe carefully</u> all his commandments which I command you today, that the Lord your God will set you high above all nations of the earth. And all these blessings shall come upon you and overtake you, <u>because you obey</u> the voice of the Lord your God" (Deuteronomy 28:1, 2).

The Laodicean church has a tremendous heritage. For centuries the Christian church mixed Scripture and tradition. But in God's providence Scripture was restored to its rightful place, and the Bible became available to the people. The Protestant Reformation began the long road back from apostasy to biblical fidelity. Studying the Bible for the first time, many longed to learn true biblical faith. Others, unfortunately, stuck with tradition, too apathetic to change.

In the fourteenth century John Wycliffe called for a reformation in the church—not just in his England, but for the entire Christian world. At a time when the Bible was not readily available to the common person, Wycliffe translated the entire Bible into English for the first time. Called the morning star of the Reformation, he taught of salvation through faith in Christ alone and upheld the Scriptures as the sole source of Christian faith and practice. His teachings had a major influence on other Reformers such as Huss, Jerome, and Luther.

God used Martin Luther to further this change in Germany. As a young priest, Luther was disturbed by the sale of indulgences by the church. This practice, which is still in use in the Roman Catholic Church today, provides for the payment of money to the church in exchange for forgiveness of personal sins as well as the sins of those supposedly suffering in the flames of purgatory. To Luther, this was bad theology. He wrote out 95 reasons why he felt this practice was unbiblical, and nailed them to the church door in Wittenberg—a common practice for posting notices in those days. This put Luther in direct confrontation with papal authority and became the spark that ignited the Reformation. In spite of the almost overwhelming power of the Papacy to intimidate those who questioned her teachings, Luther stood firm to his two great convictions— that salvation was by faith in Christ alone and that the Scriptures are the only standard for Christian faith and practice.

The Struggle to Change

Even when people realize that change or reformation is necessary, it is not easy. The devil sees to that! Of course, the church didn't get into an apostate condition overnight. It was a gradual fall over centuries. It couldn't be changed overnight, either. In fact, the changes were surely almost imperceptible to any individual at any point in time. It is somewhat like the growing-up process of a child. The child may not notice much change. But when he or she makes a visit to Grandma's after a year lapse, Grandma exclaims, "Oh, how much you have grown!" Similarly, a person might not have noticed much, if any, change in the church because the change was usually gradual. But over time the church had gone so far from the path to the kingdom that many didn't even remember what the path looked like.

During the early period of the Reformation many of the unbiblical teachings of the church that had crept in over time were repudiated and abandoned. The list is long and included prayers for the dead, veneration of saints and relics, cerebration of Mass, worship of Mary, purgatory, penance, holy water, celibacy of the priesthood, the rosary, the Inquisition, transubstantiation, extreme unction, and dependence upon tradition. In fact, the Protestant Reformers were nearly unanimous in identifying the papal system as the "man of sin," the "mystery of iniquity," and the "little horn" of Daniel 7. They saw it as the entity that was to persecute God's true people during the 1260 years of Revelation 12:6, 14 and 13:5, and before the second coming of Jesus.

Reformation Stops Short

The full reformation of the Christian church was not accomplished in the sixteenth century. The Reformers made much progress, but they did not rediscover all the light lost during the apostasy. They took Christianity out of deep darkness, but it still stood in the shadows. They broke the vicelike grip of the medieval church, gave the Bible to the people in their own languages, and restored the basic gospel. But many other Bible truths, such as baptism by immersion, immortality as a gift given by Christ at the time of the resurrection of the righteous, and the seventh day as the Bible Sabbath, were waiting to be discovered.

The successors of the early Reformers failed to advance in Bible knowledge much beyond their predecessors. In fact, many so-called Reformers did not study further to seek more forgotten truths. So were established the many different denominations in the Protestant world. Those who followed each Reformer camped around these great individuals, but would not accept any further light than their leader had discovered. God's plan was surely for each generation to build on the truths already uncovered until the entire truth of God's Word would be restored. But, unfortunately, as current events indicate, many of the followers of the Reformers did not advance in biblical understanding, have even "fallen away" from the positions of the Reformers, and are now on their way back to Rome.

Time for the Remnant

God describes the church that would flee from the apostate church after the time of the end in 1798 as the "remnant." "And the dragon was wroth with the woman, and went to make war with the remnant of her seed, which keep the commandments of God, and have the testimony of Jesus Christ" (Revelation 12:17, KJV). This verse contains a description of the last remnant of God's chosen line of loyal believers—His loyal witnesses in the last days just before Christ's second coming.

Another description of the last-day church is given by John in Revelation 14:12: "Here is the patience of the saints; here are those who keep the commandments of God and the faith of Jesus." The remnant at the time of the end cannot be easily mistaken. The Bible describes them in specific terms. They "keep the commandments of God" and "have the testimony of Jesus Christ." They have the responsibility of proclaiming, just before Jesus returns, God's final message of warning to the world (Revelation 14:6-12).

One characteristic of the remnant is having "the faith of Jesus." God's remnant people are characterized by a faith similar to that which Jesus had. They reflect Jesus' unshakable confidence in God and the authority of Scripture. They believe that Jesus Christ is the Messiah of prophecy, the Son of God, the Saviour of the world. Their faith encompasses all the truths of the Bible—those that Jesus and the apostles believed and taught.

Accordingly, God's remnant people will proclaim the everlasting gospel of salvation by faith in Christ. They will warn the world that the hour of God's judgment has arrived. Like Elijah and John the Baptist, the remnant will "prepare the way of the Lord." They will proclaim the soon-coming Lord. They will be involved in a great worldwide mission to complete the divine witness to humanity (Revelation 14:6, 7; 10:11; Matthew 24:14).

The second characteristic of the remnant is that they "keep the commandments of God." In any generation those who return to the Lord will keep His commandments. Genuine faith in Jesus commits the remnant to follow His example. "He who says he abides in Him," John said, "ought himself also to walk just as He walked" (1 John 2:6). Jesus kept His Father's commandments, and the remnant, too, will obey God's commandments (John 15:10).

Inasmuch as they are the remnant, God's last-day church will practice what the early church preached. And their actions will harmonize with their profession. Jesus said, "Not everyone who says to Me, 'Lord, Lord,' shall enter the kingdom of heaven, but he who does the will of My Father in heaven" (Matthew 7:21). Through the strength of the indwelling Spirit they obey God's requirements—all 10 of the commandments that describe God's unchanging moral law (Exodus 20:1-17). Obviously this includes the restoration of the fourth commandment—the seventh-day Sabbath.

A third characteristic of God's end-time remnant is that they possess "the testimony of Jesus." John defines "the testimony of Jesus" as "the spirit [or gift] of prophecy" (Revelation 19:10). The remnant will be guided by the testimony of Jesus conveyed through the gift of prophecy. This gift of the Spirit was to function throughout the history of the church, until "all come to the unity of the faith and the knowledge of the Son of God, to a perfect man, to the measure of the stature of the fullness of Christ" (Ephesians 4:13).

The Bible says that when Jesus returned to heaven after His first advent He "gave gifts to men" (Ephesians 4:8). In five places the New Testament names some of these divine gifts to the Christian church (Romans 12:6-8; 1 Corinthians 12:4-11; 1 Corinthians 13:1-3; 1 Corinthians 14; and Ephesians 4:11-16). It is significant that only the gift of prophecy occurs in all five places. Our Lord Jesus knows the need for continuing contact with His people as they face the perils of the end time. Our God, who has communicated with His people down through time, could not abandon us at the very end, right before the most climactic event since the Creation. We know that "the Lord does nothing, unless He reveals His secret to His servants the prophets" (Amos 3:7).

Such prophetic guidance makes the remnant a people who proclaim a prophetic message. They will not only understand prophecy and teach it; they will have the gift of prophecy in their midst. The revelation of truth that comes to the remnant helps them accomplish their mission of preparing the world for Christ's return.

That is God's biblical picture of His last-day church. His people stand on the platform of the Reformation and search deeper for a more biblical faith. The Sabbath has been recognized and restored. Man's condition in death has been understood. The prophetic end-time picture is much clearer.

They have recognized and more clearly understood the biblical principles of healthful living, and modesty in dress and adornment. It is God's plan for His people to be continually advancing, "growing in grace and in a knowledge of their Lord and Saviour, Jesus Christ."

But alas, just as the Israelites in the Old Testament, and the Christian church in the New Testament, had times of apostasy and backsliding, so God's remnant church, the one with "the truth" and the gift of prophecy is called by Him "lukewarm" and "miserable, poor, blind, and naked." Why can't we learn from the past? Has the church become lax in its faithfulness because of a deeper commitment to God, a study of His Word, and a prayerful desire to prepare for a place in His kingdom? Sadly, no. Many now live, eat, dress, and act like the world that we profess to be leaving. Guarding the edges of the Sabbath and walking the narrow way don't seem that important. Some are beginning to scoff at the idea of an imminent Second Coming. Some are playing music in church that suits their own tastes and entertains them and makes them feel good, with very little thought of actually "worshiping" the Creator of the universe. And, as one might expect with such changing attitudes, there is more attention to materialism and less commitment to mission and concern for the needs of others.

Early in the history of the Remnant Church we were called to give attention to the Laodicean message: "The perils of the last days are upon us. We have been asleep, and our lamps are going out. We now need a thorough consecration, a deeper devotion, to the work. The Lord has shown me the corruption existing even among Seventh-day Adventists. Satan, the originator of every evil, is Christ's personal enemy. If our eyes could be opened, we should see him working with his specious devices upon the minds of men whom we think are secure from his temptations, and who feel themselves secure. Are we prepared for the trials that await us? When the lying wonders of Satan shall be manifested, will not many souls be ensnared? Let us arouse and do our duty. We must individually draw near to God, repent of our sins, our lukewarmness, our selfishness, and give back into the Lord's treasury the goods He has lent us in trust. Faith in God and in the teachings of Christ our Saviour will be revealed, if it is in the heart.

"The Laodicean message is applicable to the people of God at this time. They are saying, 'I am rich, and increased with goods, and have need of nothing;' and they know not that they are 'wretched, and miserable, and poor, and blind, and naked.' Christ, the True Witness, declares, 'I know thy works, that thou art neither cold nor hot; I would thou wert cold or hot. So then because thou art lukewarm, and neither cold nor hot, I will spew thee out of my mouth.' How is it, brethren? Have you not been giving up to self-indulgence, rather than growing into greater self-denial? Have you not backslidden upon health reform? Has the light which God has been pleased to give His people been cherished? Have not life and health been sacrificed through the indulgence of appetite and carnal lusts? Will my brethren consider this matter carefully, and see if they have closely followed the self-denying Saviour?

"There has been a great departure from God in this matter. There has been a loss of zeal for the truth, and the light contained in the 'Testimonies' has been disregarded. May the Lord help you, my brethren, to come into a position where the animal powers will not predominate over the moral and the spiritual. May your eyes not be blinded by self-indulgence, so that you cannot discern between the sacred and the common. God forbid that the precious truth should be held in unrighteousness, and that you should dishonor God and the truth by a corrupt and unconsecrated life. Study your true position before God. At this time, when the prayers of faith should be going up to God, you are not ready to lift up holy hands, without wrath and doubting. Have you not a work to do, to seek the Lord with humiliation of soul, with fasting and prayer? Is it not time, high time, for you to awake out of sleep, and shake off this carnal security? 'Seek ye the Lord while he may be found, call ye upon him while he is near.' This privilege will not always be granted us, therefore we should make diligent use of our present opportunities. 'Let the wicked forsake his way, and the unrighteous man his thoughts; and let him return unto the Lord, and he will have mercy upon him, and to our God, for he will abundantly pardon." Then make no delay. The gracious promise is yours today. Set your heart and house in order. God sees the defects in your character, and He desires that you should see them, and feel your great need of the help which He alone can give" (*Review and Herald,* December 18, 1888).

The Church Militant

But the church changes near the end. The faithful wake up and, through the power of the Holy Spirit, begin in earnest the work of completing the gospel commission. There is a recommitment to the values and principles of the Bible, and a desire to become fit to live in the company of holy beings in heaven.

"The life of Christ was a life charged with a divine message of the love of God, and He longed intensely to impart this love to others in rich measure. Compassion beamed from His countenance, and His conduct was characterized by grace, humility, truth, and love. <u>Every member of His church militant must manifest the same qualities, if he would join the church triumphant.</u> The love of Christ is so broad, so full of glory, that in comparison to it, everything that men esteem as great, dwindles into insignificance" (*Christian Education,* p. 76).

As the Laodicean church gives way to the militant church there are both "good" and "bad" people in the church. Some are growing colder, and some are growing warmer. It is not a perfect church. "Let every one who is seeking to live a Christian life, <u>remember that the church militant is not the church triumphant.</u> Those who are carnally minded will be found in the church. They are to be pitied more than blamed. The church is not to be judged as sustaining these characters, though they be found within her borders. Should the church expel them, the very ones who found fault with their presence there, would blame the church for sending them adrift in the world; they would claim that they were treated unmercifully. It may be that in the church there are those who are cold, proud, haughty, and unchristian, but you need not associate with this class. There are many who are warm-hearted, who are self-denying, self-sacrificing, who would, were it required, lay down their lives to save souls. Jesus saw the bad and the good in church relationship, and said, 'Let both grow together until the harvest.' None are under the necessity of becoming tares because every plant in the field is not wheat. If the truth were known, these complainers make their accusations in order to quiet a convicted, condemning conscience. Their own course of action is not wholly commendable. Even those who are striving for the mastery over the enemy, have sometimes been wrong and done wrong. Evil prevails over good when we do not trust wholly in Christ, and abide in Him. Inconsistencies of character will then be manifested that would not be revealed if we preserved the faith that works by love and purifies the soul" (*Fundamentals of Christian Education,* pp. 294, 295).

Yes, Satan brings unconverted people into the church to cause problems. But this should not cause us to become discouraged or disheartened. It is part of the last great struggle in the battle of the spirits. Our part is to study diligently to know God's way. We must then focus our attention on His will and way. <u>"Has God no living church? He has a church, but it is the church militant, not the church triumphant.</u> We are sorry that there are defective members. . . . While the Lord brings into the church those who are truly converted, Satan at the same time brings persons who are not converted into its fellowship. While Christ is sowing the good seed, Satan is sowing the tares. There are two opposing influences continually exerted on the members of the church. One influence is working for the purification of the church, and the other for the corrupting of the people of God.

"Although there are evils existing in the church, and will be until the end of the world, the church in these last days is to be the light of the world that is polluted and demoralized by sin. . . . There is but one church in the world who are at the present time standing in the breach, and making up the hedge, building up the old waste places; and for any man to call the attention of the world and other churches to this church, denouncing her as Babylon, is to do a work in harmony with him who is the accuser of the brethren. . . . The whole world is filled with hatred of those who proclaim the binding claims of the law of God, and the church who are loyal to Jehovah must engage in no ordinary conflict. . . . Those who have any realization of what this warfare means, will not turn their weapons against the church militant, but with all their powers will wrestle with the people of God against the confederacy of evil" (*The Faith I Live By,* p. 305).

Some individuals focus on the presence of the "tares," and suggest that those who are serious about their faith should leave the church and associate only with those whom they perceive to be "on the straight and narrow." They fail to see the big picture of the great controversy. They fail to understand that under the "shaking," it is the "tares" who leave the remnant church, not the "wheat." To make it real plain—the bad guys are the ones that leave. "God has a church upon the earth who are His chosen people, who keep His commandments. He is leading, not stray offshoots, not one here and one there, but a people. The truth is a sanctifying power; but the church militant is not the church triumphant. There are tares among the wheat. 'Wilt thou then that we . . . gather them up?' was the question of the servant; but the master answered, 'Nay; lest while ye gather up the tares, ye root up also the wheat with them.' The gospel net draws not only good fish, but bad ones as well, and the Lord only knows who are His" (*Testimonies to Ministers,* p. 61).

One church member recently told me that his church had no problems. He said that in his church everyone loved everyone else and that no one was critical or judgmental. Further on in the conversation he revealed that his church was very tolerant of the views and lifestyles of others. But we can't come to the point where we become like the bad guys or tolerate them "just as they are." "The Lord desires us to realize that it is of great importance that we stand in these last days upon the platform of eternal truth. Those who think that the church militant is the church triumphant make a great mistake. The church militant will gain great triumphs, but it will also have fierce conflicts with evil that it may be firmly established upon the platform of eternal truth. And every one of us should be determined to stand with the church upon this platform" (*The Upward Look,* p. 152).

I do not want to spend any more time talking about the unconverted in the church. According to Jesus, they will be with us until the angels do the work of separation. We have some evidence that this will occur when the Sunday law agitation begins. For when there is a real threat of persecution the unconverted leave immediately. Then, in the power of God, the church will move rapidly to finish the work.

An Army With Banners

Just as some of the lukewarm are getting colder and falling away from their "first love" experience, another group is getting warmer, more involved, and preparing for the Second Coming. Many of these are young people—youth—who are making a tremendous contribution to the advancement of God's work. It was predicted that this would happen. "With such an army of workers as our youth, rightly trained, might furnish, how soon the message of a crucified, risen, and soon-coming Saviour might be carried to the whole world! How soon might the end come—the end of suffering and sorrow and sin! How soon, in place of a possession here, with its blight of sin and pain, our children might receive their inheritance where 'the righteous shall inherit the land, and dwell therein forever;' where 'the inhabitant shall not say, I am sick,' and 'the voice of weeping shall be no more heard.' Psalm 37:29; Isaiah 33:24; 65:19" (*Education,* p. 271).

This greatly increased level of youth involvement in ministry is definitely a positive sign of the end. There are literally thousands of youth today who are involved as student missionaries, taskforce workers, church builders, and evangelistic workers. The student literature sales ministry is being revived with hundreds selling magabooks as well as the standard books. Global Mission pioneers now number over 20,000! And the Thousand Missionary Movement, with training centers in the Philippines and the United States, is training youth workers in a short intensive course and sending them out by the hundreds for a year's work in various parts of the world. The converts won by this group are a major part of the progress of the work in the Southern Asia-Pacific Division.

Another oft-used quotation involves the laymen of the church. "The leaders in God's cause, as wise generals, are to lay plans for advance moves all along the line. In their planning they are to give special study to the work that can be done by the laity for their friends and neighbors. The work of God in this earth can never be finished until the men and women comprising our church membership rally to the work and unite their efforts with those of ministers and church officers.

"The salvation of sinners requires earnest, personal labor. We are to bear to them the word of life, not to wait for them to come to us. Oh, that I could speak words to men and women that would arouse them to diligent action! The moments now granted to us are few. We are standing upon the very borders of the eternal world. We have no time to lose. Every moment is golden and altogether too precious to be devoted merely to self-serving. Who will seek God earnestly and from Him draw strength and grace to be His faithful workers in the missionary field?" (*Testimonies for the Church,* vol. 9, pp. 116, 117).

This also is being fulfilled as thousands of laymen are becoming involved in the various divisions of the world field. In January and February 2001, Adventist Laymen's Services and Industries laymen took time off work to conduct evangelistic meetings in India and the Philippines. They worked for several weeks with local pastors and laity, and the Lord gave a rich harvest of nearly 20,000 souls baptized. Similar experiences of lay participation are seen throughout the world, most notably in Central and South America, Africa, and Asia.

It Is Written television ministry has dedicated a two-year period to conduct public meetings in ten major cities around the world. Thousands have already been baptized—numbers way beyond expectations. Three Angels Broadcasting Network, with a satellite footprint that covers virtually all the world, carries the last-day message 24 hours a day via television. And Adventist World Radio also has a broadcast footprint that now covers virtually all the world.

God's Side Is Winning!

While it is clear that much more work needs to be done and that which remains may even be the hardest part, by the grace of God we are making progress. When the Adventist Church was organized in 1863 with 3,000 members, there was a ratio of only 1 member for every 367,143 people in the world. By 2001 that ratio had changed to 1 member for every 521 people in the world. That is a ratio 704 times better than when we started! And baptisms have now reached an average of over 3,000 per day!

Another amazing phenomenon today is a seemingly spontaneous interest in the Bible Sabbath. Around the world those involved in evangelistic outreach encounter those who have already investigated the topic and are now keeping the Sabbath. There may have been a television or radio program that started the interest. Many have read some printed material that sparked their interest. And others are reading their Bibles and have independently come to the conclusion that the seventh-day Sabbath is a marker of true Christianity.

Those who criticize the remnant church and spend their full time taking potshots at it risk becoming blinded by Satan as to what is going on around the world in the work of evangelism. I am personally very encouraged and excited and wish to do more myself in the ongoing work of God. Let's praise God in the manner that He has encouraged us. "The greatest praise that men can bring to God is to become consecrated channels through whom He can work. Time is rapidly passing into eternity. Let us not keep back from God that which is His own. **Let us not refuse Him that which, though it cannot be given with merit, cannot be denied without ruin.** He asks for a whole heart; give it to Him; it is His, both by creation and by redemption. He asks for your intellect; give it to Him; it is His. He asks for your money; give it to Him; it is His. 'Ye are not your own, for ye are bought with a price.' 1 Corinthians 6:19, 20. God requires the homage of a sanctified soul, which has prepared itself, by the exercise of the faith that works by love, to serve Him. He holds up before us the highest ideal, even perfection. He asks us to be absolutely and completely for Him in this world as He is for us in the presence of God" (*The Acts of the Apostles,* p. 566).

As more and more people become involved, the last message of warning will swell to a loud cry that will enlighten the whole earth. Ellen White described that time with these words: "Servants of God, with their faces lighted up and shining with holy consecration, will hasten from place to place, to proclaim the message from heaven. By thousands of voices, all over the earth, the warning will be given. Miracles will be wrought, the sick will be healed, and signs and wonders will follow the believers. Satan also works with lying wonders, even bringing down fire from heaven in the sight of men. Thus the inhabitants of the earth will be brought to take their stand" (*Evangelism,* p. 700).

The Church Victorious

Someday it will all be over. The last sermon will be given. The last evangelistic meetings held. The last Bible study shared. The last character developed. Probation will close; and all will have made decisions for or against being a part of the kingdom of God. John saw, and even heard, a vast group which included these at the end time. He says, "And I heard, as it were, the voice of a great multitude, as the sound of many waters and as the sound of mighty thunderings, saying, 'Alleluia! For the Lord God Omnipotent reigns! Let us be glad and rejoice and give Him glory, for the marriage of the Lamb has come, and <u>His wife has made herself ready.'</u> <u>And to her it was granted to be arrayed in fine linen, clean and bright,</u> for the fine linen is the righteous acts of the saints" (Revelation 19:6-8).

In spite of what we see here now, by the eye of faith we can see a better world is coming soon. "Now the church is militant. Now we are confronted with a world in darkness, almost wholly given over to idolatry. <u>But the day is coming when the battle will have been fought, the victory won.</u> The will of God is to be done on earth as it is done in heaven. The nations of the saved will know no other law than the law of heaven. All will be a happy, united family, clothed with the garments of praise and thanksgiving,—the robe of Christ's righteousness. All nature, in its surpassing loveliness, will offer to God a tribute of praise and adoration. The world will be bathed in the light of heaven. The light of the moon will be as the light of the sun, and the light of the sun will be sevenfold greater than it is now. The years will move on in gladness. Over the scene the morning stars will sing together, and the sons of God will shout for joy, while God and Christ will unite in proclaiming, 'There shall be no more sin, neither shall there be any more death'" (*The Ministry of Healing,* p. 504).

All who are a part of the church victorious will themselves be individually victorious. So what is necessary for our individual victory?

1. **Develop and maintain faith in God.** "And this is the victory that has overcome the world—our faith" (1 John 5:4).

2. **Keep your eye on the prize.** "Forgetting those things which are behind and reaching forward to those things which are ahead, I press toward the goal for the prize of the upward call of God in Christ Jesus" (Philippians 3:13, 14). "The effort put forth to overcome,

though requiring self-denial, is of little account beside the victory over evil" (*Christian Education,* p. 122).

3. **Prayer and communion with God.** "And all things, whatsoever you ask in prayer, believing, you will receive" (Matthew 21:22). "True prayer takes hold upon Omnipotence and gives us the victory. Upon his knees the Christian obtains strength to resist temptation" (*God's Amazing Grace,* p. 86).

4. **God's grace and our effort.** "We are unable of ourselves to pursue a right course. It is only by the grace of God, combined with the most earnest effort on our part, that we can gain the victory" (*ibid.,* p. 327).

5. **Make a decision to be victorious.** "The victory can be gained; for nothing is impossible with God. By His assisting grace, all evil temper, all human depravity, may be overcome. . . . You may be overcomers if you will, in the name of Christ, take hold of the work decidedly" (*ibid.,* p. 39).

6. **Commit everything to God.** "The kingdom of heaven is like treasure hidden in a field, which a man found and hid; and for joy over it he goes and sells all that he has and buys that field" (Matthew 13:44). "Sacrifice all to God. Lay all upon His altar—self, property, and all, a living sacrifice. It will take all to enter glory" (*The Faith I Live By,* p. 359).

7. **Be willing to suffer.** "All who desire to live godly in Christ Jesus will suffer persecution" (2 Timothy 3:12). "Ye must be partakers of Christ's sufferings here if ye would be partakers with Him of His glory hereafter. Heaven will be cheap enough, if we obtain it through suffering" *(ibid.).*

8. **Unite divine power with our effort.** "It is not our heavenly Father's purpose to save us without an effort on our part to cooperate with Christ. We must act our part, and divine power, united with our effort, will bring victory" (*Christian Temperance and Bible Hygiene,* p. 16).

9. **Be willing and obedient.** "If you are willing and obedient, you shall eat the good of the land" (Isaiah 8:19). "Feeling our inefficiency we are to contemplate Christ, and through Him who is the strength of all strength, the thought of all thought, the willing and obedient will gain victory after victory" (*Christ's Object Lessons,* p. 404).

10. **Resist the devil.** "Therefore submit to God. Resist the devil and he will flee from you" (James 4:7). "Satan trembles and flees before

the weakest soul who finds refuge in that mighty name" (*The Desire of Ages,* p. 130). "It is only by the grace of God, combined with the most earnest effort on our part, that we can gain the victory" (*Counsels to Teachers,* p. 544).

There is no hidden mystery to our gaining the victory. And yes, there will be a great multitude that are victorious. Of course, it will be relatively small compared with the billions who have lived on earth. But, by the grace of God, the victorious will at last stand on the sea of glass. That day cannot be far off. "Transgression has almost reached its limit. Confusion fills the world, and a great terror is soon to come upon human beings. The end is very near. We who know the truth should be preparing for what is soon to break upon the world as an overwhelming surprise" (*Testimonies for the Church,* vol. 8, p. 28).

CHAPTER 18

Time and Eternity

In my stewardship studies of late I've been thinking a lot about the eternal perspective—the bottom-line reason for why we are here and our involvement in the great controversy. We were all made for a person and we were all made for a place. Jesus is that Person and heaven is that place. Ecclesiastes says that God has put eternity into the hearts of men, and we are not satisfied with this world. Nor should we be satisfied. God has given us a longing for things eternal. Jesus said, "I'm going there, to heaven, to prepare a place for you and I will come back and take you to be with Me, so that we can be together for all eternity." He was speaking as a bridegroom to His bride-to-be. These are words of love and romance. A bride is told by her bridegroom that He loves her with all his heart. Then he goes away to prepare a home for her. How much time do you think would pass without her thinking about him and about this place he's gone to prepare? I'm sure that not an hour would go by without her anticipating this and looking forward to being with him again.

How does this topic relate to the battle of the spirits? It reminds us, you see, that this world is not our home. Scripture says we're aliens, we're strangers, we're pilgrims (see Hebrews 11:13). We are ambassadors for Christ. While we are here we are to represent the values and beliefs of His kingdom. That's what we are here. The homes that we live in here on earth, even these physical bodies, are like rented motel rooms that may be ours for 75-80 years, 40-50 years, or maybe only 10 years. Whatever length of time, God knows that the earth, in its present state, is not our permanent residence.

As I thought about this in relationship to stewardship, I wondered, What is the single greatest deterrent to generous giving? I believe the answer is succumbing to the allusion or belief that this earth is our home.

Scripture tells us that the carpenter from Nazareth has gone to build our true home. He's been building for 2,000 years, and He has a tremendous advantage when it comes to things like building—He's omnipotent. He can do anything and everything. How great do you suppose our true home is going to be? Jesus said, "I go to prepare that place for you" and that is our true home. But it's difficult for us to grasp because of the paradox that our true home is a place we have never been. Yet, to all who have a relationship with Jesus Christ based on our belief in His work on the cross, that is our home.

People tend to spend their lives longing for the person of Jesus and longing for this place called heaven, but they don't always know that is what they're longing for. They move restlessly from relationship to relationship, maybe seeking that one true relationship for which they were made—the relationship with that person, Jesus Christ. They spend their time moving from location to location, from place to place. I believe that it is in search of that place for which we were made and for which God is preparing us. So people look for some place new and better—a bigger house, a different city, the suburbs; a new, safer, nicer neighborhood, with better schools. That dream house in the country. That idyllic mountain chalet. That perfect little beach cottage.

Matthew 13:44, in a single verse, captures the heart and soul of following Jesus Christ. "The kingdom of heaven is like treasure hidden in a field, which a man found and hid; and for joy over it he goes and sells all that he has and buys that field."

Picture this average guy, leading a routine life, walking along by himself. Suddenly he discovers something that forever changes the course of his life.

In the time Jesus was here there weren't that many roads. So if you were going from one place to another, you would frequently cross the property of another person. It was OK to do that. This average guy has a staff in his hand, and as he crosses a field he pokes it into the ground and hears a thud. He wonders, "What's this?" So he gets down on his hands and knees to investigate. He digs with his hands and finds a rich treasure. He quickly realizes that the current landowner likely has no idea that this ancient treasure is even there. In other words, this is unclaimed treasure, and whoever owns the land owns it. This treasure captivates him. It becomes the stuff of his dreams. He becomes single-minded about it. He determines he is going to buy this field no matter what it costs, and, in fact, it costs him everything. He experiences the ultimate paradigm shift. He takes on a new perspective. He now sees life through different eyes.

In this example, Jesus is taking something we value—a temporary earthly treasure, found in the field—and uses it as an analogy to what we should value, which is the eternal heavenly treasure. This is the kind of paradigm shift that we need, because God is just not interested in raising up donors. He's interested in raising up disciples—disciples who will follow Him wholeheartedly.

Every time I go on a mission trip to different parts of the world, my vision expands and deepens. If you ever have such an opportunity, don't hesitate—take advantage of it. On a recent trip to India I experienced many things that opened my eyes. I saw again the level of world need and the level of investment opportunity out there for the kingdom of God.

Let me ask you a question about this man in Matthew 13; the man who found this treasure. Are we supposed to feel sorry for this guy? Think about what it says. He sold all that he had to buy this field to get the treasure. It cost the man everything. He had nothing left of what he originally had. It cost him everything! Should we pity him? No, we shouldn't pity him. We should envy him because what it cost him paled in comparison to the value of the thing that he obtained—the greater treasure. And that treasure above all treasure is the Person of Jesus Christ.

Investing our earthly treasures in the kingdom of God is all a matter of cost-benefits ratio. Of course there's a cost, but the benefits far outweigh the cost. There is no joy, therefore, like the joy of giving. You notice what it says about the man. **The key word in this passage is joy.** "For joy over it," he went and sold all that he had. It does not say "in his misery he went and sold all that he had" and the unbelievers went out and had all the fun. No. That isn't what it says. "In his joy." This is a man who is captivated by joy.

In Matthew 6:19-21 Jesus says, "Do not lay up for yourselves treasures on earth, where moth and rust destroy and where thieves break in and steal; but lay up for yourselves treasures in heaven, where neither moth nor rust destroys and where thieves do not break in and steal. For where your treasure is, there your heart will be also." He then goes on to talk about the eyes (the good eye and the bad eye), and the two masters. You can serve only one master, He says. You can't serve both God and money. And you must choose which master you will serve.

I want to focus on the two treasures. Do not store up for yourselves treasures on earth, Jesus admonishes. Well, why not? What is Jesus' rationale? We might expect Him to say, "Don't store up for yourselves treasures on earth because that's the wrong thing to do." Then He goes on to say, "Do store up for yourselves treasures in heaven." But what's His line of argumentation? When He says, "Don't store up for yourselves treasures on earth," why not? Because they won't last. It's a completely pragmatic argument. Moths, rust and dust, and thieves breaking through and stealing—it's not going to last! In other words, His argument for not laying up for yourselves treasures here on earth <u>is not that it is wrong, but that it is stupid.</u>

Let that sink in. This is like the book of Proverbs—dealing with wisdom and foolishness. The book of Proverbs is not simply a book of right and wrong. It's a book of wisdom and foolishness. It's a great book for teenagers and a great book for all of us who are tempted to do wrong. Sometimes being told that something is the wrong thing to do isn't enough to persuade us, because that's an appeal to our righteousness. Sometimes we just don't have enough of that to go around. <u>So God doesn't just appeal to our sense of righteousness; He also appeals to our sense of wisdom.</u> Don't lay up for yourselves treasures on earth because, folks, they are not going to last. And even if they did, we're not going to!

Imagine our lifetime on earth is a dot and from that little dot extends a line that goes out into all eternity. So if you're smart, are you going to live for the dot or the line? We should live for the line, and that's what Jesus is saying.

Then in verse 20 He says, "Do store up for yourselves treasures in heaven." Significantly this passage does not say that we shouldn't store up treasures for ourselves. In fact, it explicitly says we should store up treasures for ourselves. This might be somewhat surprising, but that's exactly what it says. Jesus is not speaking against us storing up treasures. What He's saying is this: "Stop storing up treasures in the wrong place and start storing them in the right place. Switch your investment strategy. Switch your repository. Switch your treasury. Move your assets over from earth to heaven and use your earthly assets as an investment in the kingdom of heaven." And guess what? They're going to last there.

John Wesley said, "I judge all things only by the price they shall gain in eternity."

So God is calling us to operate in our own best interest. Store up for *yourself*. Sometimes we think that God never calls us to do anything for our good. That He is just concerned about His own glory. Of course He calls upon us to do that which is for His glory. But God created the universe and us in such a way that when we do that which is most to God's glory, we are simultaneously doing that which is for our best good as well. Do you believe that? That is a fundamental principle.

I'm not talking about prosperity theology. I'm not talking about a health and wealth gospel. I believe such an attitude is a curse on the church today. The problem with the health and wealth gospel is that it's a half truth. The truth is that it is ultimately in our best interest to follow God and give generously to His kingdom. The problem is that we too often think that it is in our immediate best interest in the sense that we're going to get a quick payoff, and we begin to treat God like a genie. We want to rub the lamp three times and call Him out and He does whatever we want Him to. If you give to the Lord, then He's obligated to give back to you. But God is not obligated to do anything. God is a God who graciously entrusts material wealth to us in varying degrees. Any gospel that is more true in California than in China cannot be the true gospel.

We need to say to ourselves, "What does God really promise?" He does promise that obedience is in our long-term best interest. And that's true for the Christian in China, who's put in prison for his faith, just as much as it's true of us, but his short-term situation may not be positive at all. He may actually be punished for his obedience to God.

This is where we need to look at the long term. Is there a sacrifice in giving? Sure, there is. But God calls us to a lot of little short-term sacrifices, because of the long-term investment reward. The only safe investments are eternal investments. Jesus is reminding us that you can't take it with you. You'll never see a hearse pulling a U-haul. You won't see it because you can't take any of your earthly treasure with you. John D. Rockefeller was one of the wealthiest men who ever lived. After he died, his accountant was asked how much money the billionaire left. His reply was classic. He said he left "all of it." You can't take it with you.

Here in Matthew 6 Jesus adds something profound—something absolutely life-changing if we can grasp it. He says, **"No—you can't take it with you, but you can send it on ahead."**

John Wesley was shown around a large estate by a proud plantation owner. They rode their horses all day and saw only a fraction of the estate. When they sat down to dinner that evening the man said, "Well, Mr. Wesley, what do you think?" John Wesley thought about it for a moment and then said, "I think you're going to have a hard time leaving all of this." Now think about that.

Missionary Jim Elliott was killed by Indians a number of years ago. His philosophy of life was expressed in those classic words **"He is no fool who gives what he cannot keep to gain what he cannot lose."** Of course some people totally misunderstand those words. I have heard them quoted accurately but misapplied completely by persons who assume that Jim Elliott was simply not concerned about gain. This is the whole point. He was concerned about gain. The entire statement is about gain. "He is no fool who gives what he cannot keep to gain what he cannot lose." He was concerned about a different kind of gain: the kind that most people aren't concerned about.

It's not really true that there are two different kinds of Christians. Some people think there are the spiritual, heavenly-minded, missionary, martyr types, with no mind for seeking profit. Then there's the ordinary, practical, less spiritual, head-on-their-shoulders, profit-seeking, business types. But there should be only one type of true Christian. Regardless of our vocation, we should always be sold out to Christ. We will then be looking for the eternal payoff in the changed lives of other people, in the glory of our Lord, and, yes, even for our own reward.

Financial planners say that when it comes to your money, don't think just 3 days ahead or 3 months ahead or 3 years ahead. That's too short-sighted. Think 30 years ahead. Think to those retirement years. Christ, the ultimate investment counselor, takes this same line of thinking and stretches it a lot further. He says, Don't just ask yourself how this is going to pay off in 3 days, or 3 months, or 3 years, or 30 years. Ask yourself how this investment is going to pay off 30 million years from now.

We have a disease. It's called mortality. We're going to leave this world. Do you want what you've done here to survive? Surely you don't want it to rot like the wood, hay, and straw that are spoken of in 1 Corinthians 3. Instead, we want it to last into eternity like the gold, silver, and precious stones.

Imagine for a moment that you were alive at the end of the Civil War. Suppose you were living in the South, but your home was really in the North. While in the South, you'd accumulated a good amount of Confederate currency. Suppose you knew for a fact that the North was actually going to win the war and that it could end at any time. What should you do with your Confederate money? Well, if you were smart, there'd be only one answer to that question. You would cash in your Confederate currency for U.S. currency, of course. You would want the currency that was going to have value once the war was over. Would you get rid of all your Confederate currency? No. You'd keep enough to meet your basic needs for that short period of time until the war ended and the money became worthless.

As believers, we have "inside" knowledge of an eventual upheaval—a worldwide social and economic change—a catastrophe—the ultimate dive in the economy. Everything in this earth is going to burn (2 Peter 3). That will reduce its value considerably. That knowledge should radically affect our investment strategy. In the investment world market gurus read the signs. If they think the stock market is going to take a downward turn they recommend switching funds into something more dependable or consistent such as money markets, T-Bills, or CDs.

In Matthew 6 Jesus speaks as the ultimate investment adviser. He says, "Here's what I'm calling upon you to do. Transfer your funds from earth, which is volatile and ready to take a permanent dive, into heaven, which is totally dependable, insured by God Himself, and is going to last forever." In verse 21 Jesus says, *"Where your treasure is, there your heart will be also."* What He's saying is "Show Me your checkbook, your Visa statement, your receipts for expenditures, and I will show you where your heart is. Wherever you put your money, your heart is sure to follow." Do you want a heart for Microsoft, IBM, or General Motors? Fine. I'm not suggesting that it's wrong to put any money there. But what I'm saying is that when you buy up shares of a stock you didn't own two months ago, you didn't care about news reports related to it two months ago. You didn't watch how it was doing two months ago. But now that you own shares and put your treasure there, your heart is there, and you've suddenly become interested in how this stock is doing now. Isn't that just a principle of life?

You want a heart for the kingdom of God? Jesus tells us exactly how to get it. I've had people say to me, "I really wish I had a heart for missions." Jesus tells you exactly how to get a heart for missions. Put your treasure there. Put your money into missions. Now money isn't the only treasure, but it's certainly a primary one. Yes, put your time and prayers into missions. Go on a mission trip. Put your life into missions. Put your money—your treasure—into missions, and you are going to suddenly be very interested in missions. As we give, we buy up more shares in God's kingdom. And our hearts will follow our money.

People sometimes ask if they should give now or later. It's never wrong to answer by saying "Give now." God is capable of creating much better returns on money invested now than you'll ever get on the stock market, or in real estate, business, or anything else here on earth. That doesn't mean that God calls on us to give everything today. It doesn't mean there's anything wrong with the stock market or real estate. It does mean that if you feel a prompting of God to give, to give more, and give radically, I hope you do. Nothing is more exciting and ultimately more joyful.

Be careful not to procrastinate obedience. If God tells you to read His Word, don't say "In another few months when I have time, I'm going to start reading His Word." If God tells you to pray, don't say "Well down the line I need to start praying." And if God moves you to give your money and invest it generously in the kingdom of God, don't procrastinate in obeying, because there will be 1,000 reasons that will come along to dissuade you and keep you from it. Satan, the evil one, is very good at giving us all kinds of reasons.

In our next conscious moment after we die, we will know exactly how we should have lived. But then it will be too late to go back and change the way we lived. God has given us His Word so we don't have to wait till we die to find out how we should have lived. We can know now. We can say, "God, You have told me to invest my life and assets in Your kingdom." We can make the choice to do it now.

Christians know the Bible clearly teaches that there is no second chance for the unbeliever, once the unbeliever dies. It's not like he can come back, with a second chance, and can live life over again and accept Jesus Christ as his Lord and Saviour. Something that we sometimes fail to realize is that the Bible also teaches there is no second chance for believers to go back and live our lives over again, either. We must live now to the glory of God and generously give of the assets He entrusted to us. They are all owned by Him. We are not owners—we are stewards. We are money managers. We are employees. We are God's errand boys. We are not the ones who own the stuff. Passage after passage of Scripture tells us that God owns it all. Yes, it's reasonable that we should take a certain amount of what God has entrusted to us and live on that. But beyond what's adequate for us to live on, we need to give above and beyond for the kingdom of God. That is something we will never regret doing. I will say very few people ever regret doing it in this world, and I can guarantee, based on what I see in the Word of God, that no one will regret it in the world to come. No regrets when we stand before the Lord and hear Him say, "Well done, My good and faithful servant."

A couple came to see their pastor and said that they wanted to give more money to the church and to world missions. "But we've always had this dream of a beautiful house out in the country, and we've been planning on building that house," they confessed. "But frankly, if we do that, we won't have money for the church and God's kingdom. We keep praying about it, but we can't seem to shake this vision that we have. We feel like God has given us our dream of this beautiful house. Are we wrong?"

The pastor thought about it for a minute and said this to them. "I don't think it's wrong. I think God has given you the dream of a perfect, ideal, wonderful home. The only problem is that you want to have that dream house here in this world." God has a dream house far beyond anything we can comprehend. That dream house is coming. We don't have to build it here. In fact, we can't build it here. Any house we build here is going to be ravaged by time, floods, earthquakes, tornadoes, carpenter ants, freeway bypasses, you name it! Even if, somehow, that house lasts, guess who isn't going to? We, in this world, but we will last through all eternity. So doesn't it make so much more sense to lay up for ourselves treasures in heaven—to give the building materials of our financial material assets to the carpenter from Nazareth right now so that He can be using them to build that house in heaven?

I recommend taking a field trip to a junkyard as a reminder of what will ultimately happen. Let me summarize by asking you a final question. Why are so many Christians today afraid to die? I think the answer to that question comes back to exactly the answer to the question "What's the greatest deterrent to giving today?" The answer is that we have made this world our home. The Bible tells us something else—we are pilgrims, aliens, strangers, ambassadors. Remember the Black spirituals? *Soon I will be done with the troubles of the world. Goin' home to live with God. Swing low sweet chariot, comin' for to carry me home.*

Let's be honest, most Christians are storing up treasures on earth. What does that mean? That means that every day of our lives as we get closer to the day of our earthly death, we are backing away from our treasures because we've laid them up on earth. Jesus says to turn around. Look the other direction and face eternity head-on. Lay up for yourselves treasures in heaven. Then every day of our lives we'll be moving toward our treasures, instead of backing away from them. He who spends his life backing away from his treasures has reason to despair. He who spends his life headed toward his treasure has reason to rejoice. "And for joy over it he goes and sells all that he has and buys that field."

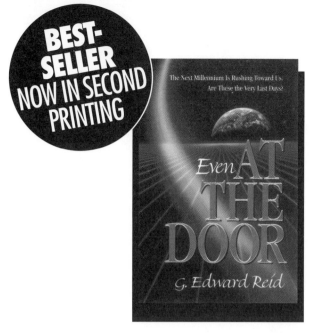